# Praise for

# WALKING WITH THE MAN

*but not to Church*

*Everald walks the talk of Jesus the Man in the way he lives his own life and his book 'Walking with the Man' provides guideposts for living. The Good Samaritan and Flynn of the Inland inspired Everald to live a life of service and compassion as was evidenced by his leadership in the campaign for voluntary assisted dying reform in Australia. Everald is not about saving souls. He is all about turning Christian values into real and practical service for humanity in the here and now as exampled by Jesus as the 'light on the hill' for Everald. This book is a 'must read' for those seeking meaning to life.*

—David Muir AM, Chair, Clem Jones Foundation and Real Republic Australia

*There isn't a page in this compelling read that doesn't engage you. I agreed, disagreed, questioned and pondered in equal measure. For any book that's quite something. You will admire 'Walking With The Man' as I do the man who wrote it. Everald's long life has been one of extraordinary achievement. Read it at a leisurely pace and enjoy a wonderful journey.*

—Greg Cary, veteran talk back radio host and author of 'A Fascinating Investigation'.

*'Walking with the Man' has been a pleasure for me to read and I warmly commend Everald's book.*

*I am not a church goer and best describe myself as agnostic, but in a real sense I have been walking with Jesus of Nazareth. I attended a Church School and rejected its religious education as it focussed too much on mysticism instead of the underlying principles of Jesus of Nazareth's philosophy. My life is based on the golden rule and I am delighted that Everald's book enthusiastically captures the core principles of Jesus who was a very good man, a man of principle.*

—Michael Springer, barrister at law
and author of 'The Flower Bed'.

*Everald's energy is irrepressible. His desire to work and walk together creating a better world is contagious. There's not a conversation with Everald nor a book he's written that hasn't kept me thinking deeply or having a giggle. To know more about his personal philosophy in life is a gift. We can all grow from his curiosity and care.*

— Rebecca Levingston

# WALKING WITH THE MAN

*but not to Church*

EVERALD COMPTON

Walking with The Man


ISBN: 978-1-923289-29-1

A catalogue record for this work is available from the National Library of Australia

Cover Design: Everald Compton and Clark & Mackay
Format and Typeset: Clark & Mackay
Published by Everald Compton and Clark & Mackay

Proudly printed in Australia by Clark & Mackay

**Other books by Everald Compton**

*Catching the Linville Train*
*Dinner with the Founding Fathers*
*The Man on the Twenty Dollar Notes*
*A Beautiful Sunset*

# CONTENTS

# WELCOME ESPECIALLY TO THOSE WHO DO NOT GO TO CHURCH

**WALKING WITH THE MAN** has not been written to change the beliefs of people who have a strong involvement in a Church.

Its primary audience is the 90% of the population whose lives have no involvement in a Church, particularly those who:

- Once belonged to a Church, have given up their involvement, and have no intention of returning.
- Have never been involved in a Church.
- Attend church at Christmas and Easter and ask themselves why.
- Are atheists or agnostics or humanists.
- Have doubts about their reason for being but are afraid to rock the boat with questions that may cause them to appear to be traitors of their faith.

My sole purpose in writing this book is to encourage my readers to take a small step forward from wherever you find yourself in your journey through life and enjoy *Walking with The Man* as your role model without feeling any necessity to be involved in a Church.

The book covers my personal journey through life in search of The Man. You will note that I am not a theologian. I am just a guy who has been going to church for ninety-three years. During that time, I have enjoyed the friendship of many wise mentors and friends whose wisdom and deeds have inspired me. I have also learned from some leaders who switched me off.

I hope the words I have chosen will accurately reflect their thoughts more so than mine.

At the conclusion of this book, my hope is that we can make five positive decisions{

- Our role model is Jesus the Man.
- The Sermon on the Mount is our guidepost.
- We face all challenges by asking 'how would The Man handle this?'
- We create a working group of up to five partners to work out how we can create a better society by following The Man.
- We empty our pockets and dirty our hands in building a new world.

## FOUR THOUGHTS

When I was a child, I spoke as a child, I understood as a child, I thought as a child, but when I became a man I put away childish things.

*Paul, 1 Corinthians 13:11*

* * *

Jesus said: 'Follow me.'

*John 21:19*

* * *

Christianity is the reproduction in our lives of the spiritual quality of Jesus of Nazareth, the creative result that takes place when he personally captures you, breathes into you his spirit and sends you out into the world to feel all that is noblest and decent in life.

*Harry Emerson Fosdick, Riverside Church, New York, 1933*

* * *

'Are you a Christian?'
'No.'
'What religion are you?'
'None.'
'What then is your reason for being?'
'I am a working partner of Jesus the Man.'
'How is this different from being a Christian?'
'I work with The Man, with purposeful intent, to create a caring and sharing society of compassion and justice. Christians tend to concentrate on being saved from their sins and going to heaven.'

*Everald Compton answering a question about his religion.*

# DEDICATED TO LLOYD GEERING, PIONEER OF A MODERN REFORMATION

**AS I WRITE THIS** book, Reverend Professor Sir Lloyd Geering is living in Wellington, New Zealand. He is in his $106^{th}$ year, very active in mind and vision and still contributing positively and thoughtfully to debates on faith and belief.

His distinguished life has been devoted to creating a foundation upon which a modern reformation can occur, not within Churches, but in the lives of non-church attenders who choose to become followers of The Man.

Over many decades, Lloyd Geering has worked positively to create a genuine possibility that such a reformation will take place, hopefully being achieved in this century.

*Walking with The Man* is my humble contribution to the inspiring revolution that Lloyd Geering has begun. It is my hope that it will, in reality, be a positive door opener for many people.

So, I dedicate it to him and acknowledge that I owe him much. He is a trailblazer who has hugely influenced my thinking ever since we first met in Brisbane in 1956.

Significantly, he has been an influential contributor to the positive decision I have made to refrain from describing myself as a Christian and to make a deep commitment towards earning the right and privilege to be called a working partner of Jesus the Man.

This quiet but persistent reformation within my soul has added depth to my attitude to life and has created powerful challenges for me in relation to the manner in which I walk the pilgrim way and strive to contribute to the fostering of a cohesive, challenging, and meaningful society.

I give thanks for the creative challenge into which Lloyd Geering has led me.

—Everald Compton
Brisbane
November 2024

# CONFESSION

**JUST BEFORE EASTER 2023,** I published a book to which I gave the title *Catching the Linville Train.*

It is not an autobiography, but it does reflect my public journey through nine decades of the history of my era.

Now I have written *Walking with The Man.*

It highlights a significant element of my personal journey and is a positive account of my experience of life in a world that was once hugely influenced by religion.

My pathway has led me to the reality of a secular scene. It is heavily influenced by political and financial ideology combined with the growing influence of agnostics, atheists, and religious extremists, plus those who believe that life has no purpose at all.

Thus we now have a society that is heavily influenced by those who adapt their religion to fit any ideology that fosters their own needs, especially that which relates to the curse of greed and the abuse of power.

Primarily, I have tried to give an honest account of how I have upgraded my thinking from traditional Christianity to one that places total and positive emphasis on the life and work of Jesus the Man.

In doing so, I reject the selfish and unjustifiable dogmas that say it is vital that I be saved from my sins so I can gain an assurance of a place in heaven where I will enjoy eternal life.

My experience is that there is a huge difference between Jesus Christ, who was created by a religion, and Jesus the Man who is a reality. He was, and still is, an extraordinary human being. He is and always will be a powerful role model for all humanity, especially me.

So here is what I hope is for you an interesting account of my journey in which the supernatural, mystical, and miraculous have ceased to influence me, but where meaningful events are a welcome experience.

Along the way, I found strength in the discovery that Jesus the Man, not a mythical god, is the great mentor of humanity. I have not the slightest doubt that The Man fosters and empowers you and me as we strive to create a caring society dominated by love, justice, and equality, not by obsession with our sins.

You will note also among my words that the traditional belief of a trinity of Father, Son, and Holy Spirit are of no relevance to me whatsoever as they simply distort the powerful presence of The Man.

My hope is that you will be my positive partner in walking through life with The Man as consistently and purposefully as possible.

In my journey I have found it to be beyond dispute that The Man is a very worthwhile companion. I am inspired by the fact that I am just one of his many working partners.

My hope is that the 90% of the population of Australia who are not Church members will experience a desire to walk with him without ever feeling compelled to attend a church.

# 1

## Discovering The Man

**MOST PEOPLE BELIEVE THAT** Christianity is a pathway to boredom.

It too often can be, especially when we experience the misfortune of listening to its principles being inflicted upon us via the closed minds of fundamentalists.

Nevertheless, whether we are aware of it or not, you and I have quietly developed a personal set of beliefs about the core of life which are our very own. They are more than likely to be different to those proclaimed as indisputable facts by whatever church we may happen to be attending.

We may not be aware of it but each one of us has been steadily forming our philosophy over our lifetime, but far too many of us have not been inclined to take the time to write down our thoughts. This is unfortunate as the very act of writing helps to clarify and verify whether our reason for being has genuine meaning for us. Be this as it may, our core values are always there in our minds directing our thinking.

I am certain also that those who have rejected Christianity and have consciously and actively become non-believers have in doing so made crucial decisions on what is our basis of life.

The exciting truth is that the very act of debating our values with others unlocks a door to the possibility of a mind-expanding journey which can lead us to become working partners of The Man, the incredible teacher who came out of Nazareth. He has for very many centuries reached out to humanity from the core of his powerful presence and has influenced us by the manner in which he walked and talked around the shores of the inland sea in Israel that we know as Galilee.

One way or another, those of us who now sincerely and actively identify with The Man have found ourselves to be on a mind-expanding journey of discovery that has established a meaningful sense of mission and purpose in our lives.

Personally, this valued experience has led me to decide, after nine decades of committed attendance at church, to express my core beliefs in writing this book. I hope my journey will be of interest and value to you. I can assure you that I have found the writing of it to be a fascinating venture of greatly expanded learning about the depth of my reason for being.

By sharing my journey with you in a humble and happy way that avoids Church jargon, I sincerely hope that it will be a mind-expanding, motivational, and entertaining experience for you, just as much as it has been a venture that has challenged me in a significant manner.

I use the friendly, down to earth, language of the Australian bush that I first learned as I grew up in the two small villages of Linville and Monsildale in the Brisbane River Valley. There, most people followed the philosophy of Saltbush Bill who simply let us know that Jesus was a good bloke who always lifted his mates out of the gutter and pointed them in the right direction.

One Bible verse confirms the message of Saltbush Bill:

'Do unto others as you would have them do to you.'

Some traditional Christians may be disturbed by my views on the core of their lifelong faith, but this book has not been written with churchgoers in mind.

Nevertheless, I apologise if my words cause you any personal pain as this is not my intention. This book is clearly intended to be read by those who do not attend church.

My aim is to interest and challenge readers, not accuse, or denigrate or preach or make people feel that, if you read and absorb my words, you will have betrayed the beliefs that you hold sacred.

Nevertheless, I have no option but to be honest with you as I do not seek to convert committed Christians to my chosen pathway. My intent is to outline some inspirational door openers to those who have placed their religion on the back-burner. My basic hope is that I can initiate a healthy and long-term discussion about where we are going with our lives.

My target market is the 90% of people who live in our society but are no longer involved in churches or actively committed to Christianity, except in a very casual fashion. Hopefully, you may be willing to review and expand your current view of religion and travel with me on what you may come to regard as a personal journey to a deeper life experience.

As the legendary Hercule Poirot, that great character created by the magnificent wordsmith, Agatha Christie, so often said:

> 'We must always use the little grey cells in our brain in the manner for which they were originally created as nothing in this world is ever as it seems to be.'

Allow me to begin our dialogue by having a happy and relaxed chat with you about the events that set me firmly on the pilgrim way. They began a long time ago in 1931 in tiny bush villages in Queensland, Australia.

Then, I will share with you my reflections on many great lives who influenced my thinking and actions as I journeyed around the world. It will be good if you too can be inspired by these powerful lives. Indeed, you may already be aware of them and have many more of your own.

This will lead us to a reflection on where my journey is now and what I hope will be its ever-expanding future. Hopefully, this will encourage you to view your own reflection on your future.

I invite you to read on with a critical eye and mutual respect.

At the end, I hope that our society will be a better place for the simple reason that many of us will have decided that The Man is an appropriate role model for life, so that whenever we face a challenge, we will instantly ask ourselves a significant question:

'How would The Man
handle this situation?'

# 2

## My Journey

### 2.1 GREEN YEARS

*My mother*

**THELMA COMPTON, WHO GAVE** me life during her twenty-first year, was a loving mother and a devout fundamentalist Christian who lived out her often illogical version of faith with huge enthusiasm and long-term commitment. She held the unshakeable belief that everything that occurred in her life, without exception, was the will of God and could not be questioned in any way. Many years down the track, I would become clearly aware that she had unintentionally blamed God for lots of things he had absolutely nothing to do with.

Thelma was a descendent of devout Lutheran missionaries from Bavaria in Germany who had been given a written charter by their Church to remove every vestige of sin from the continent of Australia. They used their first ministry on the Darling Downs in Queensland as their launchpad. She was very proud of the fact that they established a strong congregation in the small town of Goombungee where they built a fine rural church which has faithfully carried out its ministry for more than a century.

She often reminded me that, when she first took me to church in Linville when I was just three weeks old, she did so because she wanted Christianity to be the basic learning experience of my life from the earliest possible moment. I have been attending one church or another quite happily as a routine activity of my life on most Sundays ever since and have enjoyed the privilege and responsibility of having a leadership role in most of them.

Even though Thelma's ancestors failed dismally in their mission to rid Australia of sin, I am grateful for her sincere initiative in making me a regular churchgoer as it set me on a pathway of discovery of the meaning of life that I have never regretted. Her passion ensured that Jesus the Man would become a cornerstone of my life from my earliest years. She also taught me that having core values in my life is a rich experience.

Importantly, it would lead me to discover that having a solid relationship with The Man did not require me to have a closed mind. Far too many Christians sadly fail to enjoy the sheer mystery of it all.

### *Methodist*

The first church of my religious life was the Linville Methodist church which has now been converted into a home for one of the locals. It was a quite plain wooden building and so its transformation to residential use has not caused any loss to the grandeur of fine architecture.

Linville was, and still is, a pleasant village where mostly lower income families live in small homes. It is located in a remote part of the Brisbane River Valley, a couple of hours drive northwest of Brisbane just off the highway that runs from Ipswich to Kingaroy.

Back in my day there were only two churches in the village – Anglican and Methodist. I don't know why the Catholics were not there as some of the residents were Irish. Thelma chose the Methodists even though she had married my dad, Herbert Compton, in the Anglican church. He was nominally Anglican.

My lasting memory of my involvement with the Linville Methodists is that of my troubled relationship with its fearsome Sunday School teacher, Miss Beacham.

I did not ever find out what her first name was. She was just the formidable Miss Beacham. She was a ferocious opponent of sin and a despiser of men, perhaps because no one in the village ever got around to marrying her. She even sued the local storekeeper for breach of promise after he very wisely and just in time had bailed out of their brief relationship. All the gossips in the town had a field day when this happened.

One Sunday, when I was still learning to write my name, she forced me to sign a lifelong pledge to never drink alcohol, informing me that, in the sight of God, the only sin worse than alcohol was to do rude things to girls. She gave me no option but to sign as she stood over me and put a pen in my hand. She declared that my failure to sign would give the Good Lord no option but commit me to the hottest of all hellfire.

Afterwards, when I tearfully complained to my mother about how dreadful Miss Beacham had been, Thelma assured me that the fearsome lady was in reality a wonderful Christian who had just led me to carry out what she irrevocably believed was God's will for me. Thelma emphasised that Miss Beacham was God's undisputed agent in Linville. My view was that if this was true, then God had made a real dumb choice.

An associated matter that confused my young mind at the time was that my dad, a lowly paid labourer at the local sawmill, and a lapsed Christian, occasionally enjoyed a beer with his mates after work at the local pub and never came home drunk. Nevertheless, Miss Beacham and Thelma prayed fervently that Herb would see the light and cease his wicked ways. Be this as it may, as far as I could work out, the Lord clearly did not seem to be too keen to take any drastic action to strike him down.

Years later, my mother who by that time was living in Toowoomba while I worked at a bank in Brisbane, sent me a telegram to let me know that Miss Beacham was dying at a hospital in South Brisbane and asked if I would go to see her as she had no known living relatives. Reluctantly, I decided that the right thing to do was to visit her at her deathbed. As I took a seat beside her she looked frail and vulnerable, but she held my hand and quietly told me that she was proud of me. I took a deep breath and thanked her for the Christian upbringing she had shared with me. She meant well even though she had a strange way of showing it.

Nevertheless, I was unable to remove from my mind just how wrong it is that so many Sunday Schools have been led by too many teachers with the attitude of Miss Beacham. Fear and brainwashing have been primitive weapons that far too many Christians of her mould have used in their efforts to win souls to the faith. Too many still try but, thankfully, their influence is usually rejected but at a significant cost to Churches themselves as they eventually and inevitably lose lots of members as a result.

Even so, Miss Beacham, without knowing it, had via threats of the devil convinced me that I must never again make any decision on any matter in my life that is based on fear of consequences. It was an important gift that she had planted in my soul. Now, when faced with any crisis, I quickly assemble all the facts, study them carefully, then make a clear decision that is based on commonsense, not fear. I do not change any decision unless I am faced with no other option.

My overall memory of my relationship with the Methodists at Linville is that, despite Miss Beacham, I discovered that there was a depth to life that went beyond the ordinary and the mundane and I must search for it.

I discovered also that I was entitled to ask questions from time to time about what ministers and teachers told me.

For instance, when I was still quite young I can remember asking one of the pastors why God caused so many good people to die while many awful people stayed alive. He, like so many others, told me that God works in mysterious ways and I must not ever question his wisdom. I often thought that those answers were simply a fob off, but they encouraged me to embark on a lifelong journey of constant questioning.

Now, whenever I think of the Linville Methodist church, I recall the many times I have been at worship in bush churches, especially around Australia and New Zealand. In years past they had a huge role in community life as they were the focal point for baptisms, weddings and funerals, plus public gatherings called to discuss a crisis etc. Often there would be a tiny graveyard beside the church which revealed the history of the community. Now, most of them are closed and this fills me with sadness as they were once the cornerstone of rural society.

Someone once wrote a hymn about them and it was special.

'Come to the church in the wild wood, O come to the church in the vale.'

They were symbols of hope, something the world is now very short of.

*No church*

We moved from Linville to an even smaller village called Monsildale, a few kilometres further up the Brisbane River, where a new timber mill had just been established. This change offered my dad a slightly better paid job and we lived in a newer house. Our happy abode was one of twelve homes that surrounded the mill, but there was no church in the town. There was no community hall either and only one shop which was owned by the mill. Neither was there a pub, meaning there was no social centre.

Thelma organised and led a Sunday School of no religious denomination which met at the tiny state school. I was there every Sunday as she valiantly tried to convince me never to question a single word in the Bible, ever. Like Miss Beacham, she was certain that such a transgression was a sin far worse than the lure of alcohol, gambling, theft, and sex. However, she conveyed the message in a much more kindly fashion than Miss Beacham ever could achieve.

Her cherished dogma about the infallibility of the Bible continued to create doubts in my young mind as the years went by. Surely those blokes who wrote the Bible two thousand years ago had made some mistakes when they wrote it all down, just as I would do with my essays at school. Were they really supermen with super minds? No.

Those doubts about the Bible have never left me throughout my nine decades. In fact, my love of asking courteous questions has expanded considerably, but this is the exciting part of any learning experience. It is filled with discovery that strengthens the core, isolates the myths, and creates never ending fascination with discovering the real meaning of it all.

The absence of a church and a minister also caused me to wonder why any community anywhere in the world actually needed a legal church entity or a clergy person of any type. Could we not be Christians without either? I steadily came to a revelation that the answer to this is Yes.

I have never forgotten that we did very well without a church or a parson at Monsildale because we were a small group of believers who met regularly and were not subjected to the overpowering presence of a priest or the legalistic domination of a Church hierarchy. We were free of religious politics and smothering dogma. Absolutely refreshing.

I was not filled with enthusiasm when we left Monsildale and returned to the rigid and oppressive ways in which Churches organise Christianity.

### *Presbyterian*

Dad then got a job at the bacon factory in Toowoomba when the timber mill at Monsildale was suddenly closed along with many other small mills that were regarded by their owners as being too small to be profitable.

It was culture shock for me to move from a village of fifty souls to a city of 50,000 and to attend worship in an historic Gothic church, St Stephen's Presbyterian, the spiritual home of most of the business and civic leaders of the Toowoomba community. Back then in 1941, with the world at war and many having a need for God to be on our side, it was generally regarded as socially unacceptable not to be seen at church on Sunday.

This was my first encounter with the reality of witnessing how far too many churchgoers feel, sometimes unconsciously, that they must be seen at church so as to enhance their wealth and community status by using Christianity as a social, financial, and political weapon of self-interest.

I would live long enough to discover that it still happens, especially in politics, where people who call themselves the Christian Right are flexing their muscles more and more as they try to use Christianity as a respectable pathway to personal power and financial gain.

At St Stephen's Toowoomba, I was enthusiastically involved, initially with the Sunday School, then in a youth group called the Order of the Burning Bush. Its name came from the Bible story of Moses seeing a bush that was on fire, but the fire was unable to consume it. In this group, I was taught that, if I followed God, it would be impossible for anything to hurt me, just as the burning bush was not destroyed. I could only fail in life if I departed from the will of God. It was made clear that, if I got into strife, it was because I was my own worst enemy for departing from the paths of righteousness.

This created a need in my soul to begin a lifelong quest to discover what the will of God actually is and how I could find and understand the formula that determines it.

Sadly, I must report that I have failed utterly in my search as I can find no evidence that God ever wrote down anything and floated it to us out of the heavens. I only ever discovered that humans wrote what they declared God had told them. Nevertheless, I am still searching for valid answers and will continue the search until the end of my days even though I know it will prove to be fruitless. Every day I become even more certain that there is no such thing as God's will. There is only the inspiration of The Man and that is a prime asset of my life.

When my schooldays ended, I joined the PFA (Presbyterian Fellowship of Australia). It was a young people's group that had a presence in most Presbyterian congregations across Australia. It would become a significant experience of my early life. The PFA trained its members to be leaders in both church and society and fostered the hope that we would all become exceptional ones. Whatever leadership skills I now have can trace their birth to the ten years of my membership of the PFA. It remains a powerful highlight of my walk with The Man.

It was during my era in the PFA that I developed the clear view that it is not possible to be a solid working partner of The Man without having a pioneering role in a never-ending quest for a better quality and purpose of life for all who live in whatever secular community I belong to.

I became convinced that no Church, nor its people, can stand apart and alone in society as an elite group who believe themselves to be God's chosen people.

### *Methodist again*

When my schooldays ended, I secured my first job as a clerk in the Commonwealth Bank as only three out of thirty in my high school class received invitations to study at what was then the only university in Queensland. I did not lament missing out on a university education as the circumstances in which I found myself caused me to set out on a fascinating pathway of lifelong learning and this included my Christian education.

This first step in my career in banking took me from Toowoomba to Brisbane where I worked at the Woolloongabba branch of the bank. While working there, I regularly attended St Andrew's Presbyterian Church in the CBD where I continued my membership of the PFA.

However, the bank soon moved me to their branch in the small rural community of Nyngan in Western New South Wales where I joined the Methodist congregation, the only other churches in town being Anglican and Catholic.

By this time, I had begun to discover that there is no such thing as a universal set of beliefs that all Christians agree upon.

The friendly but clear divisions between Presbyterians and Methodists became evident. I enjoyed the debates on their varying attitudes to both theology and service. This was made easier by the fact that the Methodists of Nyngan welcomed me most warmly and openly into their ranks. It also caused me to understand why many Christians keep moving around until they find a congregation of any religious denomination in which they can genuinely feel that they belong and are sincerely accepted. Beliefs actually take second place to the warm feeling of belonging.

This experience set me on yet another path of discovery as to what it really was that I personally believed and practised. This has been an essential experience in preparing the basics of my beliefs. Was I a Methodist or a Presbyterian or a fundamentalist or modernist, and was there a wiser and deeper alternative to all of them? These fascinating questions remain with me to this day and will forever more.

But this ever-expanding realm of understanding introduced me to two wonderful role models whom I wanted to follow.

The Methodists taught me about the life and work of John Wesley who founded their Church four centuries ago, while Presbyterians led me to another giant of the faith, George McLeod, founder of the Iona Community in Scotland. These two modern disciples influenced me more than most biblical characters. I have included chapters about both.

*Presbyterian once more*

A couple of years later, I returned to Toowoomba where I renewed my membership and revived my fellowship with the Presbyterians at St Stephen's.

For the first time, I became a lay preacher.

There were many small congregations spread across the surrounding farmlands of the Darling Downs that struggled to find and maintain a minister and needed volunteer preachers to stand in to fill the gaps. This new experience pulled me up with a jolt.

I became aware that my personal understanding of the Scriptures was inadequate for this challenging task, even for preaching to a dozen people in a little bush church on a hot summer day. This discovery set me on an adventure of reading and study which continues to this day as my sense of personal inadequacy as a promoter of The Man remains with me.

I didn't realise at that time what a long-term commitment my role as a lay preacher would become. Eventually, the National Assembly of the Uniting Church in Australia would formally appoint me to be a lay preacher for life and I would live and serve long enough to become the longest serving lay preacher in the Uniting Church nationwide.

At this time in my life, I came to encounter the full depth of enmity between Protestants and Catholics, not only in Australia but worldwide, especially in Northern Ireland. What concerned me was that most of the denigration was fostered by Protestants and I had to acknowledge that we did have a holier than thou attitude towards Catholics.

I vividly remember an experience one Saturday evening when my ultra-fundamentalist grandmother tore strips off me for taking a Catholic girl to the movies at the Empire Theatre in Toowoomba. She was a lovely redhead, attractive and intelligent, who worked with me at the Commonwealth Bank. We enjoyed a grand movie 'Gone with the Wind' but my mother expressed to her mother her concern that I had got myself a Catholic girlfriend.

Grandma summoned me to her home and told me in no uncertain terms that I had committed the ultimate sin. She declared that there was no place in heaven for Catholics or anyone who fraternised with them. I was in dire danger of hellfire unless I repented immediately.

In addition, I was banned for one week from the roast dinner which was held for her entire family at her home after church every Sunday. I was instructed to stay at my home and eat sandwiches of bread and dripping. I gave every sign of repentance, but I sneaked down to the local corner store and bought myself a hot pie with peas and mashed potato on top.

The crisis was resolved a few weeks later when I changed my occupation, leaving the profession of banking to become a public accountant, having qualified by evening studies to gain what is now known as a CPA. I was appointed to a position in a small accounting practice in Brisbane which required me to move away from Toowoomba once more.

An even more challenging world awaited me, socially, financially, politically, and in my faith.

I faced it with both excitement and gratitude and soon found that I would encounter some challenging experiences, all of which would prove to be character building.

## 2.2 MISSION

*The PFA changes my life*

This new chapter in my journey led me to become president of the Presbyterian Fellowship of Australia for the Southeast Queensland Region. There were more than fifty congregations in the region that had PFA Groups. I made it my business to visit every one of them and come to understand what young people hoped for in their journey of faith.

I concentrated my efforts on leadership training and used the example of St Paul as a leader who aimed to spread the message to every nation of the known world. Years later, I would come to seriously question whether Paul advocated the right message and to form the opinion that he did not, but there has never been any doubt in my mind about his magnificent communication skills, leadership ability and total commitment to his calling.

The experience affirmed my conviction that no one could be a passive partner of Jesus of Nazareth. My basic beliefs were useless unless they motivated me to use all my skills to do as much as I could in the manner that a committed partner should do.

It was largely attributable to the results achieved in my leadership in the PFA that the Presbyterian Church of Queensland appointed me in 1956 as organising secretary of St Andrew's War Memorial Hospital which was to be established on Wickham Terrace in Brisbane as a totally new medical institution. I was responsible for raising its funding, supervising its construction, and enlisting the skilled medical and nursing staff who would be vital to its success.

This task meant that I had to travel throughout Queensland visiting many Presbyterian congregations to raise funds to establish the hospital. I learned much more about religion and Church politics in those three years than at any other phase of my life.

At the time, a wise old parson gave me some splendid advice that would prove to be helpful in achieving the results that were necessary.

'Before you go to any congregation, do some research about the minister. Find out what his theology is – happy-clappy, fundamentalist, moderate, conservative, liberal, reformer. Then check out the key lay leaders to find out if they are with him or against him. Then adapt your fund-raising strategy so as to talk their language. You do not have to become a chameleon to do this. Just hit the right buttons to give them personal reasons to support the hospital in accordance with their beliefs, without in any way fiddling with the truth of your message.'

I had some challenging encounters that were often humorous as they revealed the many interpretations that people applied to the Scriptures and their faith experience. The scope was vast. No matter where I went in my campaigning around the world in the years that lay before me, I found that this broad diversity of beliefs not only abounded mightily but was often beyond reality.

I especially discovered that far too many Christians loved their money far more than their God. Much too often, I found that their public expression of faith covered everything except the manner in which they gave or did not give their money to the mission of their Church.

I discovered there can be no doubt that far too many people want a God who conforms exactly with their ingrained views of life and can be trusted to provide them with anything and everything to which they aspire.

However, my most vivid and happiest memory of my time at St Andrew's Hospital is the spirit of volunteer service that was the vibrant core of the mission to build a Presbyterian hospital. There were at least a thousand volunteers who worked regularly at fund-raising, promotional activity and organising the construction, staffing, equipping, and opening of the hospital. I remember with great affection the many devoted women who hand made every piece of linen that the hospital required on its opening day. And they met the total cost personally.

There was a genuine sense of calling to create a Christian presence in a caring institution. Never again would I experience this in any other Church project anywhere in the world. Now, in most Church institutions, volunteers have gradually been replaced by professionals with skills in every walk of life but little sense of calling. This has been to the detriment of fostering a compassionate society, thereby losing a quality of life that been of real value.

### *St Philip's, Aspley*

I met Helen at a PFA youth conference at Alexandra Headlands in 1954. When we married and built our first home at Aspley, we worked together to establish the Aspley Presbyterian church as a new congregation called St Philip's. The initial meetings were held in our home (even though we had only sparse furniture at that time, causing most of our guests to sit on the floor).

The new congregation consisted mainly of young families who wanted their children to have a solid Christian education and so it grew quickly in size and enthusiasm. I was elected an elder and session clerk (leader of the elders) and the representative elder of the congregation at the Queensland state assembly of the Presbyterian Church. A memorable sixteen years of active involvement followed in a positive atmosphere until Church Union throughout Australia caused us to merge with the local Methodists to create the Aspley Uniting church.

Those years of growing a new congregation were a very positive experience that enabled me to learn much about why people get involved in growing a new church congregation and what they expect from this experience. Above all, I discovered how to encourage members to develop and grow their own personal beliefs and commitment. This of course only had personal meaning because my own faith grew in its depth and outlook.

The memory that remains with me is my conviction that the pioneering work of creating a new congregation is most effectively done by lay people, not the clergy. It was our friends in the PFA who helped us to find Presbyterians in Aspley who were interested in joining the new congregation at St Philip's. A large team of them joined with us in knocking on every door in the suburb in our successful quest to get this new church moving forward.

Those who governed the Queensland state assembly and the regional presbytery of the Presbyterian Church only sent a minister to work with us after we had proved that this new congregation was a certainty to be established. They had given us little encouragement as they appeared not to want to take the blame if we failed in our efforts. They seemed to worry that its possible failure could cause a blot in their religious careers.

Even back in those days, the attitude of self-preservation of the bureaucrats who administer Churches clearly indicated that the rot was already setting in. This will eventually begin the demise of Churches as the prime advocates of the faith and mission of The Man. More about this later.

## 2.3 WILDERNESS

*Church Union*

I had a leadership role nationally in establishing the Uniting Church of Australia as I was convinced that it was essential that the Methodist, Presbyterian, and Congregational Churches in Australia should combine their resources and influence so that a new and growing Church could have a significant impact on the life of the nation.

My role in this significant venture of Church Union was acknowledged a long time afterwards when I received an AO in the Australian Honours List of 2022. The citation recorded my leadership activities in the founding of the Uniting Church.

However, it is with much grief and agony that I acknowledge that my inadequate endeavours have helped to contribute to the undeniable fact that Church Union has been a sad and disappointing experience for many. To be more blunt, the history of the Uniting Church in Australia outlines the fact that Church Union has proven to be a disaster. It has been based on establishing a massive bureaucracy while neglecting the grass roots where people live, move, and have their being.

The Basis of Union, was originally a revolutionary and inspiring document, theologically and organisationally. However, it was pointlessly watered down to appease small but dissident elements within the ranks of Presbyterians, Methodists, and Congregationalists, who eventually walked out after the final vote was taken. This made it a legal impossibility to revert to the original powerful version. Almost half a century later, the Uniting Church is now on the brink of its death throes because it has no spine, no conviction, no mission. It currently stands for very little that is of consequence and few will mourn its departure from either the national, state, or local scenes.

The burden of its overbearing governance has been massive despite the high hopes with which we all went forward from the opening day.

I was present and voting when the final decision was taken to create Union at the national assembly of the Presbyterian Church at Scots church in Melbourne. I had been a representative elder at two state and two national assemblies of the Church, where long and painful battles were held to bring Union into being. I had also served as national chair of the Uniting Church Association, a powerful group of elders who toiled hard for a Yes vote.

When the winning vote numbers were announced, and after the Continuing Presbyterians had walked out, we were joined by Methodist and Congregational colleagues who had met on the same day in churches nearby and had likewise voted Yes. Scots church was jam-packed and the crowd spilled over to block the Collins Street footpath. Our moderator announced that the new Uniting Church of Australia had 2.5 million members even after some renegades had left.

Now, almost half a century later, and even though the population of Australia has grown significantly in the meantime, the most recent census shows nominal membership of the Uniting Church is only 700,000, most of whom are over seventy years of age. It is a shocking legacy of what should have grown to be an absolute powerhouse in building a more caring nation.

Not long after reading this book The Uniting Church in Australia might well be dead, and few will lament its demise. What are some of the key issues?

It has not walked with The Man.

In reality, it is a temple of rules, regulations, and strategies that have created a rigid administration similar to a political dictatorship, with The Man nowhere to be seen.

There have been two main reasons for this.

Firstly, there has been a decline in the quality of the life and work of congregations. Secondly, greater concentration was given to the development of centrally controlled community service projects that have not involved Church members in any personal way.

Let's take the latter first.

Right across Australia, the Uniting Church has established a formidable number of charitable institutions, building on that which was inherited from the Presbyterian, Methodist and Congregational Churches. At the time of writing, these include hospitals, schools, aged care services, early childhood education centres, workshops for the handicapped, city missions, and well-known national entities like Lifeline and Blue Nursing and a multitude of social mission activities managed by numerous governing bodies that employ a wide range of competent professionals.

Most of their funding comes from governments not from Church members. Indeed they are simply government agencies that pretend to be Christian.

The issue that we face is that, while most of those professionals are genuine and competent carers, there are not many who are practising Christians. In addition, very few members of the Uniting Church who are active out in the congregations are involved as volunteers, the opposite to the case when St Andrew's Hospital was established.

The reality is that health and safety laws, plus an absence of basic qualifications as carers, prevent many volunteers from participating. But the key problem is that the leaders of each institution find that the involvement of volunteers is an organisational nuisance, therefore they discourage it. This means that these Institutions are not faith-based ministries. They are charitable institutions that do a good job. Long after the Uniting Church fades into history, they will continue to serve society as secular expressions of caring.

Indeed, if the Uniting Church were to wind up today, those institutions could continue under one administrative umbrella and would become the largest charity in Australia.

However, the first issue that I am raising is the most important.

Congregations have been allowed to die with little effort being made either to save them or grow new ones. Evangelism has become a lost art.

Especially sad is that the quality of ministers has dropped over all with many regarding their ministry as a five day a week profession that has concentrated only on carrying out the required formalities. There is little passion for the cause. Because there is no zeal for growth, the Uniting Church has lost a whole generation of potential members. This result has been caused by sheer negligence. Most attendees are now oldies like me.

As I write these words, I want to weep, but I am compelled by honesty to acknowledge that I have no option but to accept my share of the blame.

As I mentioned earlier, I am an elder and lay preacher in my Church. By resolution of the first assembly I was appointed in those roles for life on the day the Uniting Church was founded, having formerly held similar positions in the Presbyterian Church. This means that I have held those two positions for a total of sixty-six years and more.

The demise of the Uniting Church happened on my watch. I am in the ranks of the guilty.

I should regard the public acknowledgement of my work as an honour, but it is far from that. I should have done my utmost to start a revolution way back in those early years and make it work effectively, but I sat on the fence. I ceased attending synods of the Church three decades ago because they were boring talkfests of false adulation that have eventually achieved absolutely nothing except to build up a lazy hierarchy.

So it is that I stand guilty along with many others.

The issue that I cannot avoid is what I intend to do about it right now.

I do have a positive plan and I am very aware that it will happen only if it is carried out beyond Church structures.

The task fills my bones with excitement.

## 2.4 ADVOCATING STEWARDSHIP

My career as a fund-raising consultant that began with my work at St Andrew's Hospital, took me to undertake many other organisational and financial challenges. An important one started when ministers and priests began to contact me seeking help in improving the finances of their congregations.

I soon discovered that this task was quite different to raising funds for a hospital.

I knew that I was dealing with the basic faith and commitment of people who had chosen to belong to a local church. It wasn't a matter of just organising a campaign to motivate people to give more money to keep their church alive and functioning. Quite clearly, their commitment of money had to have a direct relationship with their growth in faith and their willingness to have a role in caring for others.

At this time in my life I wrote a book on the subject called *Where have the Christian Stewards Gone?* There was only one printing and it sold out.

I then designed a campaign that I called a Thanksgiving Program. It challenged Christians to give willingly and generously to their local church as an act of thanksgiving for their growth in faith. They also made a commitment to pastorally care for others in their congregation and encourage them to do likewise.

Many congregations across Australia and New Zealand that were part of the main religious denominations (Catholic, Anglican, Presbyterian, Methodist) retained my services. Groups of congregations in a city or region then asked me to organise programs where they learned to practise stewardship together.

This especially occurred in the Anglican Church where a bishop would undertake to lead a Thanksgiving Program that would involve every parish in his diocese at the one time. The ones that I led in Australia were organised in the dioceses of North Queensland, Rockhampton, Grafton, Newcastle, Bathurst, Riverina, Wangaratta, Ballarat, Gippsland, and Bunbury, also in New Zealand at Nelson, Christchurch, Napier, and Hamilton.

I also organised a nationwide Thanksgiving Program for the Presbyterian Church of Southern Africa. This covered the Colony of Southern Rhodesia (now Zimbabwe) as well as South Africa. The campaign was difficult to organise as both Nelson Mandela and Robert Mugabe were reaching the height of their revolutionary powers and many white people and minority tribes were very unsure of their future.

As the years rolled by, I came to realise that I was just upgrading the financial and human resources that would keep congregations and their buildings open and operating and help them pay for their priest. I was not encouraging and organising people to become involved in the human needs of the society that surrounded them beyond their church. Indeed, I have come to a firm belief that a congregation is not a genuine congregation unless it gives to humanity more than it spends on running their church. Rarely does this happen anywhere in the world.

Gradually, it dawned on me that I would be a better steward if I became personally involved in enhancing the attitude of community service by people who did not go to church and will never do so. This is actually 90% of the population here in Australia.

Now, my clear calling is to find a way for non-church goers to relate personally to The Man without feeling any compulsion to go anywhere near a church.

This is a work that is very much in its infancy. I am aware that I am fast running out of years in which I can achieve worthwhile results.

Nevertheless, I press on as the challenge fascinates me enormously.

It is obvious that my homeland nation of Australia needs a cornerstone of values that define our lives. I am certain that those values can be discovered and enhanced in the life and work of The Man.

## 2.5 SAVING CATHEDRALS

My work in advocating Christian Stewardship enabled me to gain a fairly high profile in Church circles. This encouraged cathedral deans to call me to seek my help in raising funds for urgent restoration of their historic buildings that were succumbing to centuries of bad weather, the march of time, and irresponsible human neglect.

I responded with enthusiasm as I have always been fascinated by the sheer majesty of cathedrals everywhere. I would sit within them in the twilight and soak in their magnificence especially at times when there were no crowds of visitors and few worshippers, thus enabling me to savor a quiet sense of peace. I could feel the presence of The Man in the silence of these huge buildings and I could meditate with depth about the state of my life and my inadequate value to humanity.

So it was that I answered yet another call and got thoroughly involved with all the vigour that I could muster.

My first assignment was Ely Cathedral in the Fens near Cambridge in England.

It has been rated by the BBC as the second most beautiful cathedral in the world. They ranked the cathedral at Chartres in France as the finest. I deliberately made a visit Chartres to find out if this was correct. I reckon the BBC ranking is correct, but not by much.

I subsequently got involved in saving more historic British cathedrals at Gloucester, Worcester, Winchester, Exeter, Bath, and Portsmouth, plus Tewkesbury Abbey. They were filled with the tombs and history of kings and queens and the heroes of wars, as well as with magnificent art.

I also worked at less spectacular cathedrals at Edinburgh in Scotland, Limerick in Eire, Victoria in Canada, and Wellington in New Zealand, plus Newcastle, Adelaide, and Brisbane back home in Australia as well as the building of a new cathedral in Darwin after the original had been totally destroyed by a cyclone along with most of the city.

Then, as usual, there came my doubts about what I was achieving.

What did all my work with cathedrals achieve for humanity?

Do people really need to worship in splendid buildings?

Do we make the world a better place by restoring them?

All of those magnificent buildings (and most are incredibly beautiful) were built centuries ago by the great, the mighty, the wealthy and the powerful, in the hope that their actions would earn them pride of place in heaven and throughout eternity. Thousands of people worked and died in their construction. Those who survived were poorly paid for their labour or skill.

Except for millions of tourists who pay their way to enter, attendance at cathedrals is now quite sparse other than on the occasions of weddings and funerals of the famous. So it is that they now serve only as sentinels of history and examples of wonderful architecture where concerts and theatre can be performed and art displayed.

Should Churches still own and use them or should they be passed over to the state for use for public events? Good question.

Growing numbers of the homeless sleep in their grounds. They remind us that their care is one of our neglected community responsibilities that should challenge us as working partners of The Man.

I often ponder as to what I have achieved in terms of real value to humanity in my life among the cathedrals of our planet.

My hope is that it has been of some value and will lead us on to fostering a better quality of community life.

## 2.6 UNDERSTANDING THE BIBLE AND HYMNS

When I was at Sunday School at St Stephen's Presbyterian Church in Toowoomba a long time ago, the proceedings always got underway every Sunday morning with a routine of the superintendent carrying in a huge Bible while we all stood with heads bowed and called out 'This is the word of the Lord.' We were then told we must read and believe everything in it or we would not go to heaven. Nothing in it could be questioned.

I once asked my teacher how it was that if the Bible was written by God as his Word for us, how did he get it to us from heaven. How did those words come to be printed in our Bible and how can we be sure that this was what God wanted?

I received no answer and was put in the naughty corner.

This happened more than once. It made me a bit of a celebrity among the Sunday School kids. It really was quite enjoyable watching the teachers squirm a bit. However, the real problem for me was to wonder why I was not allowed to ask God a question. He gave me a brain so why could I not use it at Sunday School.

However, I made up my mind that I would continue to ask questions and I did so despite reprimands that continued through my adult years. Eventually, I reached a point where I decided that not much in the Bible is a provable fact. Even so, I recognise that it is the only significant record that we have of the coming of Christianity into our world. I formed the view that each chapter of the Bible should be read and careful thought then be given as to what is the essential message of the chapter. The words by themselves mean nothing.

Gradually, I recognised the obvious and became certain that the Bible was in truth not written by God at all, but by men would claimed that God had revealed its words to them. And he revealed it to them many years after the actual events that are described.

For example, when I was in Egypt a decade or more ago, I visited the place where Moses is said to be buried. There the monk in charge told me that the Old Testament account of the life of Moses was written five centuries after his death. How can anyone claim that it is accurate?

Nor can we claim that the Four Gospels, written forty or more years after Jesus's death were the Word of God when none of the writers knew him personally.

I now regard the Bible as a very special companion on my journey as it is the primary source to which you and I can go in search of the truth about our relationship with The Man.

History records that when the Bible was first created, many legitimate books about the faith were rejected by the Roman Emperor, Constantine. At the time of his deathbed conversion to Christianity, solely for political reasons, he doubted the personal loyalty of some of the authors without ever reading any of them.

Thus it is that I have come to the writings of great Christians who have revealed their relationship with The Man to us regularly over two thousand years. I have written many chapters about them in the pages that follow. I find their comments to be of more depth than those contained in the Bible as the writers of the Bible era were people who had no access to education and limited skill in the art of communication.

Allow me to now say something about hymn books.

I have always loved and cherished the splendid music of most hymns but, from an early age I have had concerns with the words. They are so ancient and mythical and childish and mawkish that they gradually switched me off as they always seemed to have no relationship with reality. The more that I questioned the accuracy of the Bible, the more I did not want to sing words of hymns that did not ring true.

At Sunday School, they always seemed to want us to sing 'Jesus loves me' when I did not want him to love me. I just wanted to do the good things that he did to help others. I had the same feelings about 'Fight the Good Fight.' I did not want to fight anyone. I sought mutual respect.

This leads me to confess that as my journey proceeded and as I tried to sing hymns at church I began to hum the wonderful tunes and try to think of new words that would identify with The Man, not the Christ. I still do this every Sunday.

I must confess that I once came to discover that the only hymn that has words that fire me up is Number 258 in *The Australian Hymn Book*, 'When I survey the wondrous cross.'

Written by Isaac Watts 350 years ago it simply and powerfully uses words that tell us only about Jesus on the cross, not the mythology that the Church has created about the end of his great life.

Then I found a few others in another hymn book called *Together in Song*. Those I got to like include the words:

'Make me a channel of your peace.'

'When I needed a neighbour.'

'Brother sister let me serve you.'

'A new commandment I give unto you.'

If I look hard enough, it is possible that I will find others.

But let me convey in conclusion a few more thoughts about the Bible and hymns.

Throughout my ninety-three years as a regular attender at church, I have respectfully enjoyed all the debates about the contents of the Bible. My major disappointment has been that far too many church members have closed minds. Sadly, I have too often discovered that their closed minds are an indication of the frailty of their faith as it is so weak it cannot survive any questioning. For them, it must be ironclad and certain.

In the same way hymns are sung by rote like parrots without giving any thought to what the words mean. The words of those hymns are just another way to sustain closed minds.

I have come to see that when people read the Bible and sing hymns it is an attempt to have their lives firmly based on certainty. They tend to fear anything that may shake that certainty.

Let me say that there is only one certainty that I have discovered over my nine decades: There is no such thing in life as certainty.

All that we have is courage. This is fostered in our souls as we walk with The Man along the pilgrim way as we endeavour to create a better world.

## 2.7 CONNECTING

As the years passed, I came to do some deep thinking about how and why I prayed. It has diminished as a crucial element of my faith as prayer seems to be used primarily when we are in trouble.

Eventually, I came to believe that the way I live my life is a never-ending prayer.

Words that I use in prayers, cannot hide, or replace the reality of what my life actually is.

Nor do I believe that I have any right to make any requests for help from The Man. Such requests are far too often an act of selfishness.

Every evening, I quietly go over in my mind how I have performed that day as a working partner of The Man and honestly reflect about that which were my failures while asking myself many questions such as:

- What good did I achieve during the day?
- What are my thoughts and actions about the events of the day?
- How can I tomorrow improve my performance in all aspects of my being?
- What new study and debate can I undertake to understand The Man and what can I do to be more effective as his partner?
- How can I find new friends to share my walk with The Man?
- How can I walk with them to change the world for the better?

Then I listen.

- I do not hear the voice of The Man instructing me to do anything.
- I do find that my power to reflect and plan and act expands mightily.

How can I adequately explain this?

I am still searching for answers, but one thing is evident:

EVERY THOUGHT AND ACTION OF MY LIFE IS A PRAYER.

## 2.8 REFORMATION

*Searching and learning and deciding on an upgraded path to the pilgrim way.*

I have never ever had a moment in my life where I decided to take up the traditional Church model of challenging its members to make a decision for Christ.

I have spent ninety-three years going to church on most Sundays and my faith has grown steadily at the same time as my questioning became more frequent.

I have never wanted or needed 'to be saved' and I never will.

My years of asking and studying and self-analysing have both been a witness to the diminishing role of Churches in society, at the same time as provoking serious questioning of the value of having ministers and theologians and administration bureaucrats at their helm.

At the same time, I have been searching diligently for my own reason for being and my need to create a far more committed relationship with The Man as I am as guilty as the Church leaders whom I criticise.

This has caused a significant reformation in my personal attitudes as well as making me realise that a revolution will be pointless unless I put it to work as an active evangelist for The Man, though not on behalf of any Church. I want to encourage my readers to walk with him as a role model without ever feeling an essential compulsion to have to attend a church.

There is now an urgency that reminds me every day that I have only a few years left to get off my backside and do constructive things to help solve the questions and challenges I raise in this book.

The seeds of my planning have been founded on what I have rediscovered on my fascinating journey along the pilgrim way by studying the lives of many great human beings whom I regard as prophets and who have significantly upgraded my views of life as the years have passed. This has enabled me to identify where I believe I am right now and relate my thinking as to where I hope and believe I am heading in my commitment to have an increasingly active role in ensuring that The Man becomes the role model of the world.

Above all, I hope that all I have learned from the very humble men and women who have shared my journey may be of value to you as you continue on your own journey.

All of this activity has led to a situation where I can assert that my desire to be a working partner of The Man has steadily and purposefully grown in depth and conviction and will continue to do so as every day of my life passes by.

I am constantly reminded as I walk with him that my commitment has grown steadily as I encountered, mainly by reading books, the inspirational people I will comment on throughout this book. Often, I would learn of them via sermons or films or, occasionally, having personal contact with those who have lived in my era.

Learning never ceases. It happened that during the time in which I have been writing *Walking with The Man* I read a great novel called *Monk Dawson* written by a fine author of religious novels, Piers Paul Read, an eminent British journalist. It is a fascinating story of a person whose religious experience went through six clear and distinct phases during his life.

The main character, Eddie Dawson, was born into a Catholic family and attended a Catholic school where he learned to be a devout Catholic. Then he chose to join a monastic order where his vocation was to teach wealthy children at a prestige catholic school. However, he soon became disenchanted as he felt his calling was to teach the children of the poor, not the rich. So his bishop moved him to become a parish priest in a poor community. There he lost his sense of allegiance to the Catholic faith as he felt the Church was doing nothing to help the plight of the poor.

So he gave up his vows and ceased to be a priest. He was a gifted author so he got a job at a newspaper writing feature articles about the great social issues of the day. But he was unhappy there too as the editors kept watering down his articles so as not to offend readers. This led him to resign and become a committed communist, earning his living doing casual work.

During this period of his life he had close relationships with two women at separate times. Both had huge mental issues in their lives and he had problems in coming to terms with his own sexuality after years of celibacy.

One left him and the other committed suicide causing him to feel a huge pain of guilt that shocked him into a reassessment of his entire being.

He approached a different order of monks to those of his earlier life and gained their permission to repeat his original vows but this group had a different view of the faith to the first one. These monks required vows of silence at all times. Communication was solely by sign language. He was required to become a humble labourer on a farm run by the order. His lengthy daily prayers were to be for others, never himself or his Church.

The book concludes with him conveying to a friend from the outside world that he was now totally at peace for the first time in his life. He felt it to be an honour to be known as Monk Dawson. He was home at last.

Reading this fine and thought provoking novel has caused me to make additions to some chapters of my book to indicate that there is not just one path to follow in seeking to walk with The Man. There can be many and they will be different for each one of us, sometimes changing dramatically and urgently.

There is no such thing as a perfect person and I have no aspirations whatsoever to becoming one.

In writing *Walking with The Man*, I have found it to be a great learning experience in itself to select which of the giants had the greatest impact on my life. There are, in fact, so many who have inspired me that I have had to make a careful selection of those who have influenced me the most. Circumstances have caused me to reluctantly omit many of my initial selection of those who helped to create a pathway for me. This is sad as they have all enabled me to make a deeper commitment to being a very active working partner of the greatest person who ever lived. Cold logistics won. Had I included them all, this book would have been larger than *War and Peace*.

Let me now tell you what I have discovered about the lives of sixty-five people whom I have happily researched in detail for inclusion in this book that has recharged me on my journey. Naturally, I hope it will be of genuine meaning to you. I have tried to relate what particular impact each one has had on me as they have been and still are powerful contributors to my transformation. They have led me to move from words to action on behalf of humanity as it is out at the coalface of life where The Man is, not locked away with holy people in Church buildings.

In fact, I have grave doubts that The Man was ever really understood in most of the churches that have closed down as far too many have been personal fiefdoms that specialised in creating closed minds as a means of staying in control of their flock.

Some of whom I have chosen to write about neither were, nor are, Christians. But I have been fascinated to find that their thinking was of a similar mould to that of Jesus and are worthy of serious comment.

Three others whom I have chosen actually taught me how easy it is to betray The Man, not that I have ever seriously contemplated doing so. I deliberately included them as their lives have provided important guidelines of how to handle occasional pitfalls that appear along the way.

Read on.

Learning from the people who have helped me discover the ground of my being has brought me to a discovery that Churches are no longer the vehicle to lead people to The Man.

# 3

# Founders Who Inspired Me

**IN CONSTANTLY SEEKING AND** welcoming inspiration from a wide variety of extraordinary leaders I can now chat with you about the first of those sixty-five special ones who hugely impressed me, often in quite different ways.

At the conclusion of each chapter, I have expressed in brief words a guidepost of what each one has meant to me.

Starting at the very beginning of New Testament times, I describe ten of the initial faith builders who powerfully influenced my life and my thinking from my Sunday School days and through my happy years in the PFA and beyond. The ten have been chosen from what I identify as the biblical influence on my life. They laid the foundations of my journey so they are the starting point of my path to humanitarian service along the pilgrim way.

Those whom I have carefully chosen are: Mary, Jesus, Mary Magdalen, James, Paul, Mark, Judas, Andrew, Pontius Pilate, and the Good Samaritan. In describing their lives, I have tried not to use biblical language or religious words. These are people worth knowing even if you are not in any way religious.

## 3.1 MARY

Without Mary it would not be possible for me to write a book about The Man.

As the world's most famous mother, I respect her as a very special person whose life is a powerful example of personal commitment to what she believed as her calling in life.

I bypass for the moment any debate about whether or not Mary was a virgin and whether it was ever necessary to create the myth of a virgin birth when Joseph could have been given a similar role to that of Mary as God's representative. It is enough to note here that a number of theologians believe the story of the virgin birth was added while the Gospels were being written. Later in this book there is a chapter about the symbol of the virgin birth.

So let us now share some thoughts about significant issues of her life.

For a long time, I have held the view that too little has been made of the huge decision that Mary and Joseph made when they fled to Egypt at a time when they feared that King Herod would kill Jesus. It meant that they valued their child's life ahead of their own security as they headed off to face the perils of an unknown land that was far away. It was a brave action which, in modern terms, should affirm to us that most refugees are a good people who are forced to react to perilous situations. They are not all a blight on society that far too many Australians now accuse them of being.

There is however a further issue to note about this incident.

As refugees, Joseph and Mary made a decision to return to their homeland just as soon as it was safe to do so. This attitude is a vision that all refugees should have in mind as a goal, simply because the land of our birth must always have a special place in our lives at all times. As a minimum, it is worth regular revisits if this is at all possible in the circumstances that may prevail at the time.

Egypt, which we often regard as a primitive nation, has always welcomed refugees, something that Australia has never done. We are the poorer for fostering our narrow attitude.

Then, many years later, Mary's strong character is highlighted by her courageous presence at the cross when she wept for her son as he was brutally put to death. Most of the friends of Jesus had run away in fear. If she too was frightened, she did not show it. She stayed there from the beginning right through to the very end even though her own life was in danger by doing so.

Harshly, her later life is recorded as having to face even more threatening incidents that caused her to flee for her life once again to a foreign land.

According to tradition, she travelled from Israel to southern Turkey to spend her final years, a huge distance in those days, probably walking all the way. There she created a small Christian community that revered her son. She is said to have died in Turkey and to be buried there. It is not publicly recorded as to who was with her on her journey or at her new home.

With great care, Christian and Muslim people have preserved and restored her home, with the approval of the Turkish government of the time. Indeed, the Turks not only allowed it to happen, they authorised it to remain open as a public monument to her for twenty centuries. This decision has not been contested by any subsequent government or any leaders of the Muslim faith.

Right now, it is open to tourists and Christians from around the world who visit it in their thousands.

Helen and I went out of our way to make sure we visited it while on a holiday in Turkey and we found it to be a moving experience as we contemplated her life and death and her devoted motherhood of the man who changed the world. The feeling of her presence remains with us as a treasured memory and we regard her home as one of the revered places of respect that we have visited during our many years of travel.

At one time, Helen and I were active members of the North Brisbane Inter Faith Group that is currently in recess for organisational reasons. I recall that at one of our meetings the local mullah told us that we should note and never forget that the Quran mentions Mary twenty-seven times. The mother of Muhammad is mentioned only once and not by name. This again reminds us of her immense stature as a person beyond the realm of Christianity.

The secular world has not forgotten her as, incredibly, there is a popular non-alcoholic drink enjoyed all around the world that is called a Virgin Mary. The alcoholic version is called a Bloody Mary. It tells us much about our society when we note that the alcoholic version is the most popular. A song has been composed that highlights it. 'Bloody Mary is the girl I love.'

However, let us raise ourselves above this every day level of social life, interesting though it is.

My personal view is that her life represents the ultimate aspiration for any woman who becomes a mother and seeks to enhance the status of motherhood as a cornerstone of a caring society.

She was humble, caring, loyal, enduring and deeply committed. A perfect example to those who walk with The Man.

Many people pray to her daily and always carry emblems of various designs that help them to feel close to her.

I think that they always will find inspiration from their closeness to her. An example of this is Bernadette Soubirous, about whom I have devoted a later chapter. She gained her sainthood from her vision of personal encounters with Mary at Lourdes.

In studying the lives of great people, there are always those who raise issues that can detract from their stature.

For example, I have met fundamentalist theologians who state emphatically that Jesus did not have a good relationship with his own family and declare that this has been made very clear by biblical references which indicate he stated that a true believer must give up his family, even hate them, in order to be deeply committed to the faith. However, that story is symbolic. It simply implies that there is no limit to the depth of our faith.

Some also claim that there is no evidence in the Scriptures that prove that Jesus loved Mary or was even close to her but it must be remembered that there are no words anywhere in the Bible that Jesus actually wrote himself.

I reckon that the bond between mother and son was solid. Their relationship as they fled Israel to take refuge in Egypt is just one instance of events that would have bonded them closely.

Who will ever know?

THE MARY GUIDEPOST

***Mary is a humble devoted person who risked her life to sit close to the cross so she could share the agony of her son.***

***She is a symbol of devotion.***

## 3.2 JESUS

The Romans crucified Jesus.

They claimed that they did it solely at the request of his own Jewish people, an accusation about which Jews have been (unjustly) chastised ever since, and probably will be for evermore. Adolph Hitler infamously used it as an excuse for the Holocaust. He declared that Jews had to be punished for the greatest crime in history.

The evidence reveals that the Roman governor, Pontius Pilate, was a smart enough politician to wash his hands of the whole affair and cause the leaders of the synagogue to publicly carry the can, an accolade for which they seem to have justly earned anyway.

The crucifixion was an event sparsely recorded by government records of the day and contemporary historians, but I accept it without hesitation.

Our primary information on the matter comes from the Gospel writers, Matthew, Mark, Luke, and John, even though there is no evidence they ever met him personally or witnessed his death. They wrote his story at least forty years after the momentous event and based their words on verbal evidence that had been passed on to them by witnesses. Whether or not they got it right or wrong does not bother me greatly even though they themselves disagree on some of the facts.

I want to record here honestly, sincerely, and clearly, that their Gospels are the sole part of the Bible that I seriously study as my prime biblical interest is Jesus alone. All the rest of the books of the Bible are interesting background reading of the history of a religion at that time. They just add padding to the core of the prime message of Jesus himself but has no deep impact on me.

Be this as it may, those four Gospels have sent the message of his crucifixion thundering through the ages as a mighty revelation of the death of a giant who has subsequently been proclaimed by billions to be the saviour of humanity.

Now, in a new world of science, technology, data collection and instant communication, census figures and polling reveal that only 25% of the world's population identify with him and the vast majority of those people are passive fellow travellers who have only a nominal association with his life and work. This has been caused by you and me persistently failing to do our best in effectively telling the old, old story of the life of a great being.

This means that others have stepped into the vacuum as the centuries have passed.

Mohammed is the only one who has assembled the numbers to seriously challenge Jesus in the record books of lasting fame. We should note with a feeling of negligence that in modern times his supporters do much more to win followers than Christians do for Jesus. Millions of Muslims are willing to die for Mohammed whereas few Christians cherish the thought of doing so for Jesus. Not that I recommend in any way that a willingness to die is a religious requirement for people of any faith.

Others, whether religious or political, pale into insignificance in the history of humanity in comparison to the stature of Jesus and Mohammed.

But there were some others of note.

Confucius, who was born many centuries before Jesus, had an expansive and creative mind as well as tremendous skills and commitment as a motivational philosopher. He deservedly rates highly, but this is confined mostly to China where Chairman Mao very skilfully used Confucian values to quietly lay the foundations for the Chinese people to accept communism as a political and financial ideology with most of them being unaware of it.

Julius Caesar had a moderate chance of maintaining long-term recognition as the creator of authoritarian governments over conquered lands, but most people do not admire him as he is also a prime example of how to win and lose power.

Mahatma Gandhi is immortal to Hindus and to the cause of freedom of expression by peaceful revolution, but his influence is mainly confined to India. Great man though he was, it is likely that he will be forgotten long before Jesus fades away into history, if ever.

Of even more note about these examples of leaders in world history is that far fewer of their followers have shown a willingness to give themselves totally to their cause as an indication of their personal devotion than have been willing to do so for The Man.

Artists and musicians and actors also have inspired us mightily from time to time and some achieve the status of gods but they ebb and flow in the public mind except perhaps for Shakespeare.

I identify with Jesus as an extraordinary person whose influence reaches deep into our souls to the extent that he is the ultimate role model of our lives and our prime hope as the beacon for the creation and advancement of an enlightened society.

Let me now comment on a crucial matter which is of great concern and disappointment to me and many others as it is a matter I will refer to again in other chapters.

No one has ever found even one single document that contains any personally written words of Jesus.

Everything we know about him is hearsay, words that others have reported as having been said by him. It would be a momentous experience of deep faith to read his own words, written by his own hands rather than read the words that the Gospel writers have put on his lips. Despite my asking this question of many theologians throughout my life in the Church, no one has ever been able to give me a reason why so many other famous individuals in the Bible wrote something down but he did not, despite his immense intellect and his ability to convey messages in simple terms.

To find such a tome would be regarded as the greatest archaeological discovery of all time, but I also believe that the finder would face a huge task in actually proving, beyond reasonable doubt, that Jesus actually wrote it.

All of the above might in some way substantiate claims that no such person as Jesus ever existed. Some see him as a mythical figure of inspirational presence and regard instances of his existence as rare but nevertheless they do occur here and there. It is worthy of note that the Muslim faith records him as a revered prophet whereas it would be to their advantage to deny his existence.

Despite this huge gap in our knowledge of Jesus's ministry to humanity, no one can now walk along the Via Dolorosa in Jerusalem and stop in quiet reflection before each of the Stations of the Cross on the way to Golgotha without having a genuine sense of being in his presence. Are we able to contemplate what each one of us would have been willing or compelled to do at huge risk to our lives to save him, had we been present on that fateful day?

I felt this on each of the three occasions that I went there and will never forget the experience.

The same applies, with a little less impact, when one visits the tiny Garden of Gethsemane where he was betrayed, as well the site of the Sermon on the Mount or the scene at Cana where he turned water into wine or the place on the little bay where he walked on the water to save Peter. This is especially so with his birth place in Bethlehem where the Church of the Nativity stands, reportedly on the site where the stable was located beside the overcrowded inn.

All of these experiences make Jesus more relevant to me than a vision of a mystical God whom we cannot see or touch or bring to reality in our minds. I will jot down more of my thoughts on these issues as this book progresses.

However, at this moment, I will state emphatically that throughout the entire realm of the search for faith that many constantly tread, the presence of The Man will never cease to have an impact on people like you and me.

I have a valued friend who is an agnostic. He sees the values of atheism as making more sense than Christianity. Like me he has walked the Via Dolorosa and he regards it as one of the treasured memories of his life, very aware that this indeed was the pathway that Jesus trod on his way to the cross. He holds the view that it is not possible for either an atheist or an agnostic to do this walk and not be intensely aware that a very special person had walked every step of this famous road carrying a crippling burden that would result in an immense change in world history.

Many of us believe that there is a power within our souls that comes from beyond ourselves and which puts meaning and purpose into our lives for as long as we live. We know that we are indeed privileged to walk with The Man along the pilgrim way. fuelled by his special manner of caring and sharing.

This does not mean that we should promote Jesus as a hero. But we can believe that he was a leader who has motivated us always to do the right things for humanity via compassion and justice.

*THE JESUS GUIDEPOST*

***Jesus is the ultimate example of infinite wisdom, inspirational leadership, profound teaching, and unlimited compassion.***

## 3.3 MARY MAGDALEN

As we are all aware, this Mary is very different from the revered one who is the mother of Jesus.

Even so, she is nevertheless a substantial and respected figure of biblical history and a person whom I have always held in high regard as one who left us some challenging messages.

Curiously, there is an interesting community that still exists in Provence in the south of France whose residents have seriously and persistently claimed for many centuries that they are direct descendants of Mary Magdalen and Jesus.

They declare they are able to prove conclusively that Jesus married her soon after the resurrection and then fled to France to avoid capture by the Romans. Some theorists of vivid imagination claim she was pregnant with Jesus before the crucifixion. I think that we can leave them to enjoy their delusions even though celebrated American author, Dan Brown, heavily speculated about it in his religious thriller *The Da Vinci Code* which is based in France and has been read by millions worldwide. In its final page it claims that Mary Magdalen is buried in Paris and the hero of the story claims to have discovered where she can be found.

The key issue is that she had a very special and respectful relationship with Jesus and splendidly represents the truth that no person, even one so lowly as a supposedly sinful woman, can be so disgraceful that Jesus would not identify with them, nor treat them as dear friends. She was a prime convert to a new life, an example of how our world will change if we have millions who choose to build a closer relationship with The Man and who will become empowered to achieve great things.

She is often referred to as being a prostitute even though this has never been definitively proven. But because of this view of her, history has revealed to us that most congregations of Christians down through many centuries have not allowed prostitutes into their ranks. Records clearly show that Church leaders have gone out of their way to humiliate them as lesser beings. This proves that far too many Churches have been in outright conflict with Jesus on this matter – to their eternal shame – and on many other issues.

This issue begs the question as to how many Christians have, in reality, ever been genuine working partners of Jesus who seek no reward.

We face the unavoidable fact that too many have just concentrated on the selfish pursuit of saving their own souls, an activity that will eventually leave most of them to be very disappointed in where their holiness has led them. The blunt embarrassment is that some Christians give the appearance of being respectable fakes. However, we can give thanks that, despite this, many other Christians are exactly the opposite in taking care to walk along exactly the same path as The Man in personally identifying with the downtrodden of humanity.

This situation regarding whatever sins Mary Magdalen may have committed gives me an opportunity to reemphasise one of the core messages of this book and identify it as one of the prime reasons why I have written and published it.

My thoughts are based on this fact:

Walking and working with Jesus the Man has no requirement to seek forgiveness for our sins.

None whatsoever.

Nevertheless, it does require us to personally take action to meet those whom we have hurt, fixing, and paying for our sins right now.

Our partnership with The Man is all about love, compassion, sharing, learning, justice, peace, generosity, and service to all humanity no matter how much others may differ from us in their religious beliefs or their social and political status.

I firmly believe that I am required to make personal reparations for every one my sins with the people whom I have hurt by those sins and pay whatever the cost of doing this happens to be, even if it is huge and very difficult to pay, or threatening to my reputation.

I am certain that would be an absolutely cowardly act for me to hide behind God and seek forgiveness. It would be not just cowardly, but gutless.

Indeed I do not ever seek forgiveness from anyone or anything except from whoever I have hurt.

Whenever I think about Mary Magdalen, I think of a solid and loyal soul who changed her ways when she met Jesus and sought to serve him to the fullest extent of her capacity to do so.

Her revered place in biblical history was assured when she went to his tomb three days after his crucifixion to care for his body. Whether it can be proven that he had risen from the dead or, alternatively, had never died of his serious wounds, does not matter one iota. She went to the tomb before any of the disciples were brave enough to do so and sought to be near the man who had turned her life around. She was seeking no reward, just the honour of being with him and of continuing to experience the spiritual power that he had stored in her soul.

In my world, she is a prime example of a penitent person who sought a new life and achieved it splendidly.

*THE MARY MAGDALEN GUIDEPOST*

***No person is unqualified to be a working partner of The Man.***

## 3.4 JAMES

For much of my life I took little interest in the life and work of James, brother of Jesus, as he had been almost anonymous in the Christian story that progressively moulded my life. Most of my preachers and teachers just ignored him. Except for one occasion, I can't ever remember hearing a sermon about James but then again, three out of every four sermons I have heard have been eminently forgettable.

I began to do some serious research about James after I enjoyed an intriguing sermon one Sunday that was based on a dispute between James and Paul of Tarsus over what was the core message of the life and legacy of Jesus.

Paul, who did not ever meet Jesus, based his entire ministry on the belief that Christianity was primarily about being saved from our sins and thereby achieving eternal life.

James, who is often referred to as James the Just, had experienced the privilege of living with Jesus for three decades, said the core message from the life of his brother was about creating sharing communities where his followers would care for one another, just as the original disciples did. Those communities would reach out to others beyond their habitat to do likewise. The powerful witness of James was about giving, not getting any of the spiritual rewards that Paul was offering.

It is on record in the Scriptures that James and Paul met face-to-face on one occasion in an attempt to resolve their differences, but it seems that they did not succeed in achieving unanimity.

Paul eventually won the public relations battle convincingly as the world accepted his version and heard very little about James. Clearly, Paul was a hugely talented, persuasive, and committed communicator while James appeared to have lacked this talent.

However, I find it astonishing that modern Christianity has not taken up the cause of James and reduced the impact of Paul. The life of James is more in tune with the state and needs of humanity today. Indeed, the biblical book of ACTS should be more about James than Paul.

James lived his faith sincerely.

However, as we know from our life experience, it is the polarisation of beliefs that is actually a mirror of life experience. We know that powerful communicators usually win the day no matter what the evidence. We have all met many committed believers who spent their entire lives caring for others without seeking any earthly or eternal rewards but did not have the talent to convince others that this was the clear mission of Jesus.

I regard it as an enormous tragedy that Paul sold his sincerely held conviction of personal redemption so well that it has fostered a dominance of selfishness in society. The prime focus of Paul's message is that we must all save ourselves and this attitude inevitably fosters greed.

The understanding I have gained from reading about James from a number of sources is that the small community he created in Jerusalem immediately after the crucifixion of Jesus was a society in which no one owned any personal property or possessions. The community itself held all the money needed for its people to survive and prosper as a way of life for all, not just a privileged few. This enabled his people to work together to create a sharing society that mirrored the life of Jesus. It was a great example how there can be a well bonded society without greed especially as they reached out to help people who were in need beyond their community.

The community that James led has been described by some critics as the model communist society that

Marx and Lenin attempted to copy and create but failed to achieve.

History has made it clear that the Marxist way of life failed because they tried to achieve a sharing society by ruthlessly gaining political power and then using it to create a ruling class that would make equality work effectively. However, in practice the ruling class looked after themselves first and did little about equality for humanity. James achieved it correctly at the grassroots level via the power of love and the compelling appeal of Jesus as a role model.

The dream of James was pure magic but, apparently, it died when James was killed by the Romans just a few years after Jesus as there were no more leaders of his quality to perpetuate it and there are very few instances of it surviving anywhere else in the Christian world today in the manner that James had planned.

This is a tragedy but a powerful question remains. Is it possible to be recreate the vision of James today?

The blunt challenge for us is this. Who among us has the spiritual power and organisational skill to lead society while accepting all the personal sacrifices that will be involved in making it successful and meaningful for all involved?

Huge question which involves significant personal cost.

No quick and easy answers are obvious and I must confess that I don't have one at this moment.

But it is a visionary thought, even though it makes me feel hugely uncomfortable. It would take a tremendous personal reformation within my soul for me to put all my possessions into the coffers of a caring community in which I would have to put my complete trust. A huge ask in which I fall short and I am aware that this reduces my value as a working partner of The Man.

Even so, I can't help wondering what would have happened if in different circumstances Paul and James had been together for a long period at the same time and same place just before Paul made his decision to begin his powerful crusade to convert the world to his selfish version of the faith.

Let me make it clear. I am firmly in Team James, not Team Paul, but James at this moment would have no option but to regard me as a slacker.

*THE JAMES GUIDEPOST*

***James lived with Jesus and understood him far more clearly than any other.***

***His vision of his brother's plan for the world is worth serious consideration.***

## 3.5 PAUL

While I am not a fan of his, it is an honest comment for me to state that Paul of Tarsus was, and still is, the greatest salesman the world has ever known or may ever know.

Indeed, I have met professional marketers who hold a carefully considered view that there is absolutely no question about his qualifications to be awarded this well-deserved accolade.

When I studied for my marketing diploma (CPM) at evening classes seven decades ago, I wrote an essay about Paul. It won me a prize (a lunch voucher). All of the class had been asked to write a thousand words on the subject of 'Who is the greatest salesman in the history of the world?'

I had no hesitation in deciding to base my essay on St Paul and confidently achieved a thousand words without having to stretch my imagination. When responding to a question by the lecturer as to why I chose Paul, I discovered that all of my fellow students and the lecturer were amazed at both the scope and manner of his enormous achievements as an evangelist in selling an invisible product. (It was notable that no one in the room other than me did any Bible reading).

I affirm that I was fascinated by his zeal in travelling to the entire known world of that time, visiting nations where he did not know the language or the people. He had no friends in those places, nor introductions to anyone who had power and influence, had no media to back him and no literature that he could hand out. Yet he won many people to a faith he passionately believed in and he did it so well that its depth did not fade. Indeed, many centuries later, there are still active Christian communities in all of the places he visited.

All of this eventually led to Helen and I making a personal journey of discovery to study one of the great successes of all of his extraordinary achievements. Thirty years ago, we chose to spend a week visiting Malta. We found it to be a remarkable experience.

Our rented villa was located at St Paul's Bay on the western end of the island where the great man had been shipwrecked when the Romans were taking him to Rome as a prisoner. We made sure that we visited all the places that revealed key evidence of his visit.

The most significant was the small underground cell where he had been imprisoned. We took time to read the local account of how he converted his jailer to Christianity and then with his help also converted the Roman governor who subsequently allowed groups of Christians to meet openly and grow in numbers. Now, no nation in the world has a greater number of Christians per head of population than Malta, nor does any nation have as many churches per hectare as Malta does. Paul undeniably sold his message solidly and permanently.

Years later, we made a visit to Ephesus in Turkey to check out the impact of his visit there which is recalled in the letter to the Ephesians in the New Testament. His time there is embedded in local folklore and his memory still revered.

The account of his conversion to the faith on the Damascus Road has become a legend, both in Christian and in secular history, as it was incredibly spectacular. People with no Christian background often refer to others who have expressed a significant change of mind on an issue as having experienced a 'Damascus Road Conversion' and most of us understand exactly what this means. Paul had decisively changed from being a murderer to being a man of God.

Paul's personal experience convinced him that Christianity is based on forgiveness of our sins. He was certain that he had been forgiven for the appalling life he had led previously and felt compelled to take that special message out to the world. He did not ever shrink from his commitment to this task.

In Christian circles, people who become evangelists and missionaries are now deemed to be walking in the steps of St Paul and their vocation is hugely honoured because of his enduring legacy. This is fascinating as nowhere is it recorded that Paul did not ever refer to followers of Jesus as being Christians. In his mind, they were followers of the Man

So, it is with a genuine sense of sadness that I must restate and reinforce the comments I have made in the previous chapter on James.

I firmly believe that the great salesman superbly sold the wrong message to all whom he met, an observation I will describe in more detail in later chapters. Even so, it is abundantly clear to me that he believed what he said and like Jesus and Peter, he died while standing fast for his deeply held convictions.

May I once more reassert my firm belief that it is wrong to base Christianity on selfishness – our desire to be saved from our sins and our need to find a place in heaven. This is not what Jesus told the world. Far from it. Jesus the Man was all about service to humanity.

Let me conclude by making a couple of personal comments on his life.

The fact that Paul completely changed from being a murderer of Christians to becoming a powerful advocate of a faith that many died for, indelibly outlines the way in which an encounter with The Man can change the life of any person.

I find it fascinating also to discover that he was very uncomfortable in the presence of women, declaring in one of his letters that a woman must never speak or pray aloud in a public place. He got this wrong too. While Churches have long pompously given power to men as leaders, it has always been women who worship in far greater numbers and with much greater commitment as well as greater talent.

Some theologians believe that Paul was homosexual, but this is of no consequence whether it be true or false. No matter what his sexual preferences may have been, he was a believer in the man from Nazareth.

Having said all of this, while I proudly walk on a far different pilgrim pathway to Paul, he remains a formidable figure whom I cannot totally dispense with and must not ever ignore.

*THE PAUL GUIDEPOST*

***I am disappointed with his message to the extent that he now does not have a major role in my journey.***

***Nevertheless, I hugely respect and enthusiastically copy his professional skills as a salesman.***

## 3.6 MARK

Saint Mark founded the Coptic Church at Alexandria, the centre of education and culture in Egypt during the first century. This new Church would grow to become a significant, powerful, and long lasting Christian presence in Egypt and beyond.

The Copts were independent souls creating their own Bible as well as having a unique set of beliefs, creeds and dogmas that differ in many respects to those of the mainline Churches of the West. Nevertheless, their statements of their faith are sincerely held. They are not controversial dissidents creating waves.

In the twenty-first century, the Copts are the largest Church of the Christian faith in the Muslim Middle East which means they are currently and regularly suffering persistent persecution. I wrote about them in my book *Catching the Linville Train* as it made an impact on me.

I visited a Coptic community in the countryside not far from Cairo two decades ago. I had a wonderful conversation with their spiritual leader who told me that he proudly modelled his life on Mark. Some months later my new found friend was killed in a violent and unprovoked raid on his church by Muslim extremists. I remember with reverence the love he had expressed towards all humanity and the way he was totally relaxed about the differences between his faith and mine, and so was I. I regard his death as a great loss to the compassionate practice of grace and peace.

Furthermore, why is it that people of one religion feel called by their God to kill believers of another faith? Their action has absolutely nothing to do with God. It is undeniably an act of pure evil.

All of my quiet research about Mark highlights the fact that he, like Paul, was an evangelist preacher, just as we are all called to do likewise even though we may have widely varying messages.

Sadly, evangelism is low in the agenda of most modern Churches and the quality of preaching has sharply declined in my lifetime. I can't pinpoint why as it is undeniable that in choosing to walk with The Man we have no option but to sell to the world whatever it is that we personally believe and that motivates us to care for all humanity.

Mark's most notable claim to fame in history is that he is the first writer of the Gospels in the New Testament. He originally wrote it in Greek, similarly to the three other authors, Matthew, Luke, and John. He was not a proven eyewitness to the events that he wrote about. He, and they, faithfully tried to pass on the powerful legend that had been portrayed to them. Of course, we have the right to debate whether or not a person who was not an eyewitness may, unwittingly, detract from the validity of Jesus's message.

Nevertheless, he was the first of the four Gospel writers in the field and was ten years ahead of the other three. There is clear evidence that they copied much his account of the life of Jesus and they added two matters which have caused the most controversy down the centuries. He did not highlight a virgin birth or appearances after the resurrection. They clearly did, wrongly I believe.

Mark was born in North Africa at a place called Cyrene in Libya, not far from the border of Egypt. It is interesting that another biblical character, Simon of Cyrene, was also directly involved with Jesus.

Mark's family migrated to Cana in Galilee and it is believed that he was an attendant to Paul and Barnabas when they took the faith to Antioch. It appears that he was present when they had a considerable dispute and separated, with Mark siding with Barnabas. This reminds us that Jesus's brother James was not the only person who fell out with Paul.

Mark finally settled in Egypt at Alexandria where he established the Coptic Church in the year 48 CE, dying as a martyr twenty years later. Pagans who violently resented his presence tied him to the tail of a horse and had him dragged through the streets for two days until his body was torn to shreds.

His head was retrieved by his followers and preserved. It can been seen to this day in St Mark's Coptic church in Alexandria. Some of the relics of his life are on display at St Mark's Cathedral in Cairo and at the San Marco cathedral in Venice, Italy.

The Coptic Church today remembers him with great reverence, not only as its founder, but as an evangelist, apostle, witness and martyr of great courage and achievement.

He was much more than that.

Many, including me, honour him as a leader who showed to us that there are many genuine versions of the old story of the life of Jesus other than those contained in the Christian Bible.

He was a beacon shining in the world to remind us that rigid fundamentalists are totally wrong in claiming that the Bible is the only true account of the faith and is, therefore, in their minds beyond dispute.

The Coptic Bible is valid, as are the many other books that should have been included in the Christian Bible but were left out by deathbed decisions of Constantine. He heavily played local politics in deliberately choosing to leave out books written by people he did not like personally even though they were of authentic quality.

I give Mark huge stature as a religious leader of vision and courage.

As a working partner of The Man you should read Mark's Gospel carefully. I find that the best way to do this was to buy a book called *The Gospel of Mark*, written many decades ago by the eminent Scottish theologian, William Barclay. It offers a series of very readable daily Bible studies that works its way through the Gospel in an enlightening manner.

Because of his expansive mind, Barclay was constantly attacked by fundamentalists throughout his eminent career at the University of Glasgow. They correctly accused him of being a modernist but the clear evidence is that he was a middle of the road theologian of huge stature who spoke with honesty as an open minded scholar.

*The Gospel of Mark* is an enlightening read that will expand the minds of all who follow The Man.

THE MARK GUIDEPOST

***The Coptic Bible is of equal standing with the Bible that I have been reading all my life.***

***There is much we can learn from it.***

## 3.7 JUDAS

This man is one of the most maligned people in human history. It is my personal belief that he has been treated very badly and unfairly.

Undeniable logic asserts that if Judas had not betrayed Jesus in the Garden of Gethsemane on that dramatic evening at the onset of the crucifixion, the Christian faith would not exist in the manner that we understand it today. It can be validly claimed that without the role of Judas as the scapegoat of the crucifixion and the resurrection, the faith would have died with Jesus.

We are saying that Judas was set up by God as someone was needed to betray Jesus. Therefore, he was chosen by destiny to do the job simply because it had to be done.

It is claimed that he committed suicide by hanging himself in shame, and he did this after throwing his thirty pieces of silver on the ground in front of the high priests at a place now called The Field of Blood. The silver has forever been known as blood money and indeed caused those two words to be the folklore of tainted assets.

Now, the calling of any person by the name of Judas is commonly used as an insult in every walk of life to describe someone who is a betrayer, anyone who can't be trusted or will sell his or her soul for money, a person who will betray you in the worst possible way.

My reading of the Scriptures leads me to believe with complete certainty that the high priests had clearly made up their minds to crucify Jesus no matter what the circumstances were. Judas was not in any way needed by them to ensure that a crucifixion could be carried out. Theologians tell us that there was no mention of Judas in early Christian history. His role as a betrayer was not recorded until many years later when Mark wrote his Gospel.

I hold the view that the Judas legend is a biblical tale created to teach a lesson that would convey to us what the gross sin of a betrayal of a friend really is.

In fact, the Gnostic Gospel of Judas actually exonerates him and claims he was instructed by Jesus to do what he did so his death and resurrection could take place. They said that when Jesus spoke the words at the last supper, 'one of you will betray me,' he knew exactly who it was because he had arranged for it to happen.

In determining the difference between fact and fiction about any event recorded in the Bible, it is important to note that even such a great believer as C S Lewis said that he rejected the view that every statement in Scripture must be accepted as an historical truth.

I could easily expand on all of the above endlessly as the Judas tale has been recorded and debated with millions of words for thousands of years and will continue for many more. But this will achieve nothing of value for believers to add to their faith. The fact is that Judas came from a respected family and was a faithful servant until this event is recorded. He is on my list of people whom I regard as having been wrongly discredited. Down the centuries, there have been far too many fall guys who have been treated the same way.

So it is that his fame, or infamy, will continue to be enhanced for all the wrong reasons.

In a lifetime of happy evenings of good theatre, I greatly enjoyed that splendid and popular musical created by Andrew Lloyd Webber that he called 'Jesus Christ Superstar.' It should be noted that the main character was Judas, not Jesus.

Also carefully read *The Gospel According to Judas*. written in recent times by the prolific and highly successful British novelist, Jeffrey Archer, in association with his friend, Frank Moloney, who is an eminent theologian and who has verified the logic of what Archer described. This Gospel is small in size, but powerfully worded, and convincingly records Archer's belief that Judas was framed.

Many other books also tell his story. You can track them down on Google.

Some of the most notable are *The Problem of Natural Evil* by Betrand Russell who uses Judas as a prime example of how evil occurs, and a short story by Jorge Luis Borges called *Three Versions of Judas*, as well as *The Passover Plot* by British New Testament Scholar, Hugh Schonfield. The latter is firm in his conviction that Judas acted with the full knowledge and consent of Jesus. More recently, controversial theologian John Shelby Spong in his book, *The Sins of Scripture*, bluntly says that the Judas story does not describe a real event. He says it was 'constructed.'

So the Judas debate will continue to fascinate us.

What cannot be denied is that he was, and still is, a famous element of influence in understanding the life and witness of The Man.

*THE JUDAS GUIDEPOST*

***Judas is a prime example of those who carry the burden of blame for the sins of others.***

## 3.8 ANDREW

'I will make you fishers of men.'

With those famous words to Andrew, Jesus launched the evangelisation of the world, including also Andrew's more famous brother, Simon Peter, as part of the team.

Both of them took their assignment seriously and they eventually achieved results that were quite extraordinary.

Peter concentrated his efforts mainly on Rome while Andrew went much further afield. There is historical evidence that he travelled from his home in Galilee to Greece, Cyprus, Georgia, Malta, Romania, and Ukraine. Relics of his missionary endeavours have been found in Spain and Scotland even though he did not visit either.

Today, Andrew is not only the patron saint of Scotland where his most devoted followers are now located, but he has been given that same honour in cities located in Barbados, Romania, Russia, Ukraine, Malta, Greece, Italy, Philippines, and Turkey. Statues, paintings, and shrines dedicated to him can be found in most of the nations of the world where people practise Christianity.

How did this happen? Andrew and his brother were humble fishermen whose education had been very sparse and they had no real knowledge or experience of the nations of the world that existed beyond the Holy Land.

The short answer is they both ventured forth in total obedience following a clear calling from Jesus to share the faith. Both were crucified for their faithful work – Peter in Rome and Andrew in Patras, Greece when both were around sixty years of age.

Like St Paul, they conquered distance and language problems with incredible bravery and skill but, quite differently to Paul they knew Jesus personally and walked confidently in his footsteps. Both were with him at the Last Supper and on the day of his crucifixion.

Peter famously denied knowing Jesus on three occasions, while Andrew quietly witnessed the tumultuous event. What I had not known previously is that Andrew was initially a devoted follower of John the Baptist and only met Jesus around the time that John baptised him.

The influence of Andrew on my life arose out of the fact that I became a Presbyterian and found that Andrew was the cornerstone of that Church. I soon discovered that the mother Church of the Presbyterian Church of Australia was the Church of Scotland. Their traditions are powered by Saint Andrew who had become the patron saint of Scotland when in 1832 Scottish leaders declared before a battle against the English that, if they won, they would dedicate their victory to St Andrew. They proudly honoured the promise.

I have five personal associations with Andrew.

When the Presbyterian Church of Queensland in 1956 decided to build St Andrew's Hospital on Wickham Terrace in Brisbane, I was appointed organising secretary, a decision that launched my long career internationally as an organiser of projects for not-for-profit and institutions.

Years later, The Presbyterian Fellowship decided to organise a major drive to enlist new members and I was invited to be its chairman. The venture was called Operation

Andrew and it was a great success. Young Christians went out to personally approach other young people to join their ranks by promoting a simple message that Jesus was a great role model to follow.

I have often attended traditional Scottish dinners on St Andrew's Day which is observed in Australia on 30 November every year. Much Scotch whisky is consumed and a haggis is piped in on a shovel of smoking peat.

At one point in my religious life I was given a small replica of a St Andrew's cross after preaching at a church that was named after him. At some point in shifting homes five times, I lost it and I miss it. It is important to note that the flag of Scotland is the cross of St Andrew.

As a keen golfer, the grand course at St Andrew's in Scotland is the holy of holies for all golfers. Sadly my golf is not of sufficient quality to be invited to play there.

Then one night I stayed in a hotel in Edinburgh that was located in St Andrew's Square. I was allocated a room with large windows right above the statue of St Andrew that dominated the square. I was able to lie in bed and look at him in the moonlight. It fascinated me to think that this great man had an influence so far from his home during an era when communications were very sparse indeed.

I remembered a Bible verse: 'The disciples went out and spread the good news everywhere.' Subsequently, I looked it up, Mark 16:19.

On that Edinburgh evening, I whispered an apology to him for my negligence in not devoting quality time to follow Andrew's example and find new followers of Jesus.

The reality is that I am far behind him in my achievements as an evangelist but still yearn to get somewhere near his quality of commitment and determination and persistence and bravery.

The fact is that congregations of mainline Churches are dying everywhere because too many are little closed groups who feel uncomfortable when outsiders arrive as their presence may force them to change their Sunday School mentality.

However, in my old age I have found that it is quite easy to invite people to adopt The Man as their role model. My weakness is that I don't do it persistently enough.

*THE ANDREW GUIDEPOST*

***Andrew was an utterly reliable servant. Jesus gave him a specific job to do and he did it. Our world needs more faithful and committed souls like him.***

## 3.9 PONTIUS PILATE

Traditionally, the world has believed that there were three bad guys in action on the day that Jesus was crucified – Judas, Pilate, and Peter.

The charges against them are:

- Judas was accused of betraying him.
- Pilate washed his hands of the whole affair.
- Peter ratted on him.

As I made clear in an earlier chapter, I hold the firm view that Judas was made a scapegoat while Peter thoroughly redeemed himself, but I find it difficult to say much that is complimentary about Pontius Pilate.

Firstly, let us take a look at his record as a person and a leader as clearly recorded in the annals of Roman history.

It is important to note that he was not a mythical person created by a religion.

He has been clearly identified as the fifth governor of the Roman province of Judaea. He was appointed to that post for a decade by Emperor Tiberius commencing in 27 CE. He had a troubled relationship with the Jewish people for the entire decade, governing them with ever increasing brutality.

Tiberius eventually recalled Pilate to Rome to be examined about the constant complaints that were laid against him. However, Tiberius died before Pilate reached home. Nevertheless, Pilate eventually appeared before the new emperor, Caligula, and as a result of this meeting he did not return to Judaea. It is not known whether he declined to return or whether it was that Caligula sacked him.

Pilate then disappeared from public view for unknown reasons and many rumours abound about what happened to him.

One historical record indicates that he committed suicide, just as Judas had done, after having publicly acknowledged his sins and repented of them.

Other records say that this is nonsense and claim that he became a Christian and took the Gospel to Lyon and Vienne, both in France. The town of Tarragona in Spain makes a similar claim. In all three places there are memorials to Pilate in churches.

Christians are usually baffled when they learn that the Church of Ethiopia venerates him as a martyr and a saint, while Coptic Christians have a feast day in his honour every June. Both of those Churches are firm in the belief that it was the Jews who killed Jesus, not Pilate.

So, where does this leave us in our search to understand this man?

Roman records show that Pilate had officially reported to Rome that he had crucified a man call Christos at Jerusalem. Those sceptics from around the world who claim that Jesus is a mythical figure are proved incorrect by this evidence from the man who ordered the crucifixion.

The Bible makes it clear that it was the Jews who forced Pilate to crucify Jesus. However, history records that Pilate alone had the power to appoint the high priests of the Temple. They owed their positions to him so it is not credible to claim that they forced him to kill Jesus. He was their master and had no obligation to do anything they asked.

He established a tradition that on feast days he would release one Jewish prisoner recommended by the high priests. So it was not odd that he released Barabbas on their recommendation on that fateful day. It was not a political stunt for him to give the Jews a choice of who would be killed that day,

The key factor is that the record shows that he washed his hands of the whole matter and so a tradition has been handed down the centuries that people could wash their hands of a responsibility just as Pilate had done. Millions of us have done exactly that on more than one occasion throughout our lives when we had a responsibility to do something. We avoided it, washing our hands and saying that the event was not our fault or was beyond our responsibility.

A few other observations can now be put on the table.

Through every age since the day of the crucifixion, the Jewish people have been persistently blamed for killing Jesus because Pilate had washed his hands of all responsibility for the atrocity. The lethal punishment that they have constantly received in many nations since then as the result of this charge can be regarded clearly as a trumped-up accusation that will probably continue.

As the result of it all, Pontius Pilate became the most famous Roman provincial governor in the history of their mighty empire.

In reality, he is one of the most famous people in world history. He is also the world's most famous hand washer. Millions learned the art during Covid19. However, the story of Pontius Pilate reminds us that when history is debated, truth is usually the first casualty.

*THE PONTIUS PILATE GUIDEPOST*

***A veteran politician once said to me: 'Everald, with whatever projects you undertake, make sure you work out beforehand who is going to take the blame if it fails. It will save you a lot of unnecessary anguish.'***

***Our parliaments are filled with people who wash their hands far too often.***

## 3.10 THE GOOD SAMARITAN

I have deliberately left my comments on this good and decent man to be the last chapter of this section of my book. Even though he is a mythical character, his impact has greatly inspired my life and yours in our work in the community and we should give him a well-deserved and special acknowledgement.

He represents one of the world's finest examples of the tradition and practice of goodwill to one another, but yet we do not know his name. I have searched far and wide and can find no theologian who ever refers to him by name.

Nevertheless, most of us can identify with the well-known accolade of life that is used whenever someone does a good deed. Invariably, people will say to them: 'You are a Good Samaritan.'

Of all the Sunday School lessons I ever heard, the story of the Good Samaritan is the one that has impressed me greatly and permanently. To me, his generous and compassionate deed is what following The Man is all about.

I reckon that practising the intent of this man is a far more important act of faith than trying to save my own soul and hoping I may get into heaven. Those two dogmas that dominate the traditional faith have always seemed to me to be ultra selfish. I give them a very low rating.

So it is that, down the years, I have often given thought to the crucial elements of this story that have become a cornerstone of my reason for being.

The sad part of this parable it is that it is set in a world where Samaritans and Jews hated one another with a burning passion and this gave me my first lesson on racism which is an appalling attitude for anyone to have about another person. I firmly rejected it from that point onwards.

The priest and the Levite who passed by the beaten man on the other side of the road painted for me a picture of a bad practice describing what I subsequently regarded as a far too common element of my daily life.

I know that I have often tried to excuse myself from any responsibilities that could cause me discomfort. There have been too many occasions on my life journey when I have been with people whom I should have helped when they got into strife but I have too often been able to find a very convenient excuse for not getting involved in any way that would help them sort out their problems.

The Good Samaritan was a totally different character.

Not only did he pay the bill for the injured man to be cared for at the inn, he promised to pay more when he returned if it was needed. He was under no obligation to do this but was quite willing to do so as it was his natural response to the needs of other people. His care for an unknown neighbour went far beyond the call of duty, especially as the wounded man is assumed to have been Jewish, who were the enemies of his own race.

Jesus was a great storyteller. In this one, he highlights what was a regular and powerful theme of his ministry in which the background of this incident is based on two compelling questions: 'Who is my neighbour?' and 'Am I my brother's keeper?'

They remain as the same powerful social questions all these years later and most of us still go to great lengths to avoid answering them.

Strangely and sadly, all my searching on the World Wide Web has revealed to me that theologians from all quarters have tried often to strongly project their own version of the meaning of the humanity shown by the Good Samaritan. They seem to regard it as important to influence the debate about the example that this good man placed before the world.

These theories are so varied that it is impossible to record them all here. However, they clearly focus on the failings of the Jewish people and their attitude of superiority to other races. Some demean the Samaritans as a very ordinary race of people of little intelligence and imagination of whom the Good Samaritan was an extreme exception.

The most interesting theologians are those who venture the opinion that the Good Samaritan was actually Jesus himself. They claim he was too humble to highlight himself as being an extraordinary man. This is a possibility that may well be correct. Indeed, I hope it is. The more I think about it the more I am sure it was Jesus.

It can be said with certainty that having captivated the world for many centuries, the Good Samaritan will continue to motivate people for thousands more as he represents bravery, decency, generosity, responsibility, and compassion. These are human assets that are quietly fading away in today's greedy world.

There are many ways in which we can be reminded of this fine person.

One is to view a striking painting of him by Rembrandt, produced in 1630. It depicts the Good Samaritan making necessary arrangements with the innkeeper for the care of the victim. It captures the basic decency of this man. Van Gogh did a somewhat similar Good Samaritan painting 260 years later in 1890 which is well worth seeing. It still draws thousands of viewers every year.

English composer Benjamin Britten created music based on the parable of the Good Samaritan to be played at the centenary celebration of the Red Cross in London in 1963. He stated that he wanted all who served in the Red Cross to have the Samaritan as their role model.

Australian author, Henry Lawson, not in any way a practising Christian, alluded to the parable in a poem he wrote in 1906. His words have meaning for us. Read them as they capture the moment:

He's been a fool perhaps.

Would have prospered had he tried.

But he was one who never could pass by on the other side.

What Henry Lawson is saying is that a poor person is more likely to be a Good Samaritan than a wealthy one. I think he has nailed it.

So it is that countless religious icons have been produced to honour the Good Samaritan and many charities have named their activities in his honour.

Long may there be good people who will follow his example more closely, actively, and often, and enjoy doing it. And, especially, may I try a lot more diligently than I do now.

In honour of the great carer, allow me to record below the Bible verses in the tenth chapter of Luke that describe his good deed.

An expert in the law asked Jesus, "Who is my neighbour?"

In reply Jesus said, "A man was going down from Jerusalem to Jericho when he was attacked by robbers. They stripped him of his clothes, beat him and went away, leaving him half dead.

A priest happened to be going down the same road. When he saw the man he passed by on the other side.

So too, a Levite. When he came to the place and saw him, he passed by on the other side.

But a Samaritan, as he travelled, came where the man was. When he saw him he took pity on him. He went to him and bandaged his wounds, pouring on oil and wine. Then he put the man on his own donkey, brought him to an inn and took care of him. The next day he took out two denarii and gave them to the innkeeper. "Look after him, he said and when I return, I will repay you for any extra expense you may have."

"Which of these three do you think was the neighbour to the man who fell into the hands of robbers?"

The expert in the law replied, "The one who had mercy on him."

Jesus told him, "Go and do likewise."

*THE GOOD SAMARITAN GUIDEPOST*

***As my friends in the bush would say: 'There is an absolute cracker of a bloke who always picks his mates up out of the gutter and gets them back on the road.'***

***You will have noted that the front cover of this book is a painting, 'The Bush Samaritan,' done for me by my friend, Noela Lowien, who hails from Kilcoy in Queensland. You will note that the bush Samaritan is female.***

# 4

# Builders Who Opened Doors

**I NOW VENTURE BEYOND** biblical times to the early centuries of the Church and the creation of other religions that impacted upon Christianity.

Reality is that these people have had a greater influence on my journey than most of the great biblical figures other than The Man who stands alone.

They are: Confucius, Mohammed, Thomas Becket, Francis of Assisi, Joan of Arc, Isabella of Castile, Michelangelo, Martin Luther, the Pilgrim Fathers, and John Wesley. Enjoy the read.

## 4.1 CONFUCIUS

You may wonder why Confucius has a place here as the first leader I comment on in my list of builders of my faith journey when we are all aware that he was not a Christian.

Becoming a Christian was never a possibility for him as he lived in China a long way from the Holy Land five centuries before Jesus was born.

A practical reason for putting him at the top of the list is that I decided I would place my builders in the chronological order in which they lived rather than try to show them in a way that may reflect their order of importance. That task would have proven to be quite difficult.

Confucius, therefore, was an easy choice to make to head the list as there are no others from all the possibilities from whom I have chosen who lived BCE. But I do have a special reason for doing so. I hold a belief that none of us can become a committed follower of The Man until we have searched the history and beliefs of the major world religions and decided that they do not measure up to him in stature and impact.

I joke not. Too many Christians have closed minds and an immature experience of life beyond their personal faith.

Above all of this, I am significantly impressed with Confucius as an extraordinary human being of huge intellect and far-reaching vision. His influence was expanded by the fact that he was a wonderful teacher. He used this talent as a communicator as a foundation for conveying with impact his very practical wisdom, thoughtful philosophy, pragmatic political theory, and rich culture to create a magnificent heritage for China (and beyond).

The impact of his presence has been immense, hugely important, long-lasting and of genuine value to followers of The Man.

His influence was profound during his lifetime which began in 552 BCE. It was revealed to the world during the extraordinary seventy-two years of his life. Not only was it faithfully recorded by scholars of merit, but he left his own written words as a permanent record, something that Jesus does not appear to have ever done.

The teachings of Confucius have been maintained as a powerful influence on the planet for 500 years longer than Jesus, so much so that Mao found it to be absolutely necessary to adopt and adapt them as his prime means of entrée to power.

It is now part of legend that Mao very cunningly used Confucius as the ideological base from which he could launch his political revolution that would lead to the establishment of the communist regime in China that remains in power to this day. He publicly and persistently posed as a devoted Confucian, constantly referring to the wisdom of the great man, particularly that which related to the core beliefs of Confucius about communal property and shared wealth. Mao knew that he was reaching into the soul of China as he convinced millions of Confucians that he was the new Confucius who matched him in wisdom.

It really did work for Mao with huge success even though he faked it all.

Even more importantly, it is interesting to note that much of what Confucius told the world was quite similar in many ways to that which Jesus proclaimed. This raises the possibility that Jesus could have learned of the philosophy of Confucius as there was communication between China and the Middle East via the great caravan traders of ancient times who loved to sit around the camp fires at night and tell their stories for many hours.

This impresses on my mind a realisation that many of the world's religions have much common ground on which people of widely different views can find many reasons for unity and foster peace without deserting our basic convictions. There is a compelling need for us to foster this mightily as we live in divisive societies, that become more divisive as the years go by.

So, even though Confucius had an incredible mind that ranged over a vast range of subjects, what in the briefest of terms is Confucianism.

First it is not a religion.

It is a realm of wise values and ethics that are of real quality for a good life.

Its five core values are these:

- Benevolence
- Righteousness
- Propriety
- Wisdom
- Fidelity

There are many more such Confucian beliefs that are worth noting as the mind of Confucius never stopped creating new thoughts, but those five are the core and all Christians can deepen their own faith by fully embracing the depth of their meaning.

I am quite certain that many Christians will have little difficulty in identifying with most of Confucian philosophy, but some of us will struggle with the Confucian practice of worship of ancestors. However, we should have no difficulty in admiring the wisdom of the finest of our ancestors.

Nevertheless, we will readily identify with the Confucian commitment to live in peace even though we are very aware that famous Christians like Joan of Arc did exactly the opposite yet she won acknowledgement as a saint.

One practice of Confucians that we should not overlook is the way in which they conduct funerals. They wear white clothing, definitely not black. And their funerals are very happy events. There is no mourning or wailing.

Let me finish with some realistic words of wisdom from Confucius that will make most of us feel a bit uncomfortable as we are all guilty of having done this deed more often than not:

> 'It is not generous to give away something
> that you do not want.'

The more I read of this great human being the more he makes me feel uncomfortable, but he adds something mature to my soul.

I think that discomfort is always meant to make us more worthy persons. The words of Confucius were never designed to demean us or make us do that which is wrong.

*THE CONFUCIUS GUIDEPOST*

***It is vital always to have an open mind with the wisdom of Confucius.***

***We should also never fail to acknowledge and understand that all religions have beliefs that are in some way beneficial to us all.***

## 4.2 MOHAMMED

Here is a great man of huge power who was, and still is, one of the great names of world history and one of the most influential leaders ever to walk the face of the earth. The lasting impact that Mohammed has in today's world is now greater than ever before.

He had a triple leadership role in his tumultuous life as a prophet, soldier, and statesman, but it is important to note also that he was a very successful merchant. This tells us that he was a significantly different person to Jesus in many ways.

He arrived on the world scene in the year 570 CE, almost six centuries after Jesus and a thousand years after Confucius, and became the founder of Islam and the proclaimer of the Quran. Even though Christians may contest this comment with indignation, it is clear that history has recorded him as being a figure comparable to Jesus in the eyes of much of humanity.

This being so, he should be regarded by Christians with much more respect than has been accorded him during my lifetime as, right at this moment in time, it is obvious that his followers are far more committed to his cause than most people who call themselves Christians usually display in their relationship with Jesus.

The significant growth in Muslim numbers may be attributable to the fact that Mohammed's message is much more clear and direct than Christian dogma which is often difficult to understand. Uneducated people could take up his teachings much more easily.

It is important that we do not fall into the trap of comparing him in any way with the ayatollahs and mullahs who now claim to follow his leadership in our world. They do not even slightly qualify to be rated even in the most remote comparison with the great prophet as he had an expansive mind, clear vision and a huge presence that enabled him to exercise power with wisdom. Indeed, they are not eligible to stand in his shadow as they give the impression of existing solely to spread terror through the world, while falsely claiming to do so in his name.

The most appalling evidence of this is revealed in the oppressive regime of modern Iran.

The Quran does not provide us with much biographic information about Mohammed himself, mainly recognising him as a great messenger of Allah. This gives us a clear message that he did not indulge in self-promotion. He was a proclaimer, not a publicist. Some historians offer the opinion that his only personal goal was to be ranked equally with both Moses and Jesus as prophets. Be this as it may, it must never be forgotten that Jesus is widely remembered and revered as a prophet in many pages of the Quran.

Mohammed's original hometown was Mecca in Arabia and it is to this city that millions of Islamic people travel every year to pay homage to him. No matter where they live in the world, most Muslims always kneel to face Mecca as they pray every day. This fact always baffles me as it was in Medina where he died in 622 at the age of sixty-two (twice the lifespan of Jesus). He had fled there to escape from many attempts made on his life at Mecca.

It is also interesting to note that among the first people to revere his strong spiritual presence and leadership skills were Christian monks located in many nations. Fascinatingly, at one point in his life, he was inspired by the appearance of the Angel Gabriel, a spiritual being who has influenced the lives of many Christians.

Unlike Jesus, he married.

At forty, his wife, Khadijah, gave him two sons (who died in their childhood) and four daughters of whom he was very proud. He took no other wife, even though polygamy was quite common in his era, but some historians claim that he had relationships with a number of mistresses after Khadijah died. This rumour matters little. However, it was the absence of a direct male heir that caused a huge dispute as to who would be his successor after his death.

Many attempts were made to kill him for a number of reasons in different places. However, in physical defence of his life and of Islam, he fought on many battlefields and was victorious on most. Except on the cross, Jesus was never in a situation where he had to fight physical battles to survive. His battles were verbal confrontations about beliefs and moral values, debated usually with those in religious, financial, and political power.

Mohammed's followers have multiplied mightily as the centuries have passed and have grown to number billions now. They clearly outnumber Christians and are expanding at a far greater rate. Generally, they are involved in most of the wars and coups that plague our modern world but so were many Christians down the centuries beforehand, especially in the Crusades.

Sadly, both faiths have always justified their battles as being fought in the name of God even though God, if he was ever asked, would deny them all.

Significantly today, when anyone derides Mohammed or ridicules him, they are very likely to be killed in severe and bloody retribution. Thankfully, most Christians do not defend the name of Jesus in the same way. In fact, we generally go out of our way to avoid doing so.

I praise Mohammed and his life's work, not because I want to ensure that I avoid a violent death but because I believe him to be an extraordinary spiritual and physical leader of a faith that is not dissimilar to Christianity. It is indisputable that he achieved things that influenced and changed the world in incredible and long-lasting ways.

He cannot be conveniently written off as a religious extremist as he was not. Clearly, he was a far greater leader than that.

The world still accepts his presence today and will continue to do so.

Let me now raise two questions about those who practice the Islamic faith today as many of their rigid attitudes baffle me and concern me.

While I respect their rigid devotion to the Quran, I am of the opinion that this creates in too many Muslims a closed mind that hinders their life experience. Why do so many allow this to dwarf their own existence?

The role to which they define and restrict their women is hugely baffling. Indeed it is totally unnecessary.

While it provides a basis for a strong family life, it denies women the opportunity to use their skills and creates a situation where 50% of the population of every Muslim nation is economically unproductive. Is this justifiable in any way and is it humane?

All of this adds to the dilemma we face in determining whether or not fundamentalist religions of any type, are of value to society in any way.

Another question arises. Can enlightened religion in any of its forms gain wide acceptance and change the world for the better in the most wise and compassionate form that is possible.

One hopes that it can and will. Life without hope, is pointless in every way. But, when we work with The Man, we are never without hope.

*THE MOHAMMED GUIDEPOST*

***The Islamic faith did not ever try to claim that Mohammed was the son of Allah.***

***They correctly revere him as a great prophet. I do exactly the same with The Man.***

## 4.3 THOMAS BECKET

He was assassinated by so-called Christians at fifty. This shook England to the core when this happened in Canterbury Cathedral in 1170.

Yet, his memory does not fade from public debate. Indeed, his murder was one of the most high-profile assassinations in the history of religion.

He was a hugely influential figure, being for a time a close friend of King Henry II, as he served as royal chancellor, and then as archbishop of Canterbury. His life story is a classic study in the annals of betrayal and there are some important lessons we can learn from it.

Firstly, we can question whether or not he was a man of genuine faith and qualified spiritually to be archbishop. The evidence is that, like most people of his era, he observed the rituals and disciplines of the Church as, without such a display of piety, it was impossible to hold any position of power in the land. In order to be appointed archbishop it was not a necessary requirement to be a committed disciple of Christ.

His life is well documented as one of huge wealth, living in several splendid residences in both England and France, owning ships and regularly throwing lavish parties to which he invited the great and mighty of the land. While it is often possible for a rich man to be a Christian, the evidence is that Thomas Becket was a nominal adherent.

Of greater significance is that he loved the exercise of power.

As noted above, he was holder of two powerful positions, first as royal chancellor and then as archbishop of Canterbury, positions that required starkly different talents. The first put him in control of both the money and politics of the realm while the second made him the pope's personal representative on all matters relating to the Church. The king hoped that in both positions he and Becket could totally control both the spiritual and financial life of the kingdom.

Whatever his sins, Becket knew that this political situation was untenable in the long term. So it was that he made the fascinating choice to fight for the independence of the Church as this gave him a greater control of power than could be achieved in the management and control of the finances of the nation. The king saw Becket as having publicly committed his allegiance the pope rather than to him, an assumption that was correct. The archbishop of Canterbury had no option but to take his orders from the pope.

Becket correctly assessed that his life was now on the line and so he fled to France but did not resign as archbishop. The king sent Becket a conciliatory message seeking peace between them and invited him back to Canterbury. Becket accepted this offer in good faith but the king had already arranged for four knights to murder him at the cathedral. The king gained more power to justify this extreme step when Becket unwisely excommunicated three influential bishops whom he believed were his enemies. They aided the king in the plot to kill him and it was quickly carried out.

An extraordinary event of the entire saga was revealed when immediately after the assassination people with serious illnesses visited the cathedral to dip their clothes in Becket's blood and claimed that they had experienced immediate cures. Word of this happening spread quickly all over Europe and caused thousands of ailing pilgrims to journey to Canterbury Cathedral.

Such was its impact that the pope declared Becket to be a saint only two years later as recognition of his miraculous power of spiritual hearing.

Some years back, I visited Canterbury Cathedral for the sole purpose of assessing the legacy of Thomas Becket. I walked the pathway that his assassins trod on their way to murder him and stood on the spot where they carried out their regal instruction to permanently remove him. I noted that sick people still come to the cathedral to kneel at the spot where he died and call out to God to cure them as they believe that the spirit of Thomas still holds power, even though a thousand years have passed.

A century ago, the respected English author T S Eliot wrote a best-selling book about this unforgettable event. He called it *Murder in the Cathedral* and based it on the written notes of a monk, Edward Grim, who was a close witness to the assassination. His evidence has been preserved in the cathedral records for all this time.

Three issues from the life and death of Thomas Becket are worthy of comment.

- He was the first leader of any nation in the world to proclaim the necessity that there must be a clear distinction between the powers of Church and State. This declaration ended his life. Unfortunately, the lesson still has not been learned by some. Britain's King Charles is the leader of the Church of England as have been all British monarchs since the reign of Henry VIII. He has no right to hold this position.
- The power of the spiritual healing as shown by the claim of the miracles of healing tells us

that the much-debated acceptance of spiritual healing is still a significant force of faith today. It cannot be denied that some devout people believe they have experienced it. At the same time, other devout people have also died and no one can claim that one was a more worthy being than the other.

- God's will was again a subject of unresolved debate after Becket died. His murderers stated that they were called by God to kill him and they could not and would not defy Him.

There is no way that you or I really want to believe in and worship a God who arranges for people to be murdered.

Like all of us, Thomas Becket was a sinner, but he was a significant leader to remember with goodwill as he was one of several important figures who took part in a slow reformation of the way in which the power of the Church in society first began to wane. The decline has continued and sometime in this century will become terminal.

*THE THOMAS BECKET GUIDEPOST*

***The circumstances of his death stirred my doubts about miracles as he was not a holy man.***

***He was an astute political leader who challenged royal authority, but fostered the division of Church and State.***

## 4.4 FRANCIS OF ASSISI

Now we meet the world's first high profile environmentalist and its most committed one.

Francis was especially noted for his care of birds and animals, a duty our modern society has forgotten as every year we render more and more wildlife extinct and care little about its consequences in wrecking the checks and balances of life on our planet.

He was one of history's finest examples of human compassion, a skill that now becomes less evident every day as the world is steadily consumed by the ever growing cancer of human greed. He did not just talk about it; he lived it day by day.

My involvement today in community service is firmly role modelled on his life's work and the legacy he has left. However, I am very aware that no matter what I do, it will fall a long way short of his eminent benchmark. Even so, he still motivates me to take steps forward in my challenge to be a more worthy follower of The Man.

Additionally, I am in awe of the personal sacrifice he made in leaving the comfort and security of a wealthy home and powerful family to take up what he believed was his life's calling. His loved ones at home were profoundly bewildered, openly declaring him to be insane when he went to live in poverty with lepers, the homeless, the poor and the rejected.

Clearly, his commitment to his calling was total and inevitably led to his early death when he was just forty-three.

What is a concise description of Francis that may adequately capture the entire magnitude of an inspirational life?

He was a Catholic friar who, eight hundred years ago, founded a religious order that he called the Franciscans. It exists and serves to this day.

Some have described him as a mystic. Others say he was simply a humble itinerant preacher who lived in poverty as he fostered his commitment to a sharing and caring society. Then there are those who regard him as a martyr for humanity.

As the result of it all, the pope of his day declared him to be a saint shortly after his death, the fastest declaration of sainthood in the history of the Catholic Church. His sainthood has subsequently been officially recognised by the Anglican and Lutheran Churches, an honour that has only rarely been bestowed on others.

The fascinating part of his life story is that he not only came from an affluent and influential family, but was an extravagant user of his family wealth. He wore the finest clothing, enjoyed the best food and wine, and would attend an endless number of wild parties as well as being highly popular with women.

His conversion experience was extraordinarily dramatic and focused on a beggar who asked him for alms, causing Francis to give him all the money he had in his possession on that day. This led to him acquiring a massive conscience about his unearned wealth which quickly led to him deciding to live with lepers, deliberately denying himself any part of his family assets. They disowned him anyway as being a social disgrace so he burned all his bridges behind him. In today's world they would declare him to be woke.

After establishing the Franciscan Order of friars who contentedly lived with him in his poverty and his ministry to lepers, he gradually spread his work to the known world especially travelling to Morocco, Dalmatia, Sicily, Egypt, Israel and beyond, using the most primitive forms of transport that were available at the cheapest possible price.

All of his relentless work, added to his spartan consumption of food as well as the consequences of a life lived among unhealthy people who knew nothing about basic hygiene meant that the early end of his life at age forty-three surprised none of those close to him. But he died happily, his last act being a valiant attempt to sing Psalm 141.

A concise comment on the message that Francis left for you and me is found in the tenth verse of the third chapter of the Gospel of Luke: 'He who has two coats must share with anyone who has none.'

He had quite deliberately modelled his life on Jesus and sought to carry out the work of The Man in every way that he possibly could. It is reasonable to state that no one could have tried with greater devotion and persistence. It once again reveals to me that I am a long way short of what is required of me in my quest to become a committed working partner of The Man and I know that I lack the courage to bring myself to even try to copy his lifestyle.

Right now, it is important that people like you and me who want to be active in unpolluting our world should learn all that we can from Francis the environmentalist who believed that it was a fundamental part of the Christian mandate for all followers of The Man to keep the world clean and beautiful.

In his view, no one could pollute the world, do nothing about it and then falsely believe themselves to be Christian.

In modern times, Pope John Paul II declared Francis to be the patron saint of ecology and implored us all to love and care for creation as a tribute to Francis and as being a powerful statement of our personal faith. This calling was affirmed by our current pope when he took the name of Francis. We can but applaud loudly.

Whenever I think of Francis, I readily recall the biblical story of the rich young ruler who declined the invitation of Jesus to give all he had to the poor and follow him. The young man walked away just as most of us would have done.

Francis did the exact opposite. Few have since made any attempt to accept the challenge. In that I regard myself a working partner of Francis. This adds to my ability to humbly regard myself as a genuine working partner of The Man.

*THE FRANCIS OF ASSISSI GUIDEPOST*

***Francis challenges me to do much more than just give my money, time, and skills to good causes.***

***I know that I must get my hands dirty and keep my mind and body hungry in helping to solve the great issues of humanity.***

## 4.5 JOAN OF ARC

Unless I am misinformed and lacking in vision, I strongly doubt that any person in the history of humanity other than Joan could ever have led the army of a nation into war with another nation, win most of the battles and many centuries later be declared a saint.

And for this person to be female and unable to either read or write, in age of crude male superiority and sexual supremacy and abuse, is an almost unimaginable event.

This extraordinary leader is famously known to us as Joan of Arc. She was born 1412 and died in 1431. Burned at the stake as a witch when she was just nineteen years old, she has since 1909, been known to us as Saint Joan.

I admire her valour and commitment to France as well as her deep Christian faith and devotion, extreme though it was, particularly her loyalty to the Catholic Church who rewarded her commitment by having her killed. However, I lament the fact that her faith led her to be a leader of, and active participant in wars that caused the deaths of so many innocent people, firm in the belief that she was doing it in God's name.

Nevertheless, she is still revered in her beloved France as they are certain she carried out her deeds because she was absolutely convinced that her destiny was to be a war leader for France and that God would ensure that she would win.

This leads us all to a debate on whether or not the God whom she worshipped would condone wars fought in his name especially when those on the other side held exactly the same belief. My view of it is that her God would never take sides in any war, especially as all records in history tell us that most wars have been based on greed, theft, pursuit of power and sheer barbarism. Not one has ever been fought for a noble purpose.

The life of Joan of Arc is extraordinary in every dimension. It is probably more accurate to say that had her tale been told in a novel of fiction it would have been ranked as a bestseller that was unbelievable in every dimension.

She was the uneducated daughter of a peasant farmer and she experienced visions of saints whom she was certain she saw quite clearly in person and who spoke to her face-to-face on several occasions. She passionately and stubbornly insisted that these experiences were genuine. This does not sit well with me as I have no belief in visions that have a supernatural dimension. I accept that every one of us can have challenging dreams of a worthy calling or challenges to act, but I reject any thoughts of personal influence from saints or from Jesus himself. Having said this, I have no doubt that she was motivated by a sense of a divine motivation to save France.

When she began her path to glory at just seventeen, she had an imposing personality that fascinated people who met her and caused her to win the hearts and minds and trust of kings, knights, generals, and foot soldiers who followed her leadership unquestioningly, often to death in agony.

Her victories in the field of battle, were spectacular even though she had not even the most basic military training. She had no doubt that her God was with her every moment guiding her to victory by helping her to make every decision correctly. The way she displayed her spiritual power and presence caused the army of France to follow her in absolute trust, powered by huge belief in her that few ever thought could be false.

Her spectacular victories in the battles at Chinon, Orleans, Loire and Reims are now part of legend, although her magic was dented severely when she lost the battles of Paris and Compeigne. Those two defeats created doubts in her mantle of infallibility and divine power.

As happens so often in life, those who once worshipped her quickly turned against her and she rapidly lost her power to command.

She was eventually captured by her enemies, subsequently tried for heresy, and sentenced to death. None of her former worshippers showed any inclination to step forward to defend her or try to seek a pardon for her.

Proof of her guilt was mainly based on the fact that she always wore men's clothing. This apparently was an unpardonable sin for any female. But it seems to me that this was a quite sensible and practical decision on her part as long dresses would have impeded her movements when riding a horse. Obviously, her enemies would have spotted her quite easily if she was dressed as a woman.

She died bravely despite the huge pain of her death by burning at the stake. Apparently, those who ordered her to be killed believed that burning chases evil spirits out of our souls so we can then be eligible to go to heaven in absolute purity.

The irony of it all is that a rehabilitation trial was publicly staged twenty years after her death. Incredibly, the court declared her to be innocent. Strangely, they also plunged the depths of cynicism by insisting that evidence at her trial conclusively proved her to be a virgin. This meant that she would be eligible to be declared a saint.

However, it took another five centuries for the Vatican to get around to doing so. No one can provide a convincing answer as to why it took so long.

Now, she is honoured throughout the world by statues, churches, schools, art, music, and literature. But I admire her as a person of mighty spiritual valour who challenged the domination of masculinity while advancing femininity, long before the Me-Too movement was ever even imagined as a means of fostering gender equality.

Above all, she was an unshakeable religious believer.

Even as the flames scorched her to death she believed her God was with her and she was about to meet him face-to-face. Her demeanour radiated a hope that stunned those who watched. Ever since the beginning of time, humans have found hope to be an asset that gives meaning to life.

I salute her as a person of inspiration, even though I despise war and certainly reject any belief whatsoever in a holy war.

Nevertheless, I can accept that men openly acknowledged and faithfully followed her leadership into war for one basic reason. They believed in their minds that she had been sent from God. Not to have followed her would have been seen as a public betrayal of the Almighty.

This once more raises the question as to why a belief in the existence of a God is necessary and is a declining thought in the minds of many when The Man can clearly be understood as a role model. This is highlighted by a growing number of people who state in any census that they no longer have a belief that God exists.

If a modern Joan of Arc appeared in today's world and declared that she was sent from God to lead them to win a war, how many people would believe her and follow her to the death?

Not many.

### *THE JOAN OF ARC GUIDEPOST*

***Joan's story provides me with certainty that, in the entire history of humanity, there has never been a war where God has called on either side to fight it out in his name and with his blessing.***

## 4.6 ISABELLA OF CASTILE

This relatively unknown person will surprise you as she is usually overlooked in all accounts of the diffusion of Christianity throughout the world.

However, the truth is that I could not leave her out as she was responsible for authorising and organising the spread of the faith to the entire continent of South America and especially ensuring that the faith was Catholic.

When Isabella was born in 1451, the Iberian Peninsula was divided into four kingdoms – Castile, Aragon, Granada, and Portugal – plus a few tiny fiefdoms dotted here and there. Strangely, none of those kingdoms were wealthy until Isabella led a movement to unite them. Her childhood was lived in modest circumstances and subsequently she lived comfortably but never extravagantly.

Numerous attempts had been made unite these kingdoms by various means but mainly by marriages and wars. During her lifetime, Isabella was involved in both of the above initiatives and in fact she broke off two betrothals so she could look for more powerful relationships.

Finally, she married King Ferdinand of Aragon They produced five children while organising a union of most of Spain under their rule and strengthening the domination and power of the Catholic Church. They did this to such an extent that historians usually refer to them as the Catholic monarchs. In fact, it was the pope of their era who officially gave them that title.

Isabella introduced the Catholic faith to South America to such a degree that it became the largest religion of any type in the entire continent, an extraordinary achievement that no one else has ever replicated.

It all began with the historic voyage of Christopher Columbus. It would not have been achieved at that moment in history if he had not found a powerful political and financial sponsor who also had vision. This was Isabella, not her husband Ferdinand. He had considerable doubts about the sanity of Colombus. Nevertheless, she defied Ferdinand and sent Columbus off to discover the New World.

The truth is that Columbus just presumed he had discovered it first, not realising that the Vikings had come there several centuries earlier.

Nevertheless, the huge achievement of Columbus began the colonisation of Central and South America, firstly by Spain but closely followed by Portugal. It was fuelled by the entire strength and influence of the Catholic Church, all organised by Isabella. It was a very significant accomplishment. Few people in history have founded a religious and political cause that spread across a dozen nations of a huge continent.

In acknowledgement of what she had done, the pope of the day, five centuries later in 1974, officially declared Isabella to be a servant of God.

This was a fall-back decision on his part as she had been nominated as a saint but the curia at the Vatican could not agree on whether she was qualified so they settled for a lesser accolade. At the time, there was a rumour in circulation that she had two children out of wedlock to princes of other nations before she married Ferdinand. There is evidence that this allegation is correct and was apparently an attempt to place her heirs in other kingdoms that could have a future role in unifying Spain. This tells us that Isabella was a ceaseless and fearless plotter who achieved results.

Another reason why the pope declared her to be a servant of God is that she was also the monarch who drove 90% of the Islamic population from Spain, mainly the Moors, back into North Africa, and used her influence to encourage other nations in Western Europe to do likewise. France was one, but their efforts came undone last century when people from its African colonies were made welcome as citizens, subsequently causing widespread racial strife.

A quite strange honour was given to her by the US in 1893, when portraits of her, side by side with Christopher Columbus, appeared on American postage stamps and remained in use for many years.

The strength of the Catholic Church in South America is now in decline, its influence waning speedily as Protestant charismatic churches grow spectacularly. People are yearning for personal spiritual strength that expresses freedom far more than submitting to the rigid authority of the Catholic Church. This decline in its power is further highlighted by the decline of the influence of the Church in the politics and government of most South American nations mainly through the growing influence of atheists and agnostics.

Earlier this century, Michelle Bachelet, a high-quality female politician, was twice elected by a landslide as president of Chile, a nation which was then 90% Catholic. This occurred despite very negative publicity about her personal life. It was organised and promoted with great vigour by the Catholic Church. They threw a lot of money at the task and felt called by God to tell blatant lies about her, all in God's name. The Church did not want a female president, especially one who had two children by two different fathers and was married to neither. Voters ignored the Church in droves as they wanted a competent president, not a religious one. The result shocked Catholic leaders to the very core

So it is that the decline of the influence of their Church in political, religious, and moral power in South America is a humiliating rebuff to Catholics. They overlooked the indisputable fact that Isabella herself, who had several lovers, had proved to be a very competent queen and government administrator, far more so than her rather tame husband. They have found no one else in any generation who could achieve her stature.

So, we can remember Isabella as a pragmatic evangelist for her Church and its politics, more so than from conviction of her personal faith. She saw her task as essential in taking her faith to the New World and she succeeded mightily.

As I mention often throughout this book, the sad fact of today's world is that most Christians are not evangelists. Their priority appears to focus solidly on saving their own souls while trying to ensure that their Church survives as a presence in society. This selfish and exclusive attitude is not smart as all Churches are highly unlikely to survive in the long term.

### *THE ISABELLA GUIDEPOST*

***Isabella was a most successful missionary, perhaps the greatest in history.***

***No one else took a religion to a continent and organised it to dominate every nation on that continent.***

## 4.7 MICHELANGELO

Surely, this talented man deserves the accolade of greatest artist of all time.

My visit to see the magnificence of the art of Michelangelo in the Sistine Chapel at the Vatican in Rome was one of the great experiences of my life. Not only can the painting he created on the ceiling of the chapel, which depict scenes from Genesis, be described as magnificent, so is the stunning painting on one of the walls. It depicts the Last Judgement.

I sat quietly in the chapel for a long time trying to take in the enormity of it all.

The only other time I have treasured such a similar experience was when I gazed for a long time at the superb *Night Watch* in the Rijksmuseum in Amsterdam.

How Michelangelo could have created that ceiling painting in the Sistine Chapel while lying on his back for many hours every day on raised planks for four long years was an incredible achievement of which we can but stand in awe. It is almost beyond belief.

The question that forever baffles me is why he did it.

Was it just to please the pope and to be forgiven for his many sins or was it because he desperately wanted to be renowned as the greatest painter of all time, or did he actually want to outwardly express the huge depth of his personal faith? We will never know, but I hope it was the latter.

What this tells us is that art and music are more permanently powerful in their spiritual influence than are sermons. They are undervalued as a means of evangelism for no valid reasons and so it is time that we did something significant about using them far more often.

Well, who was Michelangelo?

He was born in Florence in 1475 and lived for eighty-nine years.

His prolific works of superb excellence went far beyond the genius that he revealed in the Sistine Chapel.

He began his artistic career as a sculptor, creating the Pietà and then David.

He followed this by showing his skill as an architect by transforming the design of the western end of St Peter's Basilica at the Vatican.

His creations as an artist are far too many in scope to be adequately covered in this short chapter of my book. But some are worth special mention. They are located in a number of cities and represent notable magnificence. The ones I can recall are The Madonna, Angel, Bacchus, The Deluge, The Creation of Adam, Jeremiah, and The Crucifixion of Peter.

And, to add to all of the above, he was a talented poet.

There have been very few who have had the privilege to enjoy all of those talents in one life and were able to reach such great heights of excellence. Obviously, Leonardo da Vinci was one, but others are hard to recall.

The exact opposite of the grandeur of his art is the deplorable fact that he led a personal life that can only be described as revoltingly decadent. One historian described him as:

> 'Rough and uncouth with domestic habits that were incredibly squalid. He ate only occasionally, consuming food that was usually unhealthy in composition. He rarely bathed and he changed or washed his clothes only occasionally. He slept in his clothes and kept his boots on.'

Some believe that this indicates he was mentally ill.

These words are ones that none of us would want on our personal CV but they are an amazing description of a legend.

These habits were not the result of him being poor as this clearly was not the case. He eventually became a wealthy man, which he deserved to be as he had created so many artistic gems. However, the truth is that he had no interest whatsoever in spending his money as he regarded it as a common commodity that debased his realm of art.

His few personal relationships with people were always remote, most probably because he constantly stank. In addition, he was by nature a solitary and melancholy person who experienced huge changes of mood and deliberately withdrew from the company of others, most of whom seemed by their presence to cause him to feel personally inadequate.

Many, but not all, historians report that he is believed to have been homosexual even though there is no firm evidence of him ever having a long-term partner or casual ones. Nevertheless, copies of letters he wrote to male friends revealed more often than not that he was gay as they contained intimate language.

So, why is it that I have the feeling that this strange man, who was as crude as he was magnificent, has had an influence on my journey?

My artistic talent is absolutely nil, my musical talent is barely higher and I have only a vague interest in poetry.

Additionally, I know little about his faith except for that which is revealed in a poem that he wrote but did not publish publicly:

> 'Neither painting nor sculpture will be able
> any longer to calm my soul, now turned

> toward that divine love that opened his arms on the cross to take me in.'

There is a lot of meaning in those two lines.

If we believe our talents are a gift that we are able to use or neglect to use either wholeheartedly or casually, we have in Michelangelo a person who used his talents with total commitment even though his personal life was a polar opposite to his genius.

I learned from him that if I do not use and expand the small number of talents gifted to me, then I am a lazy and an irresponsible person, not worthy of the company of The Man as I seek to walk along the pilgrim way.

I lay great importance on the lesson I learned from Michelangelo that financial wealth, though tempting and desirable, is neither a worthy nor necessary asset of my life. All that you and I need is to have the benefit of financial independence combined with a happy sense of personal responsibility and shared pleasure.

Most of us will agree it is not appropriate or meaningful to have money flaunted or wasted or hoarded or worshipped. It is a basic physical asset to be used primarily for sustaining and enhancing life and for sharing with others as we endeavour to enjoy the finer elements of our existence.

The evidence is that Michelangelo does not seem to have enjoyed any of these special elements of life except for a pride in his work.

Nevertheless, out of a primitive lifestyle came extraordinary beauty for humanity to enjoy forever. We have had the privilege of enjoying it.

*THE MICHELANGELO GUIDEPOST*

***The gap between genius and insanity is as thin as a razor's edge.***

## 4.8 MARTIN LUTHER

Little did Martin Luther know that he would change the face of Christendom in the greatest tumult of its history when he nailed his theses on the door of his church at Wittenberg in Germany five hundred years ago and declared: 'Here I stand, I can do no other.'

It would take some time for the princes of the Church in Rome to take serious notice of what he had done and gain an understanding of his capacity to destroy them, but he eventually triumphed in his personal revolt against an utterly corrupt and thoroughly decadent Catholic Church by sheer persistence despite having much abuse relentlessly heaped upon him.

The Reformation he started is now recognised as the longest and most enduring revolution of any type in world history. Most rebellions last just a few years and quietly fade away but his has been, deservedly, very different. For example the communist revolution begun by Lenin in Russia in 1917 has lasted only one century and is now quietly fading away as China moves steadily from a Marxist philosophy to become what is in reality the practice of state capitalism.

Karl Marx said that Christianity was the opium of the people. This may be true but, despite all its problems, it has lasted longer than Marx believed it would.

There is now an undeniable challenge to follow up on what Luther achieved and start a new type of

Church. This time it must be a total revolution in which those who follow The Man can find new ways to meet, believe, grow, and act in a manner that religious leaders are currently unable to provide or even imagine.

It is interesting to consider why Luther's Reformation did not happen like a bolt of lightning. It took another fifty years beyond his actions at Wittenberg before it became an identifiable, formidable, and undeniable movement of change. However the Churches of the world have never been known to act with speed about anything. But it is noteworthy that it was the publication and distribution of Luther's books and writings beyond Germany to France, England and Italy that made it unstoppable and long-term.

I was disappointed, and still am, when I first read extracts from some of Luther's sermons. I found his theology to be primitive but it was, nevertheless, a genuine improvement on the brutal theology that was inflicted on people in his time. For instance, he believed in the existence of witches and the necessity of having them burned at the stake.

He had appalling thoughts about Jews and their role in the crucifixion, calling for them to be persecuted. We should note that some historians regard him as the ultimate anti-semite and many claim that Hitler's slaughter of Jews had its initial basis in Lutheran theology.

He also constantly told everyone that doing good deeds were unimportant in our lives and would never get us into heaven. He pleaded with his flock to be selfish and concentrate solely on repenting of our sins, saving our souls and making sure we get into heaven.

While I found all of this to be offensive, I was also fascinated to note that Luther had an enormous personal fear of death and judgement, especially after he survived a lightning strike in a storm during his student days. Thereafter, everything in his life seems to have been focussed on how he would face the inevitably of his death. His faith was very personal, not communal.

All of the above proves to me that theology is a movable feast, especially as many lay persons like me work on developing our own philosophy of life. This enables us to remove the unnecessary elements of mystery that too many followers of Jesus have embedded in their faith, without having any evidence that Jesus actually identified with what their Church told them.

One other matter of contention that I want to lay at Luther's feet is that he was the author and publisher of the first vernacular catechism. I remember having to learn the Presbyterian version by rote in Sunday School. I despised catechisms then and have an even lower opinion of them now as they were written for observance by closed minds and are an utter irrelevance.

There has always been much mystery about the life and work of Martin Luther, but this makes him a more interesting character.

Born in Germany in 1483, Luther originally studied to be a lawyer but made a huge life change to become a priest who steadily climbed up the ladder of Church bureaucracy to be recognised as a famous theologian, author, hymn writer, university professor and Augustinian friar before being declared a heretic by his pope.

Many theologians and historians now question whether he in reality did nail his ninety-five theses on the door of a church at Wittenberg. There is no historical on-the-spot account of it having occurred. It appears to have been identified as a starting point of several legends spread by his followers. They were responding in his defence after he was persecuted and excommunicated by the pope of the day who had also tried and failed to demean his work and extinguish any threat of a Reformation setting their religious empire on fire and spreading it to the world.

His final excommunication by Rome came at the end of a very long heresy trial that has not been revoked or pardoned in any way after his death, but it inevitably opened the door for the establishment of a powerful Lutheran Church. This was a good event that enabled many others to do likewise and free themselves from the yoke of Rome.

Centuries later, it would have a direct impact on my life.

Wilhelm Guhr, my great grandfather was a Lutheran missionary sent from Bavaria to Australia to establish the Lutheran Church on the Darling Downs in Queensland 150 years ago. His written charter informed him that he was to 'remove all sin from the Darling Downs.' He utterly failed to achieve his calling as an exterminator of sin. In fact, the reverse has clearly happened. Sin is still being practised mightily. Nevertheless, I am heartened by the fact that a search I did of Church records notes that he had made a valiant attempt to banish it from the face of the earth, but it proved an impossible task.

Luther gave the Catholic Church another high profile hit in rejecting their practice that priests must be celibate.

After the Church in Rome terminated his vocation as a priest, he married and set an example for Churches everywhere that it was not a heresy for a holy man to marry. Luther made it especially dramatic by marrying

Catherine who happily resigned from an order of nuns to share her life with him. Their union produced six children.

His presence as a powerful person in Christian history is undeniable. It means that his legacy gives us a platform to continue to have an impact on the world by working to foster a basis for more change. Not just within the Church in Rome but within every Church on the planet as every one of them falls short of the mark.

It is not credible for anyone to declare that another reformation is impossible. That which Luther began actually continues to change the history of the world and has created the current yearning for another revolution.

Its time has now come and it will create dramatic change as it will happen outside of Churches, causing them to fade away to eventually become a pale and irrelevant presence in society.

Even more importantly, working partners of The Man will create a greater relevance for him to be translated into community cohesion, human compassion, and individual responsibility to create a caring world.

Luther most probably would not approve, but he lit the first spark.

*THE MARTIN LUTHER GUIDEPOST*

***Luther has given me courage to challenge the masters of Churches and to create conditions whereby they will change their ancient and rigid ways, no matter what the personal cost.***

***He also spoke these clear words about God. 'Whatever your heart clings to and confides in, that is really your God.'***

## 4.9 THE PILGRIM FATHERS

Every year in November, the citizens of the United States of America celebrate in thanksgiving the memory of a revered occasion in their history when they pause to honour the arrival of the Pilgrim Fathers and do so with greater enthusiasm than the manner in which they enjoy Christmas only a month later.

The arrival of these deeply religious people in what is now the State of Massachusetts in 1620 and their immediate act of thanksgiving for their safe arrival in their new homeland is now a central theme in the history and culture of the United States.

Americans feel both a spiritual and patriotic need to repeat this celebration annually.

Most families throughout the nation enjoy a feast together during which they give thanks for their good life and prosperity which they believe comes to them as a direct gift from God. The millions of turkeys that are slaughtered in preparation for this day every year do not have the same feeling of reverence for the will of the Almighty.

The pilgrims fled from England to escape religious persecution they unhappily experienced from the king and the Church of England and believed they could re-establish God's kingdom in its intended form in a New World. They clearly believed that their God had travelled with them on their long and perilous journey across the Atlantic but they soon discovered that they were not able to create a nation that would fulfil their dream of what God's kingdom was intended to be. Indeed their mission was to ensure that everyone who followed them to America must take up their religion and adhere to their version of God's will. That intention in itself was clearly an act of domination of others similar to that which they escaped from.

However, it is interesting for us to pause and study the background details of why this happened as there are important lessons that we can learn from the disappointment they actually inflicted upon themselves.

Their history shows they held unbending religious beliefs that were both Puritan and Calvinist and they stridently opposed the trappings and traditions of the Church of England and its powerful hierarchy whom they considered to be quite pagan. They originally left the established Church and became known as Separatists worshipping in democratic congregations controlled by the laity, not the clergy. This makes them pioneers of what we know in modern times as the Congregational Church.

Their breakaway activities subjected them to even more persecution to the extent that they decided to flee from England to live in the city of Leiden, in the Netherlands. But language difficulties and the political instability of the Netherlands caused them even more grief even though they were not being persecuted there. They felt compelled to move again. Firstly, they considered seeking refuge in South America before considering North America, especially Virginia and New York, as better options. Finally, they chose to go even further north to what is now known as Massachusetts.

Their journey to freedom took them firstly from Holland back to Plymouth in southern England, travelling there in several small boats before boarding the Mayflower whose captain was willing to take them to the New World at a price they could afford to pay. He was unaware that his old boat would attain huge fame as the legendary ship of American history.

They had an extraordinarily difficult journey across the Atlantic through exceptionally bad weather while various infectious diseases also took their deadly toll. Nevertheless, they continued on their pilgrimage only to record that on arrival only forty-two of the original contingent of 102 pilgrims survived the journey for which their God had called them. Their painful experience had been such that they had no option but to throw 60 bodies into the Atlantic.

At the very moment they stepped onto the soil of their new homeland all of them fell to their knees and gave prayers of thanks to their God that he had delivered them to their new world where they were committed to create his kingdom in accordance with his will.

The American people will never cease to regard them as the prime cornerstone on which their nation was founded. Many fall to their knees every Thanksgiving Day as a symbolic act of identification with the Pilgrim Fathers, even those who go nowhere near a church at any time during the year.

Despite great and numerous problems and challenges, including wars with Indians, the Pilgrim Fathers eventually founded a solid colony at a place they called Plymouth Rock which is now formally recognised by Congress as a national monument in their honour.

While I have often been personally demeaned for my faith, I have never suffered any serious religious persecution so I really have no understanding of what it means to be harassed in such a way that would cause me so much suffering that I would have had no option but to flee my native land. Often, I have been strongly criticised for the way in which I have publicly put my beliefs into action in the community but I have never been threatened physically nor ever feared for my life.

Perhaps, this has made me a lessor person. At ninety-three, I probably will never find out what such an experience of religious intolerance would impact on me even though I often think about how I would go about handling it.

What I do find to be questionable is that these Pilgrim Fathers, who were devout servants of the Lord, settled permanently on land in America that had clearly been occupied by indigenous Indian tribes for thousands of years before their arrival. Even more worrying is that they initially stole it from the Indians with violence.

For people who unshakeably believed that the Bible was the Word of God and to be obeyed to the letter, they clearly broke one of the ten commandments, 'Thou shalt not steal,' and thought nothing of it because they knew they were God's people and the Indians were not, so this made it all okay. They were in no doubt that they were his chosen race carrying out his clear command to establish his kingdom.

Sadly, in their view, the Indians were simply a hurdle their God had sent them as a test for true believers to overcome.

The undeniable fact is that God's people had no right whatsoever to rob Indians of their land and destroy their lives. Fortunately, they did sign a treaty with them in 1621.

However, I must admit that Christian pioneers in Australia did exactly the same thing without showing any semblance of conscience or remorse.

This means that I am in no position to criticise the Pilgrim Fathers even though I was not one of the original settlers in my native land of Australia. But I do have a responsibility to at least acknowledge that great injustice was carried out by my ancestors who were among those who followed the example of the Pilgrim Fathers and did so with significant brutality for which there can be no excuse.

Despite this great wrong, the Pilgrim Fathers committed themselves to creating a new life in a Christian community that was isolated in a hostile land. They eventually succeeded in their courageous endeavours, displaying a deep commitment to walk with Jesus the Man.

It is a dedication of faith that I have never tried to copy but now I have real difficulty in identifying with their fundamentalism.

I must admit that they present a disturbing element of my journey to discover a genuine faith but I must give thanks for their continued presence in my thinking even though it causes me much soul-searching.

After all, soul-searching is a constant element in walking with The Man as his working partner and is a character-building experience that I try never to avoid.

*THE PILGRIM FATHERS GUIDEPOST*

***The Pilgrim Fathers tried to follow the example of Jesus's brother, James, who founded a Christian community soon after the crucifixion. They made a huge effort to make it work successfully but politics soon took over.***

***Nevertheless, all fine visions are worth a go even though they often fail.***

## 4.10 JOHN WESLEY

This great preacher, who also had superb organising and motivational skills, was the revered founder of the Methodist Church in England four hundred years ago.

His powerful but unorthodox ministry shook the Church of England out of its state of complacency. He created the first significant breakaway group from the Church which itself had broken away from Rome with huge encouragement from King Henry VIII. He needed a Church that would give him permission to divorce wives from time to time but Wesley had finer motives in mind.

The Methodist Church had its foundations in what Wesley called The Holy Club that he founded and led while studying at Oxford University. The club's members undertook an intense study of the Scriptures and then devoted a great proportion of time visiting and helping prisoners in jails while also acting to give sustenance and hope to the poor.

History now records that the new Church which Wesley created has spread worldwide with the same evangelistic fervour that was part of his DNA from his Oxford days.

This was quite a comeback for a man who began his career in Christian ministry as a missionary to the new American colony of Georgia where he was a huge failure in most things he attempted to do, returning to England in disgrace, but with humility and purpose. But this experience may be regarded as the lesson of his life that he was determined not to repeat.

The clear difference between Wesley's new Church and other Churches that began at that time was the great social conscience that Methodists throughout the world gladly inherited from Wesley. Following his example,

Methodist Churches were from their earliest days involved in caring for the homeless, hungry, sick, and persecuted. He made it clear that it was absolutely pointless to have your soul saved unless you then served the physical and social needs of humanity as a natural response of caring generated by your faith. How true this is and how rarely it is that modern Churches make any attempt to have their members follow Wesley's example and practise it personally.

So it is that I am now very proud that I have a direct link with John Wesley in my role as a lifetime elder of the Uniting Church in Australia which was founded almost fifty years ago as a union of Methodist, Presbyterian, and Congregational Churches. Wesley's forty-four sermons are formally recorded in the Constitution as one of the cornerstone beliefs of the faith of the Uniting Church along with the Westminster Confession of Faith.

I must confess that I have not read all of his sermons, even though as a lay preacher I have an obligation to embrace them as a basis for my preaching. Actually, a few of them are more than a bit boring, but I especially revere the one he preached about money. It is called: 'Earn all you can, save all you can, give all you can.'

It deserves to be recognised as one of the great economic philosophies of history. Its powerful simplicity is its great strength as is its very practical economic basis. Even those who have minimal education in economics can understand it and respond to it positively as it is represents a smart way to live.

Wesley had a ministerial lifestyle that was very different to that of most religious leaders. He served only briefly as a vicar to a Church of England congregation. The remainder of his ministry was as an itinerant preacher travelling constantly by horse from congregation to congregation, encouraging their growth, deepening their faith, and advising them on how to better care for people in trouble and need, whether they are Christians or not.

Until late in his life, he discouraged his people from acquiring buildings saying they were unnecessary because worship was best held in the open air. This was actually a pragmatic necessity in his case as great crowds came to hear him preach everywhere he went, often in thousands, meaning that buildings could not hold them. On one occasion 10,000 came to hear him and he addressed them without the aid of a loudspeaker.

However. Methodist chapels finally began to appear but their architecture was modest as Wesley wanted to use money to help people not construct lavish buildings. It is a pity that he ever changed his mind about buildings as many people down the centuries have come to revere buildings more so than the faith that was preached and sung in them.

Like all of us, Wesley was a man of human failings. This reminds us that far too many of us claim to be Christians while going to great lengths to cover up our failings.

He had huge personal difficulty in relating to women, not only publicly, but especially in his private life. He made proposals of marriage to no less than five women but was afraid to proceed further into marriage for reasons that he confided to no one. One of them caused him to leave Georgia in haste when she created a public scandal of his betrayal of his promises to her. On another occasion, he caused a high-profile scandal by travelling throughout Ireland on a mission in company with a woman as his constant companion, but not sharing a bed with her. He finally married a widow, but their marriage lasted only eight years, mainly because he was rarely at home. Thus, he left no heirs.

He died in 1791, aged eighty-eight, a very honoured figure in the life of Britain.

His final words to relatives and close friends on his deathbed are famous in Methodist folklore worldwide: 'The best of all is God with us.'

His brother, Charles, a huge asset in his ministry, was the creator of thousands of wonderful hymns, which he played and sang at most of John's evangelistic crusades, often improvising on the spot. He was an indispensable ally, much underrated by historians, as he was also a talented poet. Some of John Wesley's critics have declared that it was the musical talent of Charles that drew the huge crowds, not John's preaching.

His Christmas carol 'Hark the Herald Angels Sing' is still a huge favourite to this day.

I hold the view that the Wesley legacy is this:

- No one is a Christian unless you have a strong social conscience which is actively used to identify with the struggle of humanity for quality and meaning of life.
- Every Christian must be an evangelist who wins new people to the family of believers. It is not a Christian act just to come to church every Sunday but then do nothing to serve the world.
- Churches must be on a pathway of constant reformation. There is no such thing as the status quo when we are walking with The Man.

My daily challenge is to achieve some identifiable results in all three aspects of his legacy even though I find it to be a huge task for which I am ill-prepared.

Most Methodists believe that an essential basis of their calling to the faith is to abstain totally from alcohol, regarding it as a huge social evil.

However, an indisputable fact is that Wesley enjoyed drinking beer on most days because it was cleaner than contaminated water that most people were forced to drink in his day when public hygiene was appallingly bad.

But he also occasionally enjoyed a glass of wine as he found that it was a pleasant complement to food.

It was his successors who falsely claimed that Wesley was a non-drinker for religious reasons. They ignored the fact that Wesley recorded his drinking habits in writing.

It is worth noting however that Wesley refused to drink whisky, rum, gin, and brandy as he regarded them as poisons of the brain. Any frank observation by honest drinkers will acknowledge that his viewpoint is not totally incorrect.

*THE JOHN WESLEY GUIDEPOST*

***John Wesley proved that a person with significant strengths and many weaknesses can achieve great things when strengths prevail.***

# 5

# Prophets Who Opened My Mind

**WE COME NOW TO** those lives whose words changed our thinking and took the first steps towards moving us on towards another Reformation which may not follow the pathway left by Martin Luther.

They were wonderful revolutionaries who have inspired or challenged me. They are: Thomas Jefferson, Mark Twain, Father Damien, Ralph Waldo Emerson, Charles Darwin, Florence Nightingale, C S Lewis, William Barclay, John D Rockefeller, and Bernadette of Lourdes.

## 5.1 THOMAS JEFFERSON

Thomas Jefferson is famous for many things:

- President of the United States of America, its second vice-president, governor of Virginia, and American ambassador to France.
- Author of its Declaration of independence.
- One of the Founding Fathers of the nation who had a leadership role in drafting the American Constitution.
- Founder of the University of Virginia and editor of *The Jefferson Bible*.

- Revolutionary who was on the British hit list as a traitor to be shot on sight.
- Giant of history who ranks in stature as one of the great minds and political leaders of all time.

When he retired from the presidency after serving two terms and returned to his old family home at Monticello in Virginia, he wrote and regularly studied *The Jefferson Bible*. It did not become public until his daughter published it via the Smithsonian Institute after his death. It generated considerable public interest and still sells in bookshops 250 years later.

I purchased a copy online recently and immensely enjoy reading it and pondering its impact.

Having been born into a prosperous and influential Christian family where the Bible was often read at mealtime, Jefferson found it to be an inadequate resource for the sustenance of his faith. In particular, he outrightly rejected significant matters that most traditional Christians regard as fundamental beliefs. He had no doubt that the traditional Bible downgraded the life and work of Jesus and needed to be rewritten in a far more concentrated and dynamic form.

Some of his rejections of Bible content are matters that I have commented on throughout this book in relation to my own journey, such as:

- Virgin birth
- Miracles
- Resurrection
- Ascension
- The Bible other than the Gospels of Matthew, Mark, Luke, John.

> With those thoughts in mind, he decided to concentrate his study of the Bible on one crucial issue, the power and influence of Jesus the Man.

Everything else about Christianity was in his view just padding that watered down the core personality, namely Jesus.

He held the firm view that there was no other reason why anyone would want to become a Christian than to focus totally on The Man. Powerful Bible personalities of the calibre of Saint Paul were of no interest to him whatsoever. He regarded them as a sideshow.

Shortly after he left the White House he took one of the many family Bibles at Monticello and using scissors he carefully cut out passages of the Gospels that Jesus the teacher was recorded as saying or that others said about him. He deliberately omitted anything about the subjects I mentioned above as he found them to be irrelevant and ridiculous.

He assembled them into chapters and adhered them to blank pages to create a book that he regarded passionately as his own Bible.

On every evening of his final years, he read one page. He would then quietly ponder how the words on that page impacted his life and could improve him as a person and a servant of humanity. He did this many times over and he confided to his family that it was a discipline that did not ever bore or weary him.

All of this happened after his term at the White House concluded. His family was of the opinion that prior to that he had been too busy serving as president to search his Bible and collect the passages that interested him most. But his friends often remarked that he had discussed this with them on many occasions and had his choices clearly in his mind for a long time. He had been on a quiet journey of discovery, just as many other believers have done in varying ways.

I can relate to his experience personally as I have been preparing to write this book for a long time and now regret that I did not get around to doing so many years ago. I think that it was because I had a feeling of inadequacy that I was not sufficiently well-educated to tackle the task. However, as I am now ninety-three, I am very aware that I am running out of years and can delay no longer, uneducated, or not.

After Jefferson's death, his daughter began negotiations in Washington with the Smithsonian Institute to arrange that *The Jefferson Bible* would be published. It sold well and caused huge debate among Church leaders, particularly theologians, as well as many thousands of rank-and-file Christians. Obviously, most of the debate was destined to be highly controversial. Remarkably, his Bible still does enjoy steady sales and American theological colleges still have it in their curriculum as a book for serious study.

It proves the point that you and I have the right to create and develop our own personal values and beliefs and do not need to be forced to rely on Church dogmas and creeds which simply attempt to close our minds and instruct us to do as we are told.

Many critics, often with considerable hostility, openly declare that Jefferson was a fake Christian, not a true believer and they go out of their way to find moral reasons to justify their claims.

For example, they point out that he was a slave owner and assert that a Christian cannot be one. This is true but Jefferson's response throughout his life was that he treated them well and provided them with generous quantities of food and clothing and shelter, much better than would have been their lot if they had avoided capture and remained in Africa. While that is a statement of fact they, and their fellow slaves scattered throughout many states of America, were never given the opportunity to decide for themselves whether they wanted to live in their own country or be demeaned by a life of slavery in America.

After his wife died, he invited a slave girl, Sally Hemings, to live with him as his mistress. She delivered children to him out of wedlock. Jefferson did not ever try to deny the relationship. His neighbours affirmed that he treated her with the same respect as had existed in his relationship with his first wife. He often debated with her the meaning of the passages in *The Jefferson Bible*.

They also accused him of being one of the key leaders of the War of Independence against England in which many people died. Some declared that a Christian can never take part in a war but history reveals that devout Christians have regularly done so, often unavoidably.

I take note of all of those doubts about the integrity of Jefferson as a person and simply reflect that I too am a sinner for different reasons and I have no right to throw stones at Thomas Jefferson.

Were he president of the United States right now, how would he have handled the hugely divided Congress which is dominated by the ultra-fundamentalist Christian Right who are so hugely divisive in all that they do? I am certain that he would have begun and won a second revolution. He would not have tolerated them.

I thank him for *The Jefferson Bible* and for the freedom of thought that I have inherited from it after having taken a long time to discover it.

He has taught me and many others that, the more we search, the more meaningful our lives become as we discover that a walk with The Man is always a mind-expanding experience that we must cherish as a priceless gift.

*THE THOMAS JEFFERSON GUIDEPOST*

***Reading* The Jefferson Bible *was a key factor in my decision to write* Walking with the Man. *Jefferson convinced me that the four Gospels are the vital key to discovering The Man.***

***The remainder of the Bible is a treasury of background information that provides a helpful setting for discovering the core issues.***

## 5.2 MARK TWAIN

The books written by this legend of American literature and folklore were not Christian in their intent or content. Nevertheless they contain highly readable comments on life and the values by which we choose to live.

Mark Twain used his natural skills of humour, sarcasm, and communication to make people think deeply about their principles, ethics, and morals as distinct to their faith. He did it at a time when most of the world thought that the relationship between Christianity and good thoughts and behavior was exclusive. He helped to prove them wrong.

I have read the most famous of his books and enjoyed reviews of his many other publications, noting that he constantly assailed the leaders of nations about the decline they either fostered or tolerated in the standards of common decency and honesty. He achieved it in a manner of vibrant communications that most Christian leaders do not possess.

He wrote magnificently about the evils of slavery, cruelty, greed, poverty, excessive wealth, political corruption, business malpractice and much more. He was particularly powerful in his disgust of the way in which negroes were treated as though they were second-class citizens. All of his comments could easily have been accepted as the words of a Christian but without the piety. His public profile on these matters made him an easy target to be personally attacked by the political establishment on a very constant basis, but he did not ever relent.

They really could do little to curb or punish him as he was not just a superb writer, he crafted words with wonderful humour which attracted millions of adoring readers. In addition, he was a spell binding orator who drew packed audiences everywhere he went and this included speeches he made far beyond America. When he visited my homeland of Australia, he was a sensation. Huge crowds followed him everywhere.

His books still sell well worldwide.

Two of them, *The Adventures of Tom Sawyer,* and *Adventures of Huckleberry Finn,* are unforgettable. The latter criticised slavery very hard. His honesty caused him to publicly acknowledge that his own father had owned a slave.

*The Prince and the Pauper* hit hard at the gap between rich and poor while *A Connecticut Yankee in King Arthur's Court* took apart the British class system. *Life on the Mississippi* captured the deficiencies in the practice of decency in the overall American culture of his time.

He was a generous person too, even when he was short of money, which was often.

A prime example of this was when former US president, Ulysses S Grant, died in poor financial circumstances. Twain wrote an exceptional biography of Grant's life and immediately gave the entire book royalties to Grant's widow and children to save them from poverty. That was as fine a Christian act as there could be.

Twain struck hard times too. He heavily invested very unwisely in too many wildcat business ventures and was eventually declared bankrupt. Typically, he spent many years paying back all his debts even though bankruptcy laws absolved him from doing so. This was yet another attitude that Christians should be able to identify with.

His nation has revered his memory by creating museums and libraries in his honour. His former home in Hartford, Connecticut, is the most famous. It is on my bucket list to visit one day as I know that the quality of his life can be absorbed there. Similarly, his childhood home in Hannibal, Missouri, depicts his early life out on the frontier of America. In those days his name was Sam Clemens. He changed it when he began to write.

The great thing about his literary skills is that he forever sought an awareness of an ever-changing world. In writing about the deficiencies of society he always directed his readers to think about creating a better future, constantly emphasising both the real and the romantic, while always advocating that any weakness can be transformed into strength.

I see him as a very special person who was a rough diamond in a hard world. He used his skills to direct his readers to seek a finer way of life, yet never be defeated by its darker elements. In many ways, he was an evangelist.

While there is no evidence that religion ever had any real influence in his life, he would have worked comfortably with The Man as they both tackled the same personal problems that we all face from time to time. Maybe, he did work with Jesus but did not make a show of it.

I recall one statement of his that could be interpreted as having a challenge for Christians.

'There are only two important days in our lives. The first is the day we were born. The second is the day we stop in our tracks and ask why we were born.'

In my view, these words outline a pathway that The Man would identify with as a basic foundation of our journey.

For many reasons, Mark Twain has a special place in my life.

If we measure him in terms of Aussie culture, he was a fair dinkum bloke picking up his fallen mates out of the gutter. He motivated them towards a new direction by challenging the way they thought about life.

This too is exactly what Jesus did.

It confirms my belief that there are many followers of The Man who are not Christians. It is not a requirement that they should be.

It will be a great benefit to society if we can find more leaders like Mark Twain to enhance our world.

*THE MARK TWAIN GUIDEPOST*

***Secular authors of the quality of Mark Twain often have a greater capacity to link us with The Man than do religious ones.***

***They use words we can understand rather than holy and pious ones.***

## 5.3 FATHER DAMIEN

Gave his life to the care of lepers in Hawaii one and a half centuries ago and conveyed to us all a clear vision of what it means and takes to have an unshakeable sense of a Christian calling which is gladly accepted totally and fearlessly. In other words, he knew his work among lepers would cause his death, yet he did not shrink from it for a single moment.

While we might enjoy debating the validity of destiny, Father Damien was unshakeably certain that this was his destiny.

Damien began his life in Belgium in 1840 as Damien de Veuster. His was a poor family and, as a result, he received only a moderate education. Nevertheless, he sought and obtained permission to study to become a Catholic priest. He did not do well in his studies but his wise tutors declared him to be an intelligent person who was dedicated to his planned vocation. He applied to become a missionary, was accepted, and then sent to Hawaii in 1873.

There he soon learned that the islanders suffered from numerous diseases brought there by foreign traders, sailors, and immigrants and from which they had no immunity. Seeing a solution to this tragedy as being his prime calling, Father Damien decided to gather whatever resources so that he could to do something about conquering the ravages all of those diseases – leprosy, smallpox, cholera, influenza, syphilis, and whooping cough.

His dedicated work in harnessing those resources is now part of inspiring legend.

He organised governments and businesses to give him what he needed and convinced them that a large grant of land in a remote part of the island of Molokai should be set aside as a quarantine settlement that he would manage personally. Over time, eight thousand very ill people came there to benefit from his care. After a tremendous effort on his part, diseases abated throughout the islands.

He accumulated many critics who found fault with everything he did. Most of them were Christians from his own Catholic Church. As is usual with too many holy people, they accused him of not spending enough time teaching the faith and also alleged that he was unclean in his personal habits. In reality, they deliberately denigrated him so they could create a respectable excuse as to why they had not done what he had done for many years before he arrived. Clearly, they would do anything they could to ensure that they would not have to join him in his work as they feared for their own lives.

Eventually and inevitably, he contracted leprosy himself and knew that he had only a couple of years to live, before experiencing an awful death.

Before he died the king of Hawaii made him a Knight Commander of the Royal Order, the highest honour he could bestow on anyone but Damien rarely wore the medal as he believed that only God could say 'well done.' Thoughtfully, the nuns who buried him placed it in his coffin.

As the result of his magnificent work, and without any effort on his part, his fame rapidly spread worldwide.

His death occurred in 1879. He had been at Hawaii for just sixteen years and his splendid life had been lived for only thirty-nine years. For most of us, this is far too short a life span but then we must note that Jesus was crucified during his thirty-third year.

Nighty-eight years later, Pope John-Paul II declared Damien to be a saint.

Some eminent people rose again to criticise him at that time but those who praised him were many more.

The pope himself noted in his official comments that Mahatma Gandhi had praised Damien fifty years earlier for his extraordinary humanitarian work as had the famous Scottish author, Robert Louis Stevenson, who had actually visited Damien on Molokai at great risk to himself, having sailed there from his home in Samoa to personally witness what he had achieved.

Years later, US president Barack Obama, who for many years lived in Hawaii and still returns regularly on vacation, publicly affirmed his deep admiration of Damien saying that Damien had given 'voice to the voiceless and dignity to the sick.'

Many books have been published about his life and work and there have been three Hollywood movies. The Belgian Broadcasting Service declared him to be the greatest Belgian in history.

He is buried near his former home in Belgium, but his hand was removed and is buried at Molokai where its location is regarded as a shrine.

Around the world, hundreds of churches and schools and hospitals are named after him and the people of Hawaii still cherish his memory.

So, what should you and I think about his devoted life and witness and what impact does it have on us as we try to walk with The Man in the manner that Damien did?

Would either you or I be will willing to serve Jesus in a place and manner that would be certain to cause us to die. This represents the ultimate challenge to us all and I reckon I would fail it. My commitment to walk and work with The Man grows stronger every year but, while I do not fear death and will gladly choose voluntary assisted dying if I ever have a terminal illness, I want to find more and more places to serve not choose one that will ensure my service ends.

This just proves that I would not be fit to stand in Damien's shadow.

The ultimate accolade to Damien is spelled out clearly is the next paragraph and it is worthy of study as we face the inevitability of death.

Damien was diagnosed with tuberculosis before he left Belgium for Hawaii so he was very aware that he had just a short life span ahead of him. His most cynical critics in the Church have publicly declared that, because he knew he was dying, he deliberately contrived to create circumstances in which he would die as a martyr and achieve world fame as the result.

This is as crude comment as it is possible to utter and is far too frequent in the Christian world.

The unshakeable truth is he was a much better person than any of his many critics. He simply chose to use his short life for as noble a purpose as he possibly could.

Saint Damien was a disciple of rare quality, quite similar to another saint, Francis of Assisi, who had died in similar fashion. Indeed, many say that Damien deliberately modelled his Christian service on that of Francis. I reckon this is a correct assumption.

Let us just note with huge respect that both were great human beings.

Indeed, the world hungers for their presence once again and more often.

THE FATHER DAMIEN GUIDEPOST

***Father Damien had two role models in his life, Jesus the Man and Francis of Assisi.***

***I have chosen several role models who inspire me in addition to The Man.***

## 5.4 RALPH WALDO EMERSON

What a magnificent mind this man had.

Ralph Waldo Emerson was like Mark Twain in his enormous communication skills, but in a different way as a philosopher concerned with understanding of the challenges of life.

I took little notice of him until far too late in my life. Only a year or so ago, a close friend pointed out to me what a great thinker Ralph Waldo Emerson had been. He alerted me as to how many profound comments he had made about the way in which we live and the manner in which we determine the ground of our being.

I began to read and enjoy his best known books, especially his essays, and found that much of his groundbreaking philosophy had disturbed and threatened the Church and its leaders, then and even now.

Here was a man who had a deeper commitment to the values and ethics that he practised throughout his life than was the convenient spiritual shallowness that resided in the lives of far too many Christians who lived with closed minds to the simplicity of their ironclad beliefs. However, the benefit to Christians with open minds is to discover that much of the philosophy of Emerson challenged Christian dogma in a meaningful and respectful way.

Emerson began his working life as a minister of the Unitarian Church in the United States but, like many of us, he began to question the existence of an all-powerful and loving God who controlled all that happened in the world and punished us when necessary. His search for a clearer understanding of God occurred when he lost loved ones from sudden illness, his young wife at just nineteen and his son from a second marriage at five years, from scarlet fever. He wondered, as many others have done, where God was when both those tragedies occurred.

He left his Church to become a lecturer in philosophy at Harvard University in Boston. From there he made an impressive impact on the thinking of humanity at large. His essays on a wide variety of human issues are now regarded as being in the highest levels of quality literature. There is no evidence that any other essays were more widely read than his in the history of literature. In addition, he wrote many books that are now regarded as essential reading in academic circles in universities 150 years after his death.

His most famous essays covered such relevant subjects as Nature, Self-Reliance, History, Poetry, Experience, Intellect, Process, Power, Morality, Virtues, Moods, Unity, Religion, Conformity, and much more, including a subject that he gives the interesting title of Oversoul.

All of those essays had within them in some form a powerful reminder that nothing we experience in life is static or true other than for a single moment. He said that it was indisputable that the world changes every day and every aspect of life changes with it. He strongly questioned whether it was honest for Churches to say that words spoken way back in the biblical era have the same meaning as in the present day. He knew with clear certainty that we can find God only in the present, not the past.

Nevertheless, while I believe Emerson's comment to be true, I am mindful that Jesus calls us to respect all humanity, so we cannot ever discard the beliefs of those who have lived in earlier days of world history. Some good is always there to be discovered.

One of his comments has had a profound impact on me.

He said that none of us can stand, thump a table, and say 'this I believe,' as it means absolutely nothing unless we immediately put the belief into action, knowing the action will cost us something of significant value.

This rings very true for me as I am very certain that many of the beliefs I have acknowledged in my Christian life are actually expressions of hot air, no matter how sincere I may have intended them to be at the time.

In terms of public impact, his greatest work is to be found in his ceaseless assaults on slavery. They had an enormous impact on subsequent actions to remove slavery that were carried out by William Wilberforce and Abraham Lincoln. He extended his work in this field to advocate the removal of racism in its many forms.

In all of his work, his understanding of the profound words of the great thinkers is evident. In his life he was impacted by the thoughts of many giants such as Plato, Coleridge, Augustine, Bacon, Cicero, Goethe, Socrates, Confucius, and countless others whose ideas he tried to relate to his era.

I am very aware that I am challenged to study my values and sense of calling as I read more of his many comments on the questionable validity of traditional Christianity.

Another comment of his that has stirred my soul is this statement:

> 'Contemporary Christianity deadens rather than activates the spirit, whereas a Christianity that is true to a greater understanding of the life and teachings of Jesus should inspire our religious sentiment.'

All of this wisdom was packed into a life lived from 1803 to 1882.

You can read most of it in *The Complete Works of Ralph Waldo Emerson*, all twelve volumes. I took one look at those huge books and settled for reading selected essays. They alone stirred my thinking profoundly and I will read more.

I have decided that any Christian who ignores Ralph Waldo Emerson makes their choice an act of fear that this great man will shake his or her beliefs to the core.

Perhaps the most important comment made by Emerson is that no one who has a closed mind and rigid beliefs is a strong person. They just make loud noises as a cover for their inadequacy.

Means that we all need to do some regular soul-searching from time to time.

THE RALPH WALDO EMERSON GUIDEPOST

***The tragedies that devastated Ralph Waldo Emerson's life changed his view of God and uplifted his focus to personal philosophy where his books taught people to find the ground of their being, free of religious dogmas.***

***This is sound advice.***

## 5.5 CHARLES DARWIN

This humble scientist of enormous talent searched relentlessly to understand the origins of humanity and all forms of life.

He has had an impact on my life and my faith which is memorable and lasting and for which I am hugely grateful. Indeed, he is one of few people in history whose scientific discoveries have impacted the entire world.

I learned the basic details of his achievements during my school days but had not studied his life and work in any detail until Helen and I went to the cinema one evening way back in our courting days of the 1950s to see an excellent movie 'Inherit the Wind' in which Darwin's advocacy of evolution was the centre piece. It stirred my soul in such a positive fashion that I immediately went out to buy a biography of Darwin's life that set out his discoveries and their impact. Then, down the years, I gradually read the most influential of his own books on the results of his scientific adventures.

'Inherit the Wind' was Hollywood's view of the famous 'Monkey Trial' that was held in Tennessee in 1925 and which would become one of the most noted trials in American history. The court action occurred as the result of the Tennessee State Legislature passing, by a near unanimous vote, a law declaring it to be unlawful for any resident of Tennessee to teach any doctrine that denied the divine creation of man as taught and clearly defined in the Bible in the book of Genesis.

A young high school teacher in Tennessee, John Scopes, had involved his class in discussing whether the theory of evolution as discovered by Charles Darwin was true or false. One student complained to the headmaster who then reported the incident to the state governor. Scopes was immediately charged and jailed as he awaited trial for his breach of a state Law. Such was the anger of fundamentalist Christians over the 'heresy' uttered by Scopes that, acting on the clear will of God, they made attempts to break into the jail and kill him. Thankfully, they failed.

Interest in the trial spread across America when former presidential candidate, secretary of state and infamous ultra-fundamentalist Christian, William Jennings Bryan, undertook to represent the State of Tennessee in prosecuting the case against Scopes.

National attention grew immensely when a legendary barrister, Clarence Darrow, a very liberally minded citizen who was financed by a national newspaper, undertook to defend Scopes. A battle of the titans began and media from all parts of the nation descended on Tennessee to cover what would become an extraordinary event.

Little will be achieved if I describe the case in detail. It would extend this book by many pages. You can read about it in a fascinating old book called *Clarence Darrow for the Defence*.

Scopes was found guilty by a reluctant jury. They had no option but to convict him as he had deliberately broken a law that clearly existed and he did not deny that he had done so.

Nevertheless, it had become clear that the jury had been disturbed when Darrow systematically and comprehensively took Bryan apart by simply and clearly outlining the proven science that Charles Darwin had presented to the entire planet on his honest research into the basics of evolution. Bryan's inadequate response was shown by his utter confusion about the issues that were under debate.

The judge fined Scopes a token amount of 100 dollars and ruled that he could continue his profession as a schoolteacher. In other words, he was exonerated.

One small exchange between Darrow and Bryan highlighted the crux of the issue at stake. Bryan took the unusual step as prosecutor of agreeing to be a hostile witness when Darrow presented the case for the defence.

During questioning from Darrow, Bryan declared that every single word in the Bible was correct and indisputable. At one point, Darrow asked how it was that, when God created Adam and Eve who produced two sons and no daughters, humanity could expand from that point. Bryan firmly pointed out that the Bible clearly states that God found a wife for one of the sons. Darrow asked where God had found her. Bryan was stumped for an answer.

Darrow thundered, 'Charles Darwin sorted it out when he proved that she was descended from monkeys.'

The Monkey Trial generated a worldwide debate that yet continues because some fundamentalist Christians still believe that the Adam and Eve story is a correct account of an exact event that undisputedly occurred. But the controversy created by the trial generated a debate about evolution of even greater intensity than when Charles Darwin first published his book.

Even though he was a person of quiet nature, Darwin shook the shallow faith of many Christians to their very core. Especially, he disturbed the feeling of security that has always made the leaders of the Churches of the world so complacent. They viewed the science of evolution as having the capacity to totally discredit Christianity. Their personal lifestyle and the permanency of their employment was under threat. They felt a huge need to destroy Darwin's status as a genuine scientist and they did their best to try to achieve this.

The discomfort of the clergy did not cause Darwin to lose much sleep, if any. His aim was to foster the world's first serious debates about the relationship between science and religion. He wanted to ensure that the debate would persist despite fundamentalist Christianity continuing to defend its rigid positions. This has been a good thing as the enduring debate has the capacity to convince more and more people of the commonsense of walking with The Man.

It is interesting to note that, while lively debate flourished around him, Darwin quietly attended worship at his local church every Sunday. His best friend in the village was the vicar who was genuinely captivated by his regular talks with Darwin about how to lead his congregation effectively to an understanding of evolution and its place in their faith.

When he died in 1882 at the quaint little village of Downe after a long period of failing health, Darwin was accorded a state funeral at the wish of Queen Victoria and her prime minister. This forced a reluctant Church of

England to supress their vilification of him and permit his burial at Westminster Abbey. Countless thousands filled the abbey and the surrounding streets to honour a man whose honesty and integrity had opened their minds and relieved them from the oppression of Churches and the closed minds of Church leaders.

The Church of England got the message that it was on the wrong side of history and so all of its archbishops, bishops, and deans felt a need to flock to the Abbey to pretend they had loved Darwin after all.

There are several highlights of Darwin's life and skills that impress me:

- His was as pure a scientific mind as could be found in the realm of discovery. He never sought personal publicity or applause. He was committed to a never-ending search for the truth. This should be a hall mark of every follower of The Man.
- There was no arrogance in his soul. This is another virtue of real value. He constantly sought counsel from many great minds to check his findings before he published them. To him, the truth stood above all things and he knew that he should always check evidence that would lead to inevitable change.
- He suffered from appalling health issues that began after he returned from his epic five-year voyage on The Beagle that carried him on his famous journey around the world. Nevertheless his unfailing commitment enabled him to write *The Origin of the Species* and *The Descent of Man*. His continuing disabilities did not deter him for one moment from writing his other great

> books and conducting an endless range of further research. He had a powerfully humble sense of calling – another hallmark of a Christian.

His life story has sent me on a satisfying journey of discovery from simply considering that there is a mystical God who is a creator and a judge of all things to discovering that the prime source of an inspirational power resides in one colossus, a person whom we know as The Man.

I am hugely indebted to Charles Darwin for creating this pathway and am delighted that his voyage on the Beagle brought him to Australia where he was able to study the clear differences in wildlife in Tasmania from that of Western Australia.

A footnote to the Scopes Trial in Tennessee: William Jennings Bryan died a few days after the trial ended. His wife told the media he was finally overcome by a tormented belief that he had failed his God badly and was doomed to hellfire. Many bigots who revered him before the trial, publicly stated that God had struck him down in punishment for his huge failure to defend God's indisputable Word. For all his faults as a fundamentalist about everything, Bryan's long career in public life reveals that he was actually a great American patriot.

Just for the record, Spencer Tracy acted Darrow in the film and Frederic March portrayed Bryan. Neither were Christians. Darrow himself once stated that his preparation to defend Scopes had been an exercise in religious education that he had unexpectedly enjoyed.

THE CHARLES DARWIN GUIDEPOST

***Darwin opened my mind to the possibility that God may have not been a creator God. I enjoy the continuing debate about the powers of God* and I find that *there are not many. It is Jesus the Man who has power.***

## 5.6 FLORENCE NIGHTINGALE

The Lady with the Lamp.

Her legend is so great it will not diminish nor fail to continue to inspire the nursing professions everywhere.

A strict Anglican from the small village of East Wellow in Hampshire in England, Florence Nightingale was the pioneer of nursing as an essential asset of society. She also led the long overdue movement for the liberation of women to enable them to work in all professions and have a chance to gain equality of pay with males, even though this battle is still to be won, even today.

She stormed into prominence when, despite enormous opposition, she took a group of nurses with her to care for wounded British soldiers in the Crimean War, establishing a hospital at what was then called Constantinople (now Istanbul).

The upper crust of British society was outraged. In their view, no dignified lady would ever choose to go anywhere near a war. They must be prostitutes pretending to be nurses. What other use could they be on a battlefield.

The soldiers had a very different viewpoint.

They received tender care for their wounds far beyond their expectations or their experience of earlier wars. As Florence moved around the hospital in the late hours of night checking that everything was being done that could be done to care for every wounded soldier, they had not the slightest doubt that she was an angel.

She returned home to pioneer the founding of new hospitals for the people of Britain and launch training programs for nurses. She created a revolution in health care and was clearly the founder of what is now the National Health Service in Britain.

Then she became quite ill and spent more than half of her life as an invalid, rarely leaving her home at East Wellow. Famously, she occupied her hours in writing scathing letters to politicians and newspapers in her endeavours to transform for the better the essentials of life.

Deservedly, she received many accolades in acknowledgement of her contribution to the welfare of humanity. King Edward VII awarded her the Order of Merit in 1907, the highest honour a British monarch can bestow. She was the first woman ever to receive it. International Nurses Day is celebrated internationally on her birthday every year.

When she died in her 90$^{th}$ year in 1910, her family was offered the honour of having her buried at Westminster Abbey. They declined as Florence had declared in writing that she was to be buried in the grounds of her beloved little church at East Wellow. This was her spiritual home and you can visit her there. Her tombstone simply bears the initials FN and nothing else.

So, what can we learn of her life as a very strict Anglican?

Despite being a revolutionary in her public life, she was a solid traditional Christian. You could question anything you chose to debate about the world at large but she would never allow you to seriously question either the Bible or the creeds of her Church. There is some evidence that she was changing her rigid views as she grew older, as many of us do. I hope that this was the case.

It was therefore quite ridiculous and insulting for the pillars of British society to have declared her to be a prostitute all those years earlier. The accusations were even more futile when it was revealed that she had a low opinion of men, whom she regarded as being a burden on society. She broke off two engagements for marriage with wealthy and powerful English gentlemen, because she could not imagine how life could be worth living if you had to share it with a dominating man.

Wanting to be a carer from the earliest years of her life, she felt a powerful calling from God to fulfil that role. She was quite certain in her mind that if you were not a carer you were not a Christian.

These are two huge issues in my own journey.

I believe in the experience of feeling a calling to undertake great challenges.

I feel a stronger presence of The Man when I make a pastoral visit to a person in need than I do when I attend worship at a church.

A personal footnote. During my fund-raising career, I had the honour of raising funds to save the collapse of the tower at her little church at East Wellow. Had this happened it would have fallen directly on the grave of Florence Nightingale. Nurses from over a hundred nations sent money to ensure it would not happen. Some of the gifts were from Muslims, Jews, Buddhists, and Hindus.

After the campaign target was achieved and work commenced on saving the tower, I went to the florist at East Wellow, bought the finest red rose they had in their shop and placed it on her grave, quietly giving thanks for a great life.

THE FLORENCE NIGHTINGALE GUIDEPOST

***More than any other, Florence Nightingale made the world aware that women are a vastly underused asset of huge potential in the constant quest for quality of life.***

***She caused old blokes like me to change ancient attitudes and to enjoy doing so.***

## 5.7 C S LEWIS

C S Lewis was an author and thinker of enormous influence. He was a profound theologian who was not an ordained minister. He was a committed lay leader of his church with a far greater knowledge of theology than most of the professionals.

Initially, I had only a casual interest in the extraordinary life and work of C S Lewis until I saw and enjoyed a splendid movie called 'Shadowlands' at our local cinema. It is a very moving tale about human relationships, particularly revealing the personal tragedy in the life of Lewis when he lost his wife Joy to cancer after enjoying only four years of a very special marriage. It also highlighted his lifelong friendship with J R Tolkien, author of *The Lord of the Rings*, who shared his sorrow.

C S Lewis was born in Northern Ireland but spent most of his life in England where he held academic positions at both Oxford and Cambridge Universities. He despised his given names, Clive Staples, and insisted that he be known to friends by the un-academic name of Jack. That name lasted his lifetime but his books all identify him as C S Lewis. I have experienced the same problem as he did when my parents gave me the totally odd name of Everald. I have spent countless hours of my ninety-three years answering endless questions about its strange origins.

An author of thirty-two books that were translated into thirty languages, Lewis was astonished when his books sold millions of copies.

The best known is *Chronicles of Narnia*, which displayed his love of mythology, fantasy, science fiction and tales for children. I am much more interested in his work in writing *Mere Christianity* and *The Screwtape Letters*. No matter what my opinions may happen to be, most of his books became highly popular on stage, cinema, television, and radio.

In his early years, his interest in and commitment to Christianity waxed and waned as he regarded his adherence to it as a meaningless chore and a burdensome duty that brought no joy, just as millions of others have experienced.

He once wrote these profound words that have impacted me solidly:

> 'Had God designed the world, it would not
> be a world so frail and faulty as we see.'

I too have battled with that one all my life until I became aware that God did not design the world. Jesus taught us how to live in it.

Then Lewis changed his mind when he was thirty-three for reasons he never convincingly explained, He nonetheless became a committed Anglican of orthodox theology, later embracing the Anglo-Catholic tradition.

Throughout World War 2, having been rejected for military service, he was a regular religious broadcaster on the BBC. One listener wrote:

'The war and the whole of life tended to seem pointless to people like me. We needed a key to the meaning of the universe. C S Lewis provided us with just that.'

His life story is both fascinating and challenging.

He served in the British Army in France in World War I and was wounded at the Battle of the Somme on the same day as his best friend, Paddy Moore, was killed.

When he returned to England, he went to visit Paddy's mother, Janie Moore, twenty-seven years his senior. She cared for him as though he was her son and he warmly accepted her as a mother figure, having lost his own mother when he was quite young. He lived with Janie for twenty-five years and, although they occupied separate bedrooms, there was much public speculation about the question of whether or not they were lovers. However, it caused him no concern. When she became stricken with severe dementia and was moved to a nursing home, he faithfully, lovingly, and caringly visited her every day until her death despite the fact that she did not have any idea as to who he was.

There was further controversy when he married an American divorcee, Joy Davidman. They did this in a civil ceremony despite significant public opposition from the Church of England which banned all marriages involving divorced persons. She was the great love of his life and a person of high intelligence and ability in many fields. She died of cancer after only a short journey of sharing her life with Lewis. He was devasted.

There was also public controversy when King George VI named him as a Commander of the Order of the British Empire, CBE. He graciously declined the honour, giving no reasons.

What this tells us is that we cannot judge Christians by the difficulties they experience in life and how they handle them. No one is lilywhite. It is the depth of commitment to the needs of humanity that defines our lives, not our social problems.

We can say with certainty that C S Lewis conveyed his personal message to the world in many and varied ways, enabling people to understand matters of great depth with ease and complete clarity.

He used to say to his clergy friends: 'Keep it simple and powerful. Always.'

The demise of many churches suggests that not many parsons have followed his advice.

He died of kidney failure at the early age of sixty-four, on the very same day as President John Kennedy was assassinated in Dallas, USA. Lewis was mourned and revered by millions as a scholar, novelist, broadcaster, and influential communicator. The world remembers him also a fine human being. So do I.

*THE C S LEWIS GUIDEPOST*

***C S Lewis was a master of beautiful words that express an unlimited imagination.***

***I yearn for this talent.***

## 5.8 WILLIAM BARCLAY

It is important that we set aside some prime time to enjoy a close look at a very special theologian from Scotland. William Barclay was recognised as a cornerstone of Christian education for Churches worldwide, especially within the Presbyterian Church of Australia where I spent most of my early years of church attendance and involvement, prior to Church Union.

He was a scholar and educator of prominence whom I discovered in the days when I was an active member of the Presbyterian Fellowship and whose powerful words I have studied from time to time for many decades. He was a superb communicator with a wonderful ability to explain the Bible to people of every denomination and walk of life. In simple language, he could tell us in great depth the basics and benefits of important beliefs and do so in a manner that ordinary guys like me could clearly understand. At the same time he inspired us to look in depth at broader matters of faith that we would be able to take seriously.

Barclay lived from 1907 to 1978 during which he lectured at the University of Glasgow for twenty-eight years after having been minister of Trinity Church in Renfrew for a decade, his only pastoral appointment beyond academia.

It was during his years at the university that he became a celebrity mainly as the result of his many appearances on radio and television in Britain, regularly relayed worldwide. His fame spread also for his prolific writing, particularly his set of seventeen Bible commentaries about all of the books of the New Testament, which eventually sold 1.5 million copies.

His words are best described as elegant and he always related his words to the circumstances of everyday life, a fact that drew many people to read or listen to his every word as he made them feel he was talking to them alone.

Some of his most popular books, other than the Bible commentaries, include:

*The Mind of Jesus, Fishers of Men, Good Tidings of Great Joy, The Plain Man's Book of Prayers, Introducing the Bible, Ethics in a Permissive Society, The Ten Commandments*, and *The Lord Is My Shepherd.*

He also wrote thirty-five other bestsellers of genuine quality. His productivity as a writer was simply prolific. It revealed to the world a huge mind that never ceased searching for the truth.

He was also a highly controversial figure, describing himself as a liberal evangelical. This caused many lesser beings to attack him by saying that it is not possible to be an evangelical and a liberal at the same time. In my view, this is an opinion only held by holier than thou fundamentalists whose faith is so weak it can only survive if it is backed by ironclad certainty. Nevertheless, it is quite sad that they still believe that their fragile faith entitles them to be God's chosen people.

I am very far from being a fundamentalist or an evangelical in the current definition of those words, but I am absolutely certain that I have an essential responsibility to go out regularly and persistently to sell my version of life to anyone who will listen. It is a basic responsibility of being a working partner of The Man. There can be no cop-out.

Many of the beliefs that Barclay expressed also caused concern for sensible traditional Christians. For instance, some of his more revolutionary statements stopped regular churchgoers in their tracks.

He made it very clear he did not believe in the virgin birth of Jesus and discredited the authenticity of the miracles described in the New Testament. He questioned whether or not it was important for Jesus to be declared to be the Son of God because this was not a necessary element in proving his impact on humanity. Jesus was undoubtedly a very special person. There was no other religious or historical figure who was anything like him. Neither was Barclay a huge fan of St Paul and he totally dispensed with the concept of hell, and much more.

After all of that, many asked him what it was he did believe. Surely, they said in bewilderment, he had to believe in some essential cornerstones of the faith that were the ground of his being.

The short answer was that he revered the actual teachings of Jesus and the words of the Gospel writers and he wrote magnificently about the golden rule. This was his ministry and it is this that drew me to him. The words of Jesus are the core of my faith (and Thomas Jefferson's). Nothing else.

He knew that millions of Christians went through a daily routine of remembering simple Christian words and beliefs without ever expanding their minds to anything that would rock their peaceful existence. In fact, many with closed minds that avoided engagement with any meaningful thought that may disturb their faith and put it on the line in many challenging ways.

What is important is the impact he had on his theological enemies. One is recorded as saying:

'I despise his theology but I thrill to the many truths I have learned from him. I listen to him and I can't ignore him.'

Barclay himself said that all sermons are pointless unless they leave the congregation with something to know, feel, do, and change. His aim was crystal clear:

'I want to make the figure of Jesus more vividly alive so that we may know him better, love him more and serve with him forever.'

He succeeded in achieving this in my life and I am hugely grateful. In absolute truth, I am immensely in his debt.

*THE WILLIAM BARCLAY GUIDEPOST*

***William Barclay was a hugely skilful teacher who had a powerful influence on my life in my days as a young Christian. He taught me that to walk powerfully with The Man I must become a teacher as well as a writer and orator.***

***I am still learning the art.***

## 5.9 JOHN D ROCKEFELLER

The richest man the world has ever produced in any era anywhere and, in my opinion, will ever produce again.

In converting his known wealth of a century ago into modern currency value we can but sit in awe of the astronomical figure, so huge as to be almost unbelievable. There is evidence he had even more hidden away. In today's values, his wealth would exceed the combined assets of Bill Gates, Warren Buffett and Elon Musk combined.

However, the most interesting factor of life of John D Rockefeller, is that, quite unlike those three, he was a hugely devout Christian, deeply committed to his faith in a manner that grew in intensity year by year despite his constantly and rapidly advancing wealth. He lived by strict moral codes based on an ultra-fundamentalist theology on all matters except the means by which he earned his money. His wealth was a kingdom all of its own, utterly untouchable, seemingly apart from his faith.

There was one rigid belief that was an exception to this personal theology.

He was unshakeably convinced that his God gave him his extraordinary financial and negotiating talents. He was certain that it would have been a mortal sin for him not to use them. In fact, he was convinced that any person anywhere who did not use their talents to the fullest extent was indeed a lazy thief and a robber of God's goodness who was rejecting the riches that God wanted him or her to have and use and grow.

Incredible as it may seem to be for one whose heart appeared to be so cold, given the mystery created by his rare personality, he also became the world's greatest philanthropist who gave away many billions of dollars in today's values to causes that he believed would enhance the stature of Christianity in society, especially via education. Indeed, he founded and hugely endowed numerous ventures that would take the faith to the world by enhancing educational institutions that would teach the faith as a priority of human existence. No other person has ever matched his generosity in sheer volume of dollars or in the exceptional use of them on visionary projects.

He was a prime case study of how huge the challenge is when anyone tries to worship both God and money. The Bible clearly states that you cannot serve two masters, but this issue did not concern Rockefeller. He stated emphatically that he did not worship money. It was his slave, not his master, and he used it to worship God in the pursuit of the excellence that God had planned for him in everything that he did.

It is a baffling exercise when one tries to understand what made Rockefeller tick.

He owned quality homes in several states which he used occasionally as he moved around his vast empire but none of them were ostentatious. When he travelled for business or with his family, he did not occupy the best suite in hotels or trains or boats. He insisted on comfort, but never gluttony or flaunting of wealth.

At home, there was a period of Bible study at the conclusion of every family meal of his entire life, as well as many times of prayer. He always prayed before negotiating any contract asking God to lead him to success. And God seemed to do this very often.

He was a committed Baptist and so it was that the Baptist Church worldwide gained mightily from his membership especially in establishing Christian universities and schools.

Notably, he totally funded the creation of three universities that he planned to be Christian, but inevitably their Christian identity slowly faded after his death: the University of Chicago, Rockefeller University, and the Central University of the Philippines (when it was an American colony). The Rockefeller Foundation that he established to fund God's work exists to this day and still significantly endows new projects.

Despite this, he was hated mightily by both rich and poor, young, and old, and black and white. Only a few became close and trusted friends.

In his early years he bought out thousands of small businesses to create his mighty financial empire, the largest of which was to become the Standard Oil Company. He destroyed the future prosperity of many of the owners of those businesses by undercutting prices and denying them access to markets. He was unmoved by the huge public criticism of this as he declared them to be people who had not used their God given talents as indicated by the weak way they established frail businesses that could not compete with him. Their fate was a judgement of God on their lack of faith. He was acting as God's servant in punishing them.

He died in 1937 aged ninety-seven and is buried in Cleveland, Ohio, where he began his incredible career. He was the eldest son of a very poor Christian family and went to work as an underpaid bookkeeper in a small company of traders so as to help keep his parents from living in poverty at the time that the American Civil War was raging. It also enabled him to frugally save a small 'nest egg' that would eventually grow to become billions of dollars

As was his stated intention, there is nothing spectacular about his grave and no signs pointing to it. Tourists have to ask how they can discover its location.

A few years before he died, he wrote a simple poem that he said would sum up his life in a few words:

'I was early taught to work as well as play,
my life has been one long happy holiday,
full of work and full of play,
I dropped the worry on the way and God was good to me every day.'

None of us are in a position to judge him and most of us, particularly me, have all fallen short of what our lives could have been had we had a higher degree of commitment and made greater use of our talents.

If you can explain to me the complexity of the life of John D Rockefeller, especially in terms of his relationship with God and his personal practice of his faith, I will welcome your comments. I am baffled by the enormity of his presence, no matter whether I judge it to be good or bad.

He was a giant in terms of achievements in business and philanthropy and in his utter dedication to his religious faith.

On balance, I hold the view that his life had much more good about it than that which was bad. He provided employment for many thousands of people and he gave away much more money than he ever spent on himself personally.

In addition, his devotion to daily Bible study and prayer for ninety-seven years reflects a personal dedication that few others have attained.

What is fascinating about this extraordinary person was his close relationship with liberal theologian, Harry Emerson Fosdick, despite the fact that it was Rockefeller's total fundamentalism that put them poles apart. Together they established the Riverside Church in Manhattan as an independent place of worship that went on to become one of the most famous churches in the world. Rockefeller believed it would attract a different market of potential believers than his own church could.

You will read about it in my chapter on Fosdick who is one of my greatest mentors. Its huge success is a fascinating exercise in bridging theological gaps.

*THE ROCKEFELLER GUIDEPOST'*

***John D Rockefeller made a Herculean attempt to disprove the words in the Bible that say: 'You cannot serve God and money.'***

*In my mind, I am still thinking about whether or not he was successful.*

*Rockefeller constantly debated this right up to his dying days.*

## 5.10 BERNADETTE OF LOURDES

I have deliberately included Bernadette Soubirous, also known as Bernardette of Lourdes, even though she is a person about whose sainthood I have considerable doubt and which I feel has done little good for the world.

I have done this for the sole purpose of highlighting the high-profile manner in which she represents the supernatural world of miracles and visions, a highly controversial mind-set about which many people like Thomas Jefferson (and me) are hugely sceptical.

I was especially repelled by belief in miracles when I first visited Lourdes in the south of France and walked with Helen to the sacred site where Bernadette declared that she had seen the Virgin Mary on sixteen occasions over several months in 1858. Heavy rain was falling on the day of our visit so we sought shelter under the canopy of a nearby bus stop as we watched a tragic spectacle.

We were absolutely aghast at the pathetic sight of deformed, blind, and other obviously ailing people screaming as they touched her statue while their families and friends were weeping and wailing for a long time as they were soaked by the rain that fell upon them as they awaited their turn. Clearly, they either utterly believed or fervently hoped she would cure them. I reckon that their success rate would have been very close to nil.

Except for the impossibility of actually making contact with him, I wanted to immediately phone the pope and command him to stop this utterly false circus, as it crudely drags Christianity into the gutter of immense human manipulation at Lourdes. All that the Bernadette shrine achieves is to enormously boost the local economy of Lourdes where most shops in the city sell 'holy' items that they state with certainty will cure you quicker than Bernadette could ever have imagined.

The Catholic Church of her time accumulated extensive records that outline how they researched in depth her claims of visions of Mary before declaring the site of those visions to be a holy shrine. However, it also became very clear to the Church that Bernadette was not a normal person, either mentally or physically.

She was very sick indeed from the moment of her birth. In the prime of her life she measured only 1.4 metres (4 foot, 7 inches) and suffered greatly from cholera and tuberculosis, following severe asthma as a toddler. She had very little formal education and had limited ability to read and write. She was also undernourished as her family lived in poor circumstances.

When she became a nun, she could only do basic tasks. Even so, she did have a talent for embroidery. However, as a person who was generally ignored, she had a considerable need to be noticed and recognised. So it is possible that the visions of Mary filled this need.

Nevertheless, she was a human being for whom The Man died. Her visions cannot be written off totally just because of the limitations of her life experience. In our world anything is possible, even if only rarely.

The significance of this is revealed by events after her death which occurred in 1879 when she was just thirty-five years old. She was buried in the local convent of the Sisters of Charity at Lourdes.

She had revealed to her friends in the convent that, in the final one of her conversations with Mary, the mother of Jesus had told her that when she died her body would be free from corruption, that is it would never turn to dust.

Because of the controversy about the validity of her visions, the local cardinal ordered in 1909 that her body be exhumed thirty years after her death. The body though slightly deteriorated was still basically intact. Two more exhumations occurred in 1919 and 1925. On both of those occasions her face was clearly identifiable even though deteriorating. Photographs were taken on each occasion so as to provide a permanent record. Many rejoiced when these findings were made public and the size of crowds making pilgrimages to Lourdes grew dramatically, with millions visiting every year to the extent that she is now almost totally responsible for the prosperity of the people of Lourdes.

As is to be expected, many others believe that her body was carefully preserved at death so as to verify the prediction. Who will ever know the truth? There have been no more exhumations in the past century.

In the meantime, Pope Pius XI declared her to be a saint in 1933 with her feast day on 16 April every year. Many books, films, music, and icons perpetuate her life and highlight her visions. There will be many more in the years yet to come.

As is to be expected, there have been other visions in other places. I have no doubt that there will be more in the centuries ahead.

Another notable one occurred at Fatima in Portugal a century ago when three shepherd boys claimed they met Mary. Many pilgrims go there too, but not the endless crowds who come to Lourdes to honour the vision of Bernadette.

But the most famous vision of all was when a brutal killer called Saul claimed he was struck from his horse on the Damascus Road. He said that Jesus appeared and spoke to him, totally changing his life so that he would become Paul the extraordinary evangelist.

While not a vision, the Shroud of Turin in Italy is another mecca of the holy as the shroud is claimed to have on it an impression of the face and body of Jesus. With Helen, I travelled to Turin to see it, but we were not in the least impressed. In our view, there is no way that the claim can be justified except for the fact that it brings tourists to Turin to spend their money.

I firmly believe that we can feel the close presence of The Man in our lives and we can find that this experience challenges us to walk with him.

I certainly feel this presence as will also be the experience of many of my readers.

None of us need holy visions and religious relics to lead us to become working partners of the Man.

## *THE BERNADETTE OF LOURDES GUIDEPOST*

***Bernardette's visions of the Virgin Mary were real to her but her experience should influence no one else.***

# 6

# Guiding Lights Along The Pilgrim Way

**NOW WE COME TO** those who brought Christianity into the New World. They were renowned modernists who did their utmost in widely varying ways to make religion relevant to today's world.

I have carefully chosen thirty of them. They contain three whom I believe have demeaned the pilgrim way. However, they taught me how to use them as a guide-post to the way in which, from time to time, we must choose between fostering our ego or be accountable for our performance as working partners of The Man.

They are: Gladys Aylward, Eric Liddell, Samuel Angus, John Flynn, Mother Teresa, Lloyd Geering, Norman Vincent Peale, Mary MacKillop, Gordon Powell, Fulton Sheen, Alan Walker, Catherine Hamlin, George Pell, Zelman Cowen, Pope Francis, A J Cronin, Mary Baker Eddy, Mahatma Gandhi, the Dalai Lama, John Robinson, William Booth, Mitt Romney, Morris West, Harry Emerson Fosdick, John Shelby Spong, Tim Costello, Scott Morrison, Brian Houston, Billy Graham, and Rosa Parks. Their lives are fascinating and there are many things to learn from their experiences.

## 6.1 GLADYS AYLWARD

Another role model of mine who is an inspirational heartwarming example of how a humble person of limited education but huge commitment, who experienced an immensely challenging but undeniable calling, can walk with The Man, and achieve real results.

Gladys Aylward had no doubt Jesus had led her to begin a very personal crusade to help convert the people of China to the Christian faith at a time when that divided nation was involved in a bitter war against Japanese invaders. This would be followed by a prolonged civil war in which the communists would take power and create a society in which Christians would be denied any role.

I became aware of her famous endeavours as a missionary when I enjoyed a fascinating movie called 'The Inn of Sixth Happiness.' Then I read her biography *The Small Woman* and decided to do some careful research into her life and achievements. One thing I found was that the movie misrepresented a number of important aspects of her life. She expressed her concern but its worldwide popularity made her famous. However, Alan Burgess, author of the book, did splendid work in conveying the real story to a widespread and receptive audience .

Her personal history is a prime example of how Church hierarchies have so often wrongly and harshly decided who was a fit person for ministry and who is not.

When she went to the offices of the China Inland Mission in London in 1930, aged twenty-eight, to volunteer to serve in China, she was told that her basic education and her theological qualifications were not adequate for the job, given that her only work experience up to this moment had been as a housemaid. Additionally, she had struggled to learn the Chinese language.

They did not even note nor consider the obvious fact that she was a totally committed Christian soul whose heart was filled with love for humanity, especially the people of China. It is a typical attitude that bureaucratic Church leaders have repeated for centuries. They have consistently held a pompous belief they are a cut above everyone else and have a compelling need to tell you that they are God's chosen people and you are not.

So it was that, after years of careful saving, she made a very brave decision to journey alone to China even though her funds were barely sufficient to meet the lowest possible costs. She chose to travel by train across Europe, through Russia on the Trans-Siberian Railway and then down to China via Japan so she could try to take up her life's calling. She was a genuine disciple this one, and a hugely humble one. On the way she was detained by the Russian army who were involved with a border war with China but very bravely escaped to continue her journey to the place where she was utterly convinced her God had chosen for her.

When she finally arrived at Yangcheng after a long and lonely journey by foot through bandit country and where the locals believed all foreigners were devils, she offered to serve and was gladly accepted by an older missionary, Jeannie Lawson, to be part of her small team at a mission house that was called 'The Inn of Eighth Happiness' as its ministry was based on eight quite simple virtues that were the longstanding folk lore of the local Chinese people.

Those virtues are love, gentleness, tolerance, loyalty, truth, beauty, devotion, and virtue itself.

The fact that non-Christian Chinese have observed them for thousands of years would have been either heartening or disturbing news for Christians who still had problems in observing them.

Her eventful life in China was one that I could spend many pages outlining to you, but it is sufficient to say that she gave it her all and was very happy doing it.

Gladys found herself in charge and alone at the mission when Jennie Lawson died one year after she arrived. She took up this challenge willingly as she expanded the work of the inn and its care of the community. Every day she went walking in the city helping those who were ill and starving or were victims of violence. She provided refuge for prostitutes and those who were alone and lost. She also played a leadership role in the city in leading the movement to remove the primitive custom that all women must have their feet bound. Often, she was the one who unbound feet while hostile males made threats of physical punishment. As you would expect, none of this deterred her.

However, her primary aim was to find orphans and care for them, a commitment that would later bring her fame.

Two important events have highlighted her life.

She fell in love with a young colonel of the army of the then Chinese president Chiang Kai-shek. They agreed to marry after the war with Japan ended. There was nothing physical in their relationship. Once, in answer to a question at a Church meeting in England many years later, she emphatically declared that she did not ever kiss him. In her Christian view, any intimacy could only happen after marriage. Sadly, the war separated them and they did not ever find one another again.

At the height of the war, Gladys had a hundred orphans in her care and she fled with them to find a safe haven but they became trapped behind the Japanese lines. With huge ingenuity and incredible bravery she found a way through the battlefields and walked with them for twenty-seven days, finding sparse amounts of food and shelter in the most primitive and harrowing conditions, to find a safety in the south of China which was beyond the reach of the Japanese Army.

Despite being wounded by Japanese gunfire and becoming severely ill with a virus, she carried one tiny orphan every inch of the way. When they reached safety and found people who would care for the children, she collapsed and hovered close to death for a month. She recovered slowly and began a new ministry once again right where she was in southern China.

When Japan was defeated and the communists took control, they sought to arrest her, so she fled the country and found her way back to England where a church supported her work in raising funds to help Christians in China who were under persecution from Mao. Wherever she spoke there were packed out rooms. She was not a talented speaker but she conversed with them quietly and convincingly. The crowds adored her.

She tried several times to gain permission to return to China but was consistently denied entry so she eventually went to live in Taiwan and served there faithfully and well, as you would expect at an orphanage in Taipei. She died there from influenza aged sixty-eight.

Shortly before her death she had said to her friends:

'I am now a Chinese woman. I wear your clothes, eat your food, speak your language, and think the way you do. I am one of you.'

She also said that her faith compelled her to have compassion for human suffering and her life was lived with a simple belief in the power of Jesus to enable us to do good if we did so with humility, love, and faith.

Those words have made a deep impression on my thinking as I struggle to make a difference in the world as I walk along the pilgrim way.

When the news media announced her death, thousands of congregations in churches around the world spontaneously held services to give thanks for her life. Someone who was inspired by her put a plaque in her honour on the door of what was the former home of her family in run down suburb of London.

What a wonderful human being she was! Any reader who seeks to be a follower of The Man will be greatly enhanced by choosing Gladys as a role model. She is, quite emphatically, a role model of mine.

*THE GLADYS AYLWARD GUIDEPOST*

***Gladys Aylward was a magnificent example of total devotion to her calling to be a missionary.***

***I hugely admire her unwavering sense of purpose.***

***Indeed, I am inspired by it.***

## 6.2 ERIC LIDDELL

I have often been inspired by the core message of great movies.

If I rank by quality the fine films I have enjoyed throughout my lifetime, 'Chariots of Fire' must find a place somewhere near the top. I am not alone in thinking this as it won the Academy Award for best film of the year in 1981.

There were two main characters in the film, Eric Liddell, and Harold Abrahams, both of whom had won gold medals at the Paris Olympics of 1924 in dramatic circumstances.

Liddell was a committed Christian from a family with a long and respected missionary tradition and Abrahams was proudly and actively Jewish. Both held a conviction that throughout their lives they were victimised because of their religion.

Eric was talented at whatever sport he tried, but particularly athletics in which he regularly represented Scotland at international meetings. He also did well at Rugby Union having often played for Scotland against England, Wales, and Ireland.

Harold specialised in athletics but was also a singer of renown who performed regularly with the Gilbert and Sullivan company.

Eric's father and mother were committed for their lifetime to serve as missionaries in China and he was born there, only going to Scotland for his education and to benefit from some western life experience. His faith was deep and, like his parents and sister, was a fundamentalist Christian. Playing sport on a Sunday was for him a mortal sin, a huge offence to God. This conviction about the sanctity of Sunday created the circumstances that would be the basis of his fame.

Both he and Harold Abrahams were selected to run for England in the 100 metres at the Olympics with Eric as the favourite as he had consistently beaten Harold at that distance.

When Eric heard that the heats of that event were to be run on a Sunday, he immediately withdrew despite passionate intervention from the Prince of Wales (later King Edward VIII) who strongly encouraged him to run. The matter was resolved only when Eric's close friend, Lord Lindsay, swapped places to allow Eric to run in the 400 metres event, the heats for which were not to be held on Sunday. The matter had caused so much controversy and criticism that Liddell felt a genuine sense of persecution over his unshakeable Christian beliefs. Most people in Britain felt that, by withdrawing from the 100 metres race, he had let down the nation. They let him know in no uncertain fashion, especially via the media who were ruthless in their condemnation of him.

Harold Abrahams had a somewhat similar problem.

A year before the Olympics he knew that Liddell would beat him at 100 metres unless he improved dramatically. So he hired and paid large fees to a professional coach, a matter previously unheard of in amateur sport. Anyone who was in any way involved must not receive payment for any reason as this was a denial of the code of honour of a gentleman in those days. It almost resulted in his dismissal from the British Olympic team, the matter only being resolved when his professional coach was banned from being in the Paris stadium for the event.

With Liddell out, Abrahams task became easier and he won convincingly.

Nevertheless, Abrahams believed that the controversy was caused not by his employment of a professional coach but because he was Jewish, a persecuted race since time began. He was certain that a pure white British blueblood would not have been treated in the same manner.

Eric was not expected to win the 400 metres as it was not his best distance and an American participant, Charlie Paddock, was the world record holder and hot favourite. It was expected that Eric would win a respectable silver medal, a poor substitute for the gold he may well have received had he competed in his favourite race, the 100 metres.

Running a superb race in an outside lane, Eric flew out of the blocks like a thunderbolt to beat Paddock emphatically, setting a new world record in the process. He firmly believed that God was with him all the way, a reward for his faithfulness. That conviction is debateable as there were other devout Christians in the race who also thought that God was on their side.

After they returned home as national heroes, Eric and Harold became lifelong friends despite the differences in their religious beliefs and even though they would live continents apart.

Harold went on to become a distinguished attorney in London and a famous sports broadcaster as well as becoming a successful author.

Eric left Scotland to return to China where he would join his parents as a missionary. He knew that this was his life's calling and he worked at it with huge dedication.

He worked there at the same time as Gladys Aylward, but they never met.

When Japan invaded China in 1936, he was captured and imprisoned in appalling conditions in a camp run by brutal guards.

He died there from a brain tumour in 1945 just a few months before Japan surrendered. He was offered no medical help whatsoever.

When the news reached them, all Scotland mourned and Harold Abrahams joined them in grief for a friend he revered as a very special human being.

Since the occasion when I enjoyed 'Chariots of Fire' four decades ago, I have given much thought to the history of persecution of people for their religious beliefs. While I have been ridiculed for my beliefs, I have never ever been persecuted for them and I probably never will be. Nevertheless I am still unsure of how I would handle it if I was in that unfortunate situation.

Would I be willing to die for my beliefs? The answer is No, but I am not proud of this answer. I am just being honest.

I would be willing to die to save the life of a member of my family without hesitation but would not do so because of my faith. It is simply the right and natural thing to do.

Does this mean I am not a true believer?

This is a question about which I am yet to find an answer.

On the issue of whether I should or should not have played sport on a Sunday, I utterly reject Eric Liddell's decision. I played sport on a Sunday throughout my life even though I greatly disappointed my mother in doing so. I don't believe that any action to glorify Sunday represents an act of faith. Every day is the Lord's Day.

Helping a person in trouble is a far greater act of faith, hence my earlier chapter that praises the actions of the Good Samaritan.

Being sanctimonious is not good behaviour, but I don't think that Eric thought of it as being sanctimonious even though his critics thought so at the time. Nevertheless, I respect Eric Liddell and Harold Abrahams enormously for the value they placed on their personal faith in an era far different to the one in which I live.

THE ERIC LIDDELL GUIDEPOST

***I will never forget how very distressed my mother was when I played in a cricket match on a Sunday for the first time. Now, whenever I recall the turmoil of Eric Liddell's experience, I affirm my conviction that bigotry about Sunday behaviour has no place in our society.***

***Nevertheless, it is impossible not to admire Eric Liddell's willingness to retire from his illustrious sporting career to work and die in China as a missionary.***

## 6.3 SAMUEL ANGUS

The heresy trials of Samuel Angus occurred over a decade that began in 1934 and are still recognised as hugely controversial events of high profile in the religious history of Australia, even though most people could not care less about any act of heresy.

Angus was charged by his brothers in ministry with having publicly proclaimed doubts about what were regarded as fundamental cornerstones of the faith.

One of his more controversial statements was that he felt it would be a more convincing and relevant truth for Christians to accept if it could be proven that Jesus was the illegitimate son of a Roman soldier. He said that if Jesus had come from the depths of human misery, millions of believers who struggle daily with the challenges of life could more readily identify with Jesus's personal quest for respect than by identifying him with the purity of a virgin birth.

The vicious attacks on Samuel Angus were extraordinary as he was not a rabblerouser. He was a highly qualified and intelligent theologian of impeccable background and integrity.

Born in Ireland, his family were much respected citizens. His intelligence won him a scholarship to Queen's University College in his home country, then to study at Princeton University in USA as well as at Princeton Theological Seminary. He also spent semesters at universities in Marburg and Berlin in Germany.

When ordained as a minister, he deliberately accepted a call to Scotch Church at Algiers in northern Africa. While there, he often visited classical religious and historical sites in Greece and North Africa, writing frequently about his discoveries.

Then he was called to Australia by the Presbyterian Church of New South Wales to be New Testament Professor at their theological college within the University of Sydney. He had a distinguished career there and spent his private hours studying the Greek and Roman religions about which he published notable books. For this highly acclaimed work, he received doctorates from the universities of Belfast and Glasgow.

Angus was disappointed to find the theology of Presbyterians in Australia to be ultra-conservative and his ever-expanding study of theology set him apart from them. He believed that they did not understand the power of the original person and messages of Jesus and questioned their rigid interpretation of the virgin birth, resurrection, and ascension. His lectures and sermons were highly publicised and often criticised by leaders in his own and other Churches.

For a decade, he was persistently questioned by the courts of the Presbyterian Church at all levels around Australia in what amounted to be endless tirades of heresy trials. None of these trials were able to ever achieve a majority opinion to find him guilty, because of his obvious academic quality, his devotion to his calling, and his warm and loving personality.

Ultimately, the General Assembly of the Presbyterian Church of Australia in 1942 formally passed a resolution to end forever all charges of heresy against him.

He died of cancer in 1943, his passing hastened by the tension and toll of unwarranted persecution by vicious fundamentalists of limited intelligence.

Despite the relentless publicity that was generated around him during the decade of his persistent persecution, the only memorial to him is a lecture hall at St Andrew's College in Sydney, named after him. They also display his portrait.

A giant of honesty and integrity who had an open mind to the discovery of all truth is now largely forgotten, but not by me.

Every heresy trial in any place at any time within any faith in the entire history of Churches has always been initiated by bigots who have had huge egos and severely limited minds as well as a total belief in their personal holiness above that of all others.

In Australia, they hounded him to death.

Many of his critics publicly stated that his death was a very appropriate punishment for his sins.

I admire the refreshing honesty of Samuel Angus and his open questioning of the virgin birth, physical resurrection, and ascension of Jesus. I struggle to find a relevant place in my journey for those 'events,' as I feel that they downgrade the open honesty of Jesus the Man whose impact on humanity has never had any need to be propped up by bigoted myths.

Vale Samuel Angus.

I wish I could have had had the privilege of meeting you and learning from your great mind the quality that always seeks the truth.

I was just three years old when your being persecuted began and I heard only whispers of gossip about you when you died.

But I heard enough to subsequently seek to learn from your wisdom.

I continue to do so.

*THE SAMUEL ANGUS GUIDEPOST*

***The treatment of Angus is an appalling example of how bigots of very limited intelligence are able to persecute great thinkers and then claim that God called them to do it.***

***Accusations of heresy should be removed from the Christian faith. It expresses the desire of too many Christians who believe that part of their calling is to punish people.***

## 6.4 JOHN FLYNN

This great pioneer, nation builder and champion of the safety of life in the Australian outback has a significant place among those who have helped me in setting a pathway to follow in attaining that which I have tried to achieve in my life.

I first learned of him at the Methodist Sunday School at Linville when I put a penny in the plate on Flying Doctor Sunday. This penny would have bought me a big ice cream back in those days.

Sadly, I did not ever meet John Flynn personally but did listen to him often on radio. Nevertheless, this motivated me to write a book about him six years ago. I called it *The Man on the Twenty Dollar Notes* in the hope that modern Australians could be aware of what he achieved in nation building, morally ethically and physically. It all happened in a career that began 110 years ago and resulted in the establishment of the Royal Flying Doctor Service, The Pedal Radio, The School of the Air, plus twenty cottage hospitals located in the remote parts of the Australian continent as well as a caring ministry of padres who visited the lonely in remote places.

Flynn was born and bred in rural Victoria, became a much-loved schoolteacher and competent local first aid man, then felt a strong calling to become a minister of the Presbyterian Church. While serving initially in country parishes, he attended the General Assembly of the Presbyterian Church of Australia when it decided to create the Australian Inland Mission to minister to those living in the 80% of the land mass of our continent where they had no churches. The assembly voted to appoint Flynn as the first Inland superintendent in 1912.

They expected him to build churches everywhere across the continent and win souls for Christ in what the Church regarded as godless country. But he chose to carry out his ministry in a different way. He found the Inland to be socially primitive with males comprising 90% of the population and very few hospitals and schools.

In particular, he found that among the few women who lived there, far too many died in childbirth because the midwife was usually the husband. This hit a personal mark on Flynn. When he was two years old and his family lived in the bush country of Victoria, his mother had died in childbirth because there was no doctor within many miles. Coming to grips with this tragedy as he grew up, he affirmed that he would do his best to make sure that it rarely happened again.

So, Flynn made his move to create what he called 'a mantle of safety across the continent.' It would become the noble purpose of his life.

He began by raising money to build his first bush hospital at Oodnadatta in northern South Australia, followed by another at Alice Springs and then twenty more across northern Australia in remote places like Coen on the Cape York Peninsula and the Kimberly in Western Australia and Birdsville in Southwestern Queensland.

Crucially, he did not ever have any money when he started to build a hospital anywhere. He believed that if he worked as hard as he could to raise funds, God would open doors that would eventually lead him to donors.

He did the same in enlisting young nurses who would be willing to leave the safety of the cities to bravely work alone in his hospitals in remote places. He enlisted many and most of them felt a real sense of Christian calling to serve in the Inland as they trusted him to find the money to meet the costs of running the hospitals. He would personally address meeting after meeting all over Australia asking for their financial commitment to the cause. He was very successful, and took no credit for this. It was God's work.

This fundraising was repeated when he founded the Royal Flying Doctor Service.

Initially, he worked strenuously to enlist the services of Alfred Traeger, a wireless buff, to help him design a pedal radio which would enable remote properties to call for help. It created a revolution in communications in the Australian bush.

Then he formed a wonderful partnership with Qantas founder, Hudson Fysh, who agreed to rent him planes from Qantas at basic cost and no profit for his company. As there were few airfields, they then had to work out how to land planes safely on rough ground in paddocks and low-grade roads without accidents. He simply believed with great conviction that if you worked your heart out and took sensible risks in the service of God, you could never fail.

The Flying Doctor rose to great heights of service Australia-wide.

Again, he caused it to happen similarly when he created the School of the Air in partnership with Adelaide Miethke. It made an enormous contribution to educating bush children in the remote parts of every state. A tremendous achievement.

He had an enormous sense of personal partnership with The Man, a vision that is not prevalent now as Churches become more professional in their approach to ministry.

He was a tremendous nation builder both physically and pastorally.

Wherever he went, he answered human needs in a very practical way while at the same time creating a caring society that was based on the life and work of Jesus of Nazareth who went about doing good and creating a spiritual dimension in the lives of all who met him.

So we have the story of an extraordinary leader who will never be forgotten.

When he died the entire nation mourned as the ABC, in announcing his death, asked their listeners to join them to observe one minute's silence to honour a great Australian. They went off the air for the only time in their history. Thousands joined them, standing silently wherever they were across the continent to say goodbye to a man who had consistently inspired them. The ABC had never done this before and has not done it since.

He is buried close to the centre of Australia, not far from Alice Springs, where thousands of tourists stop every year to pay homage to the man who gave life and purpose to a harsh and primitive continent while he gave also gave it a human heart. His funeral was the first ever to be broadcast to the entire nation and its listening audience was a record at that time.

At every General Assembly of the Presbyterian Church of Australia, held every three years, delegates would ask him how many souls he had saved. He would invariably respond by saying that he knew of none who were saved spiritually but there were many who thanked God that Christian doctors and nurses and padres had reached out to them in time of great need and they revered God for this every day.

Here was a great Australian who showed the world that there are many special ways in which people can walk with The Man to create a better world.

Some critics falsely claim that Flynn ministered only to white people while ignoring the needs of Aborigines. It is quite simply not true. He met Aborigines on every property that he visited as this was where many of them earned their living. He knew and respected the fact that they had their own religion that came from thousands of years of culture.

Above all, he was wise enough not to try to turn them into white people.

Many Indigenous people walked from their remote tribal lands to attend his funeral at Alice Springs and have an active role in honouring his life.

Eventually, they provided the huge stone that stands atop his grave. It is now a permanent sentinel to the spirit of a caring nation.

*THE JOHN FLYNN GUIDEPOST*

***John Flynn was a magnificent example of a born leader who became a powerful working partner of The Man. He believed that his primary calling was to be a carer, not a preacher. Nevertheless, he was also a fine preacher.***

## 6.5 MOTHER TERESA

She was a saint whose life was marked by both huge commitment and public admiration of her work while at the same time creating considerable criticism and controversy.

Mother Teresa's work among the poor of India was once described by eminent British broadcaster and author, Malcolm Muggeridge, in a tribute he wrote about her, *Something Beautiful for God*.

At the time when Muggeridge visited Teresa in Calcutta, he was a high-profile atheist but she made a huge spiritual impact on him. He did not say the spiritual impact was Christian but he calmed down his ridicule of all faiths considerably. He decided that whatever it was about her, it was in his view a life that transformed his core beliefs.

For many decades, the world readily identified with her as Mother Teresa. Now she is Saint Teresa of Calcutta.

She died in 1997, aged eighty-seven, after a high-profile life. She had been born in Albania in 1910 but went to Ireland at eighteen to pursue her vocation as a nun. She then moved to India where she spent most of the remainder of her life.

She established a Catholic order which she named the Sisters of Charity. It grew in its outreach to a peak of having 4,500 nuns, doing work in 133 nations. Creating and managing the social and spiritual impact of an institution of that size and scope was an extraordinary organisational feat.

Teresa and her team were committed to giving wholehearted service to the poorest of the poor. This involved caring for the sick, the dying, the poor, the hungry, the homeless, the lonely and the rejected.

However, she drew considerable criticism for her high-profile opposition to contraception in any form whatsoever and abortion for any reason. In pragmatic terms, her opposition did not make any sense in a nation that is hugely overpopulated. She was determined to stick with strict Catholic dogma on all matters.

More concerning were the primitive conditions that existed in her shelters for the dying. It was often claimed that she did little to prevent people from dying as she concentrated on ensuring they had a beautiful death at peace with God when many of the deaths were not beautiful at all. She celebrated suffering as being something that brought each one of us closer to Jesus.

She took no notice of the constant criticism that was raised against her about these issues and the matter was ignored by the Vatican when she was declared a saint.

Teresa was particularly criticised for accepting large donations of money from people of doubtful reputation who wanted to bask in her fame, such as from the scandal ridden British entrepreneur, Robert Maxwell, who took his own life as he attempted to evade conviction for corruption.

So, where does this leave us in our assessment of Saint Teresa in our list of revered spiritual heroes?

I have always believed that if bad money can be used to help people in crisis situations without having to condone or praise the activities that produced the money, then I will use it. However, I always made a public statement saying that the money had been received and exactly what legitimate purpose it had been used for without praising the donor. We know that Jesus was ridiculed because he had friends who were tax gatherers and prostitutes.

Her emphasis on people having a beautiful death rather than doing everything she could to keep them alive causes doubts in my mind about the genuine validity of her work.

It may have been a pragmatic decision made by her in the knowledge that if the dying person was revived in one of her homes, they would certainly die quickly when they left her care to return to their life of perpetual poverty and hunger. If this is indeed the case then it seems to me to have been a quite cold-blooded action that was without compassion but who can stand in judgement of her decisions. You and I were not there to participate in the challenges she faced every day and we are probably relieved that we were not.

Furthermore, I for one would never offer to work and live in the conditions in which Teresa lived for many decades in Calcutta and where members of her order live worldwide. So I am not qualified to judge her.

I believe that when she was awarded the Nobel Peace Prize, as well as the Order of Australia, she had earned those honours.

Above all, she gave to us an example of what it means to dedicate one's life so totally dedicated to serving the poor.

She described her life in these simple words.

'By faith, I am a Catholic nun whose heart belongs entirely to Jesus.'

The Vatican acknowledged this when they declared her to be a saint.

However, it should be noted, her recognition as a saint caused controversy as some of the Vatican hierarchy strongly opposed it because the Devil's Advocate, appointed by the pope to undertake the traditional task of proving she was unworthy, had strongly recommended that she be denied it because she did not try to eliminate suffering from the lives of those who sought her aid. He said that she fostered suffering as an essential religious experience and he is reported to have asked the pope to condemn such a belief as being false.

His name was Christopher Hitchens, an eminent atheist. He did not remain quiet when the pope rejected his findings.

Few of us are qualified to sit in judgement.

But we are all aware that there is no person anywhere in the world who has lived a life of total purity. We all make huge mistakes and show poor judgement from time to time. The challenge for us is to admit them and to lift our game.

This applies to all of us who choose to become working partners of The Man and base our lives on him as our role model. We will all on occasion fall short of the mark as we never lose our frail humanity.

Be this as it may, very few of us will qualify as saints. I don't think many of us will aspire for the honour.

*THE MOTHER TERESA GUIDEPOST*

***Mother Teresa drew huge worldwide attention to a theological question. She believed that if a person was doomed to die as a result of poverty and hunger, she must ensure they have a beautiful death in full communion with God.***

***Her critics said her duty was to try to give them a life. She said the plight of the poor was so vast it was impossible for her to solve it. Was Teresa right? I think not.***

## 6.6 LLOYD GEERING

You will have noted that I have dedicated my book to Lloyd Geering (more correctly, the Revd Professor Sir Lloyd Geering).and have made some remarks on my relationship with him in the opening pages of this book.

Geering is a New Zealand Presbyterian who as an ordained minister became professor of theology at Knox College at the University of Dunedin in New Zealand, then at the University of Queensland, and finally in New Zealand again at Victoria University in Wellington.

He became a national and international public figure when, fifty years ago, he was tried before the courts of the Presbyterian Church of New Zealand on several charges of heresy. It became a very high-profile trial covered daily by radio and television, together with massive newspaper coverage. The heresies for which he was charged were similar to those that Samuel Angus had faced decades earlier with the Presbyterian Church of New South Wales. Like Angus, he was found to be not guilty by a considerable margin.

I met him on many occasions when he was at the University of Queensland and when he subsequently visited Brisbane on a lecture tour after his heresy trial, he was a guest in my home. Since then, I have read his many books that helped me greatly on my spiritual journey.

To give you an idea of Geering the man, I include a comment on a publication that was issued recently by the scholars and staff of the Westar Institute on his birthday at one hundred and five.

It is a reprint of a highly debated commentary that he had written several years beforehand and which he had entitled: *How My Thinking has Changed.* It caused yet another stir among fundamentalists who again publicly condemned him.

In considering its words, it is important to note that for years before his birth his parents had given up their Christian beliefs and had ceased to attend any church. This meant that he had no connection with any Christian organisation until his university days when a friend took him to a Presbyterian church. This led him to join the Student Christian Movement in 1937, a decision that entirely changed his plans for his life.

So we can briefly assess its impact, it will be best if I directly quote from some his written words and make a short personal comment about each, shown in brackets:

'I have never once preached that Christ's death on the cross achieved our salvation as I regard that sort of orthodoxy as quite outmoded.'

(In my early days as a lay preacher I did preach sermons about the crucifixion being the path to salvation, but have not done so during the past fifty years.)

'My sermons expound Christianity as a way of life based on the moral teaching of Jesus of Nazareth.' (Spot on)

'The New Testament is clothed in the mythical thinking that was current in the ancient world but is no longer relevant today.' (Absolutely)

'The resurrection and ascension of Jesus into heaven can no longer be taken at face value.'

(I have always been unconvinced of a physical resurrection but very certain about a spiritual one. An ascension into heaven is simply unbelievable.)

'Christianity cannot claim to be the only true spiritual home for humanity and then judge all others to be false.'

(This traditional Christian claim of superiority is actually one of complete fundamentalist arrogance which The Man himself would reject.)

'Jesus is not someone whom we should worship as the divine Son of God. This practice belongs to the world of ancient mythology, the chief proponent of which was St Paul who did not ever meet Jesus in the flesh.'

(I do not worship Jesus. I have the huge privilege of walking and working with Jesus the Man whom I hugely respect as the cornerstone of my life.)

In my earlier life, funerals celebrated the departure of the deceased to a better life in the next world. Now, most funerals are a celebration of a life that has come to an end. (I rejoice in the change.)

I have never thought it necessary or even desirable to reject Christianity as some atheists delight in doing. I remain very grateful to the Christian tradition.

(So do I. It is the very fabric of my life, even though I rarely use the words of the Christian tradition in describing the basis of my faith. I prefer to reject all the creeds and doctrines and simply state emphatically that I am grateful for having enjoyed the privilege of walking and working with The Man along the pilgrim way.)

I could record many more of Lloyd Geering's comments but these to me are very decisive ones that can generate the most respectful debate.

May I say in closing that I am hugely grateful for having enjoyed the privilege of meeting Lloyd Geering and learning much of genuine value from him.

Years ago when he stayed for a few days with Helen and me at our Aspley home we found it to be a mind-expanding experience as it also had been when we had the good fortune to attend meetings that he led on other occasions.

He has a wonderful mind and huge clarity in communication both as a speaker and a writer, as well as extraordinary grace under pressure when faced with a hostile audience, an event that occurs more often than not.

He challenged my thinking in so many open and honest ways that made me feel able not to fear that in some way I was denigrating Jesus.

I sincerely feel that I have grown enormously in my relationship with The Man in ways that I may never have discovered without the leadership of Lloyd Geering.

His impressive life has so far lasted a splendid 106 years and counting.

At ninety-three, I am quite clearly just a young lad by comparison, thirteen years his junior. I am very aware that I am far behind him in mental capacity and expanse of thinking.

It is unlikely that there will be many more years in his long life, but in whatever that may be, I am certain that if I can also stay the course I will gain many more new thoughts from him that will continue to expand my mind.

*THE LLOYD GEERING GUIDEPOST*

***Lloyd Geering has added to my ability to act with courage and grace when under heavy fire.***

***Especially, he took the mythology out of my practice of religion and showed me a commonsense pathway of discovery to find my reason for being.***

## 6.7 NORMAN VINCENT PEALE

As a young man filled with ambition I read and immensely enjoyed Peale's bestselling book *The Power of Positive Thinking*.

I soon found out that I was one of many millions of young guys throughout the world who had done likewise. This motivational book sold 75 million copies. Not many authors ever achieve such success with their book sales.

I was so impressed by its clearly stated and sensible comments that I read it three times in a decade and firmly and permanently decided that negativity was a self-inflicted burden that Jesus never intended anyone to carry. It is a decision I have never ever regretted as I have discovered that it is always best to look at every situation positively and push negatives out of any debate until I reach the point that there is absolutely no other alternative but to surrender.

Norman Vincent Peale served as pastor of the Marble Collegiate Church in downtown Manhattan for more than half a century, and his popular ministry there caused it to become one of the most famous churches in the United States of America, matching in fame the Riverside Church of Harry Emerson Fosdick.

Forty years ago, I attended a Sunday morning service there as I had been given an introduction to meet the famous preacher by Gordon Powell, an eminent Presbyterian minister in Australia who was a long-standing friend of Peale. He invited me to meet him for coffee at the conclusion of the second church service on the Sunday I was in New York. On every Sunday he preached twice, with two thousand people attending his services. It was a large church and there was a sizeable basement that handled the overflow.

As I listened to his sermon, I was hugely impressed by his ability to connect with the congregation to the extent that everyone felt he was talking solely to them with a very personal message that would lift their souls. He held the packed church spellbound, especially when he skilfully added a lot of wit into his message, generating constant laughter.

The great man greeted me warmly in his office as he made and served our coffee. We had an interesting discussion about why people flocked to his church and what they hoped to hear so they could face the world positively in the week ahead. He said that throughout history Christians have always sought to find leaders to whom they could personally relate. This told him that he had an enormous responsibility to meet the expectations of those who regarded him as a prophet even though he worked persistently at creating the image of being a light-hearted conversationalist.

As I rose to leave, I asked if he would give me a parting word of advice.

He said without hesitation:

'Never ever end a day with the last words that pass between you and the one you love being those of anger.'

Great advice. Helen and I have carefully observed it.

Many of the great and mighty have publicly criticised Peale, accusing him of having only one message – live positively. I had asked him if he would mind commenting on the validity of those critics.

He did not deny that his ministry was mainly focussed on positivity but he said that he always chose sermon topics that were based on issues of life that people were experiencing that very week. He said that he could not find any time in the life of Jesus where he had spoken negatively. All of Jesus's comments were designed to uplift people's lives.

I reminded him politely that some of his more famous comments had departed from positivity and had ventured negatively into the world of politics.

I was referring to comments he had made via high profile public broadcasts when he had asked his listeners not to vote for John F Kennedy to become president of the United States of America in 1960 because he was a Catholic who would be subservient to Rome.

He had said on another occasion that presidential candidate Adlai Stevenson must not defeat Ike Eisenhower because he was divorced.

Pointedly he had also opposed abortion and demeaned homosexuals.

In a friendly tone, he reminded me that we all make many mistakes in life, some of them huge. He then confided that he had subsequently phoned both Kennedy and Stevenson to apologise. He said that genuine repentance was a source for adding positivity to the soul.

I knew that I had been privileged to meet such a famous and influential person as Norman Vincent Peale. I was greatly impressed when Gordon Powell called me on my return home to say he had received a letter from Peale thanking him for sending 'such a fine young man to visit him.'

Peale was not a hot gospeller.

He rarely called on his congregation to repent of their sins. He simply gave them sound advice on how to live well and to achieve this by being powered by the influence of Jesus who came out of Nazareth to create a positive world.

There can be no doubt that this is a wonderful message to a troubled world.

*THE NORMAN VINCENT PEALE GUIDEPOST*

***I grew up in a church environment where sins and the necessity of being forgiven for them dominated my life. This sense of negativity hindered my growth as a person.***

***Norman Vincent Peale has had a key role in putting positivity into my life. He has guided me along a path that put new purpose into my sense of vocation.***

## 6.8 MARY MACKILLOP

Australia's only canonised saint of the Catholic Faith.

In our earthly understanding of matters religious, Mary MacKillop achieved what is generally regarded as the highest honour that a Christian can aspire to receive by way of public recognition.

An extraordinarily influential person, spiritually and politically and organisationally, she was a tremendous contributor to the expansion of modern education in which Christianity is the cornerstone and a Church is a powerful sponsor and controlling influence. Her personal achievements in establishing Christian schools have had very few peers anywhere in the world.

Even more remarkable is the indisputable fact that she was the only person in the history of the Catholic Church anywhere in the world who was excommunicated in disgrace, then redeemed, and subsequently declared a saint. It was a comeback greater than that achieved by Lazarus when he made it back from the dead.

She was born into an impoverished family at Fitzroy in Melbourne in 1842, her father having been trained as a priest, but had then declined to take his final vows. She began her career as a shop assistant before becoming a teacher in a Catholic school at Portland in Western Victoria. She then moved to Penola in South Australia where the local parish priest helped her to start a small school, the first of many that would follow. This tiny school building still stands today and I have visited it to pay my respects to this great Australian. It still stands as a memorial to her life's work.

While at Penola, she founded 'The Sisters of Saint Joseph of the Sacred Heart.' They are an order of nuns who vow to live in poverty and devote their lives to the education of the children of the poor. She was its first member and its initial Superior. The order in its later years eventually became fondly known by the loving handle of 'The Joeys.'

It quickly spread nationally, establishing schools across the continent, but did so far too rapidly. This led to it encountering extreme financial difficulties which caused several Catholic bishops, most unwillingly, to have to pay her debts. Nevertheless, she stoutly refused to allow the Church to take control of her schools.

Over a period of time, she defied them and this caused one of the bishops to excommunicate her and close most of her schools. She was reinstated a year later and reopened them all but even more high-profile fights with bishops and cardinals continued throughout her life. They were never able to conquer her and indeed they grew to fear her.

The strain of it all eventually took its toll and she suffered a severe stroke while visiting Rotorua in New Zealand where she was extending her 'empire' which now consisted of schools, convents, and charitable institutions.

She died shortly afterwards at sixty-seven.

Ninety years later, Pope Benedict declared her a saint. This was celebrated before a huge mass held at Randwick Racecourse in Sydney and later repeated at St Peter's Square at the Vatican.

Her virtues were highlighted by a huge sense of charity to her neighbours and an affectionate but determined nature.

What was it about her faith that led her eventually to be the most revered Catholic that the nation of Australia has ever produced?

- An acute sense of the creative purpose for which she lived.
- A powerful belief that if you educated children at a Catholic school they would grow up to be committed Catholics for the rest of their days. This did not always work in reality as rigid education in a Church school often switched its students off for life. Nevertheless, it was for her a noble goal that was well worth trying.
- A great love of the poor, being committed to the goal of giving them all a basic start in life. More often than not, she waived their unpaid fees.
- Proof that women could establish, manage, and succeed in creating great institutions without being dominated by males. In the case of Mary MacKillop, she regarded most of the males who led the Catholic Church as dead weight in her saddle bags. History provides much evidence that she was absolutely correct in making this assumption.

Florence Nightingale held the same view about all males, no matter what their education was.

I remember her with respect whenever I drive past one of her most famous schools, All Hallows School in my home city of Brisbane. It is located on high ground at the approaches of the Story Bridge and dominates the area as a prime example of her powerful presence.

Even more importantly, the Joeys continue to this day to carry out her deep commitment to the education of the poor.

THE MARY MACKILLOP GUIDEPOST

***Mary MacKillop had no need to seek help from 'Me Too' movement to win her battles against the male-dominated hierarchy of the Catholic Church. She did not flinch during any of the battles she won over them.***

***More women in church life can copy her skills and determination. Hopefully, male-dominated churches will quietly fade away.***

## 6.9 GORDON POWELL

Now we can talk about my good friend in Australia who had arranged for me to meet Norman Vincent Peale in New York.

When planning this book, I decided that I would include a chapter or two about ministers of religion who were personal friends and whose ministries were important milestones of my journey. I have chosen to base the chapter not just around Gordon Powell who had the highest public profile of them all and then mention some of the others in the same context.

It was a great learning experience for me to enjoy a close friendship with Gordon Powell as he was in his era, which began in the 1950s and lasted for decades, the finest radio evangelist and influential Christian author in Australia at that time.

At a young age, he was called to be minister of St Stephen's Presbyterian Church in Macquarie Street, Sydney, located just across the street from the New South Wales State Parliament. Many people call it the Presbyterian cathedral of Australia. His popularity as a preacher resulted in the church being packed out for the morning and evening services every Sunday.

However, his greatest impact was when he commenced a lunchtime church service every Wednesday that began at 1.15pm and finished at 1.45pm on the dot. It was so popular that you needed to get there early or otherwise you would struggle to get a seat. Its greatest impact was that radio stations located across the continent broadcast it later in the week. This was back in the days when technology did not enable direct broadcasts because of the huge cost involved. Cassettes of the service had to be despatched to fifty stations by express freight on Wednesday afternoon. They played it the following weekend. Ratings revealed that thousands listened in and were hugely impressed with the engaging way in which Powell conveyed his Christian message so concisely.

He broadcast from Sydney every Wednesday lunch hour for many years and continued this lunch time ministry when he was called from Sydney to become minister of Scots Church in Collins Street, Melbourne. There it enjoyed similar success for many more years. On several occasions at both churches he invited me to read the lesson.

His impact was also felt through his skill as a writer. His many books were bestsellers. The most popular were: *Happiness is a Habit*, *The Secret of Serenity*, and *The Blessing of Belief*. They enjoyed good sales but not in the same volume of numbers as those of Norman Vincent Peale. They did well considering that Australia has only a fraction of the population of the United States.

In the same era that I enjoyed the ministry of Gordon Powell, I was privileged to have a valued friendship with Fred McKay, successor to John Flynn, about whom you have read in a previous chapter. Fred was a very down-to-earth character who talked the language of the Australian bush in a way that enabled people to think of Jesus as a good bloke. He, like Flynn, believed that he was called to shower humanity with genuine Christian love. Fred and I met often down the years and worked closely together to establish John Flynn Place in Cloncurry in Queensland as well as to restore the Presbyterian Mission Hospital in Pusan, Korea that had fallen on hard days.

We spoke by phone just a week before he died.

He said: 'God gave you special leadership talents Everald. Keep on using them in all the work you do so as to contribute to making the world a better place.'

A very special leader, who was rightly proud of his Māori heritage, was Archbishop Sir Paul Reeves, governor of New Zealand, and formerly the Anglican primate of New Zealand. I first worked with him when he was the Christian Education director of the Anglican diocese of Auckland and again when he was bishop of Napier. He had huge charisma and great communication skills as well as a powerful belief in the very necessary removal from the planet of racism, inequality, and injustice. This made him a constant target for critics who publicly accused him of being a socialist, a communist, a radical and a heretic. Some of his critics were Christians but they did not deter him in the slightest from his belief that his calling was to be a revolutionary pastor of the oppressed in the same fearless manner as Jesus. He was a giant.

A brief mention of two others:

John Fairlie Forrest, minister of St Stephen's Presbyterian Church, Toowoomba in the days of my youth who taught me many principles of leadership, and the Anglican bishop of Grafton, Gordon Arthur, who was my mentor in teaching me the basic principles of stewardship and the organisation of stewardship in parishes. Both of these dedicated pastors were modern prophets in their deep conviction that Christianity was the cornerstone of society and that the pastoral care of good stewards was a vital element of being a disciple. I owe them both much. They were memorable partners on my spiritual journey.

Of special memory is Scott McPheat with whom I grew up in the PFA. He was a spellbinding preacher who became minister at St Andrew's Presbyterian Church in Brisbane, Auckland Presbyterian Church in New Zealand and St Stephen's Sydney after Gordon Powell had moved to Melbourne. His life came apart after his marriage failed. Almost overnight, he totally lost his Christian faith, resigned as a minister, and walked away from his life's vocation. I called him as soon as I heard the news and invited him to lunch. He declined graciously and said:

'Everald, it is all gone. There is nothing there. Absolutely nothing.'

'What caused this tragedy to occur, Scott?'

'None of it makes any sense anymore Everald. It has all proven to be a complete myth.'

We parted as friends and he died soon after. Scott's comments hit me for six. I could readily accept that God is a myth. But Jesus the Man, never. His reality is indisputable.

Allow me to finish with two more inspirational comments about Gordon Powell.

He was the founder in Australia of Alcoholics Anonymous and very active in its work throughout his life. He was convinced that alcohol was a major threat to humanity but believed it was pointless to condemn it with fiery sermons from the pulpit. He had to get his hands dirty right down in the dark places where people were hurting from its impact and set a practical pathway for them to recover and enjoy a good life. He did not ever cease to try to achieve this aim.

In his later years, his final parish ministry was as minister of the Pawling Presbyterian Church in rural New York State in the US, where most of the congregation were quite substantial and influential people. On one of my journeys to the United States, Gordon invited me to join him in a round of golf at Pawling's famous golf club where the final hole is a Par 8. (I took a 10).

I stayed overnight with him at the manse, a splendid colonial mansion with a significant heritage listing.

A former minister at Pawling a century earlier, was the father of legendary author Llew Wallace who wrote by hand that great novel, *Ben Hur*, page by page, in what was my bedroom that evening.

Gordon said to me: 'Drink in the aura of this historic room Everald. One day, you will write books of the same quality as *Ben Hur*.'

I am still trying diligently to make his forecast a reality. The only certainty is that I will never stop trying.

*THE GORDON POWELL GUIDEPOST*

***Gordon Powell spread calm and peace. He taught me never to get stressed about anything, and convinced me that The Man always faced his enemies with calm.***

## 6.10 FULTON SHEEN

The greatest communicator that Catholics have produced in my era, perhaps ever.

Hugely talented. So much so that in his career as a writer, broadcaster, and lecturer in the decades from 1920 to 1980 the fame of Fulton Sheen in the United States was such that most Americans knew his name far more readily than that of the pope. They also knew that his messages made much more sense than the best that any pope could offer. He also created far greater inspiration than the rigid discipline that most popes could ever convey.

Fulton Sheen was born in Illinois in 1895 and lived a distinguished life of service to broad range of people until his death in 1979.

Educated at the Catholic University of America, then St Paul Seminary in Minnesota and the Catholic University of Louvain in Belgium, he spent most of his life lecturing in Catholic universities. He greatly expanded the theological thinking of the work of St Thomas Aquinas so as to emphasise that the words in the Gospels were powerfully related to personal moral decisions and to the great social issues that all of us encounter day by day.

Commencing in 1930, he became the prime religious radio broadcaster in the US for his programs *The Catholic Hour* and subsequently a hugely popular television program called *Life Is Worth Living*. Both had a minimum of thirty million viewers every week. Today, those programs still hold the title of the most widely viewed religious programme in the history of television, far more than the achievements of today's hot gospellers.

So successful was his evangelism that he won an Emmy award and *Time Magazine* put him on its front cover as Man of the Year, declaring him to be the most influential Catholic of the twentieth century, anywhere in the world. There are not too many people, Christian or secular, who can achieve an impact of this scope.

Side by side with his broadcasting, he wrote thirty-four bestselling books and his weekly broadcasts were reproduced in pamphlets that were distributed throughout the Catholic Church in millions of copies, with many going on request to other religious denominations.

One particular book is especially worth reading in the quest to discover The Man. He called it *The Cross and the Beatitudes*. It is only a small book but it is powerful as it outlines seven verses from the Beatitudes and relates them to seven of the last words spoken by Jesus as he was dying on the cross. I have found the seven verses from the Beatitudes to be a challenge for all of us who seek to become meaningful partners of The Man:

Blessed are the meek for they shall inherit the land.

Blessed are the merciful for they shall obtain mercy.

Blessed are the clean of heart for they shall see God.

Blessed are the poor in spirit for theirs is the kingdom of heaven.

Blessed are they that hunger and thirst after justice for they shall have their fill.

Blessed are the peacemakers for they shall be called the children of God.

Blessed are they that mourn for they shall be comforted.

He used his fame to speak at hundreds of functions to raise many millions of dollars to finance Catholic missions world-wide. In doing this, he visited all 129 dioceses of his Church within the US. It was an exceptional commitment and contribution to an important outreach of his Church.

In his later years, he was appointed as bishop of Rochester but he resigned after only three years in the job as he correctly decided that leading a diocese was not his calling. His Church corrected the error and make him an honorary bishop so he could continue to write, broadcast, and give lectures, a task that he continued to do extraordinarily well.

However, his health steadily declined and he passed away quietly one evening in his chapel.

Thirty years later, he was considered by the Vatican for recognition as a saint but he did not qualify as his record failed to reveal that his outstanding service had created any identifiable miracles, a prime fundamental rule of the Catholic Church for attaining sainthood. Instead, the pope declared him to be a Venerable Servant of God who was of heroic virtue.

This was a really insulting decision, although it would not have disturbed Fulton Sheen in the slightest. He had done his utmost to serve alongside Jesus of Nazareth by faithfully using his skills of communication that he believed were a gift from his God that he felt compelled to use to the utmost of his ability.

A significant element of his ministry was that he persistently and powerfully was an advocate of family life as being a hallmark of a great society. He often told couples that there were three people in their relationship. Jesus would bind them forever. Right now, most youth crime across the planet is a product of dysfunctional families. The world desperately needs another Fulton Sheen to tell the world of the strength of family life in sustaining a stable society via its enhancement.

Clearly, he was born with an inbuilt skill to speak in a manner that was naturally sincere while being totally motivational and compelling. People of all ages and ethnic backgrounds relied on his uplifting and relevant messages to guide them on how to live well by overcoming adversity in a positive manner. He did not win them by telling them they were sinners in need of repentance. He gave them keys to a better life.

Such was his personal magnetism, he convinced people of the stature of Henry Ford and Claire Booth Luce to reject their lives as non-believers and become devout Catholics. There were many more like them.

It is important to note that throughout his life as a religious celebrity, he remained hugely humble, easily approachable, and warmly caring.

His place in history will be as one who can be used as a beacon to all who hope to follow in his footsteps as great communicators.

He is a golden benchmark for every one of us to become better advocates of faith and hope in every aspect of our lives, particularly in the manner in which we endeavour to invite new people to walk the pilgrim way with The Man.

By observation of the long tradition of Catholicism, I have not regarded the Catholic Church as having evangelism as a powerhouse of their presence in the world. Catholics always seemed to advance in size by sheer growth in the numbers of Catholics who believed it was their duty to produce large families and who then faithfully did their best to encourage their children to be very disciplined in their adherence to the Church.

Fulton Sheen magnificently broke the mould. He set out to be a modern version of St Paul as an evangelist and he achieved this goal and far more. Importantly, he did not follow the Catholic tradition of telling people they must unfailingly believe what their priests said. He enabled people to want to believe by personal choice and understand why they did so. He did his best to answer the thousands of questions sent to him by his listeners via the media and the post office.

I am cheering a great life of huge talent used so splendidly.

*THE FULTON SHEEN GUIDEPOST*

***Fulton Sheen's skills of communication were extraordinary and I have constantly sought to learn them. He taught me that words alone were not enough to make a difference. It is the way they are communicated that is vital and they must always have a persistent theme that is easily understood.***

***His was family life. He knew that it is the core of our existence. He made it his message.***

## 6.11 ALAN WALKER

Alan Walker was a visionary, a very special leader of people, a talented organiser, and a dominant personality of Australian religious history.

He was in his prime during my youthful years and so I learned much from him about the basic principles of courageous leadership and responsible risk taking even though I did not ever meet him personally. But I listened to him speak on radio and at public meetings on several occasions.

Founder of Lifeline in Australia, Alan Walker was a wonderful modern example of the manner in which Jesus of Nazareth reached out to people in crisis. He inspired followers like me to do likewise.

Lifeline was a project of the Methodist Church that was created by Walker in Sydney in 1963 as a means of enabling people under stress to gain urgent help that also had a strong core of follow-up caring.

It all began when he received a phone call at his church office from a very distressed man who would not reveal his address or any other contact details. He killed himself just days later because he felt there was no institution in the community that could help him face his personal crisis with urgency. It moved Walker to action.

He set up a crisis phone line quickly while he spent two years planning and preparing how Lifeline could be established and be enabled to work effectively in providing help 24 hours a day. This involved enlisting and training 150 voluntary counsellors who would work in an old building he rented as a telephone hub. It also entailed much work in forming partnerships with medical and other institutions to whom crisis victims could be referred. In addition, he formed a Trouble Team who would drive their own cars to the homes of people who called in and needed immediate assistance.

There were 100 calls made to Lifeline on the opening day and this has grown enormously with Lifeline centres now established and operating in every capital city and major regional cities. Sixty years later, the records show that 11,000 people have worked as volunteers for Lifeline across the nation. Every year Lifeline receives 500,000 distress calls, a clear indication of how mental illness, especially depression, has spread throughout the community. Lifeline is an outstanding example of how committed Christians can play a huge role in the care of humanity.

Lifeline was one of many ventures in which Alan Walker would become involved, revealing that he was an achiever in every way.

He was a high-profile superintendent of the Wesley Mission in Sydney for twenty years and served on the team that organised the formation of the World Council of Churches in 1948. This experience inspired him to establish the National Christian Youth Convention in Australia. Then he became the initial world director of evangelism for the World Methodist Council.

Awards flowed in recognition of his achievements.

He was awarded the Order of the British Empire in 1955. This honour was upgraded in 1981 so that he became Sir Alan Walker, and received the Centenary Medal in 2001. He became a national icon. His admirers invented friendly names to describe him: Mr Methodist, The Methodist Pope, Conscience of the Nation.

In the 1950s he led the Mission to the Nation, a well-planned crusade organised by the Methodist Church. It held rallies across the continent at which Walker was the keynote speaker. I attended one of them and was hugely impressed at his ability to hold the crowds spellbound. He motivated them to serve the needs of their fellow Australians in whatever ways their talents could possibly be used.

His plea to Australians was to affirm that our nation must have Christian principles as the cornerstone of a society in which decency, goodwill, honesty, and justice should prevail and caring become the fabric of our personal relationships. Of course, Australia has moved on dramatically from those days. Christian principles are no longer the dominating force of social life. The values of other faiths now have an influence. Different communities find comfort and inspiration from teachings that are Jewish, Muslim, Hindu, Buddhist, Mormon, etc.

Nevertheless, when the Mission to the Nation had completed its schedule of meetings, I formed the opinion that it had been a worthwhile exercise in down-to-earth social evangelism which should be organised annually. However, apart from the Billy Graham's rallies, we have allowed this form of evangelism to lapse significantly. This has been an irresponsible oversight by far too many of us for far too long.

Apart from the great exercise for humanity that Lifeline now is, I regard Mission to the Nation as Alan Walker's finest hour as a leader of change. He sowed the seed for congregations everywhere to serve the community. He had many such fine hours.

There have not been many Australians who have had his skills as an activist, broadcaster, evangelist, social commentator, theologian, and achiever for good. He took Christianity out of his Church into new spheres of ministry and let us know in no uncertain terms that we all must be constant leaders of change. Above all, Walker ranks equal with anyone whom I have written about in this book as a disciple of utter commitment, dedication, enthusiasm, and ability, serving with huge personal conviction in the service of The Man.

His personal power was awesome. He set an example to others to follow him in breaking new ground. And they did.

One is Tedd Noffs who set up the Wayside Chapel in Kings Cross to care for and attempt to rehabilitate people who are victims of drug abuse.

Another is Bill Crews who took over the Ashfield Uniting Church in Sydney when it had only a handful of members and was about to close. He transformed it into a dynamic congregation that cared for the hungry and homeless and mentally stressed. His Exodus Foundation has now extended this great work far beyond Ashfield. More will follow.

When we ponder why people want a helping hand through crises I am reminded of the verse in Matthew 6:37: 'Can any of you by worrying add one hour to your span of life?'

We are a world of worriers. All of us need people like Alan Walker to enhance our lives.

*THE ALAN WALKER GUIDEPOST*

***Alan Walker taught Christians not to wring their hands and pray about the sad state of the world.***

***He challenged me to take up causes and act decisively on them without waiting for God to tell me what to do.***

## 6.12 CATHERINE HAMLIN

A highly skilled doctor, Catherine Hamlin's revolutionary medical work in Africa has been significantly courageous and magnificently innovative. However, little is known of her and her work on the world stage, especially in her home country of Australia. Hopefully this will change.

Based in Ethiopia for many decades where she did most of her humanitarian work as a doctor, she also used it as a base from which her work could encompass neighbouring nations. In all, she served the people of Africa for sixty years, during which time she personally looked after and restored the health of most of her 60,000 patients, mainly women who had injuries and ailments associated with crude medical assistance at childbirth.

She did it all at no cost to her patients, relying totally on charitable donations to keep going while denying herself the wealth she could have earned quite comfortably as a medical specialist in her home city of Sydney.

Her huge contribution to humanity is clear evidence of committed service by a Christian doctor. She was a devout Anglican from Sydney who firmly believed that her destiny was to go to Africa as a working partner of Jesus and she acted on it wholeheartedly.

Born in Sydney in 1924 and raised in a Christian home, she graduated in obstetrics and gynaecology at the University of Sydney in 1946. She married a New Zealand physician, Richard Hamlin, in 1950 and together they dedicated themselves to serving the people of Ethiopia. It proved to be a remarkable partnership.

They established the Addis Ababa Fistula Hospital in temporary premises until a new site could gradually be established as a significant medical hub that would subsequently establish associated hospitals in five regional centres.

Fistula is a childbirth injury that mainly affects women in Africa. Its physical presence has been evident for thousands of years and was previously regarded as an unexplainable fluke of nature.

Catherine died at Addis Ababa in 2020, having been widely honoured for her work as a highly skilled medical practitioner. She had become a Companion of the Order of Australia and a holder of the Centenary Medal of Australia. The government of Ethiopia had presented her with their most prestigious honour, the Eminent Citizen's Award. There were also awards of doctorates from seven universities located on three continents.

She was twice nominated for the Nobel Peace Prize for Medicine.

A much-debated honour was bestowed on her when *The New York Times* declared her to be the 'modern day Mother Teresa.' This was quite odd as there is no genuine comparison of their relative work. Teresa helped people to die in peace in crude surroundings whereas Catherine enabled women to live normal lives with their families.

She chose to work in Ethiopia as she felt that God had given her skills to take up this special calling, something a committed Christian could not fail to take up. It was her deep faith that powered her onwards and upwards for six decades.

This book records the lives and work of several others giants who felt the same calling to serve their God in remote places and in hostile working conditions just as Catherine Hamlin had done with huge courage.

Father Damien was an outstanding example of such dedication as was Florence Nightingale during the Crimean war. Back in ancient times Andrew and Mark went to faraway places to spread the Gospel as was the calling of many whom I have not included simply through a lack of space.

Hopefully, many more will do likewise as the years roll on through a rapidly changing world of bewildering technology and religious decline caused by little effort being made to create a new Reformation.

For as long as people like Catherine Hamlin choose to walk and work with The Man, there will always be those who will see clear visions of human challenges and feel called to act on them with the utter conviction that is the fibre of their total being. Long may it continue.

THE CATHERINE HAMLIN GUIDEPOST

***Because she was female, Catherine Hamlin's great work in Africa has not been acknowledged as it would have been had she been male.***

***This has happened constantly throughout the history of Christianity yet Churches have survived mainly through the tireless work and devotion of women. History will eventually show that it was men who have destroyed Churches.***

## 6.13 GEORGE PELL

You have every right to ask me why, after writing so many positive chapters about inspirational people, I am now writing about such a controversial figure as George Pell.

The fact is that the practice of Christianity has experienced many dark days throughout its history. It is important that we recognise that there will inevitably be people who declare themselves to be working partners of The Man but then use their status for many acts of personal gain or the acquisition of political, social, and financial power.

So I decided to write about George Pell, Scott Morrison, and Brian Houston as a reminder of what can often go wrong in the practice of religion.

I am very aware that this may not be a Christian thing for me to say, but I must openly confess that I have little respect for George Pell. I should feel some sense of discomfort for writing those words, but such a feeling evades me persistently.

Nevertheless, there is much we can learn from him as we endeavour to have a Christian faith that is distinct from that of the Church and retake its place as a moral and ethical cornerstone of the world.

It is my sad view that George Pell eminently represented all that is wrong with the way in which Churches carry out their failing ministry today, especially within the Catholic Church where he became a significantly powerful figure of considerable influence. More importantly, he made a huge contribution towards ensuring that Churches will, during this century, be hugely diminished as a respected centre of influence in society.

He was a perfect role model for people who want to become churchmen in clear preference to being Christian. There is a huge difference. He believed that the Church must survive no matter what, even though it diminishes Christianity in the process. Indeed, Pell gave the clear impression of believing that the Church was beyond criticism in any way about any matter.

Like millions of others, I watched his career with more than just passing interest for decades as he gradually progressed upwards through the ranks of the Catholic Church to become a prominent public leader of immense status. I gained the firm opinion that he chose to become a priest solely because it was a clear pathway to personal power and influence, more so than any alternative career he could have chosen.

If you think I am wrong in my harsh judgement of him, may I suggest that you watch the meticulously prepared ABC television documentary 'Revelation' compellingly presented by Sarah Ferguson. It reveals his selfish ambition and confirms his secret life as a paedophile. There is no doubt that he had a role in causing some of his victims to take their own lives. Others now lead sad lives, tormented by endless mental trauma and hugely diminished self-confidence.

The documentary reveals that it was Pope Francis who initially saved him from being brought to justice by promoting him to the Vatican to manage its chaotic finances. Pell did have the financial talent to sort this out, and it had an added benefit in that it made him number three in the Vatican pecking order of power. Only the pope and the secretary of state had more power. Pell had reached the pinnacle of his career but he could never have been elected pope given his appalling history of suspected child abuse.

However, Pope Francis did his best to keep him away from the full impact of the law in Australia and in doing so he made a huge error of judgement.

There were four criminal trials in which he was charged with paedophile activity, overpublicised by the media to the extent that in truth it was not possible for him to receive a fair trial as there was huge public bias against him, even if justified.

The record shows that he served a jail sentence until his conviction was overturned. Contrary to the statement by the pope that Pell was found to be innocent, he was released only because the accusations against him were not proven beyond reasonable doubt.

Despite there being civil lawsuits pending between him and other victims, he escaped once more to Rome where he died at eighty-one. His body was returned to Australia where his funeral created public protests but was attended by many influential citizens who revered him.

No Australian Catholic has ever risen to a position of such power in the Church as he did. Nor has any Australian priest been surrounded by so much infamy.

History records his journey from being a schoolboy in Ballarat in Victoria to Oxford where he gained his doctorate. He rose from priest to bishop and then to archbishop twice, Melbourne and Sydney, becoming a cardinal and finally getting to the pinnacle of Catholic hierarchy in the Vatican. He deserves an achievement accolade for all of that. Few can or will emulate it.

Certainly, it will be a long time before another Australian priest of any religious denomination surpasses his record. However, let's look for a moment at his theology and publicly stated opinions. They are difficult to understand and always controversial.

First and foremost, he was a rigid archconservative in his beliefs and his politics. There could never be any doubts about where he stood on any issue.

At every point in his career he robustly opposed long overdue reforms for the Church, hotly criticising the refreshing initiatives of Vatican II and criticising the actions of Pope Francis. He was loudly and unreasonably opposed to the ordination of women and any relaxation of the celibacy of priests.

In politics, there was good and bad in his record.

He strongly supported the need to show compassion to refugees while also being a passionate climate denier. Extraordinarily, he opposed family planning as he believed it could cause a decline in the numbers of Catholics who could support the Church. His cynical attitude towards Jewish people was a matter of controversy but he did advocate closer interfaith relationships, particularly with Muslims. His attitude to LGBTQI+ was hostile as was his condemnation of divorced persons, except when domestic violence was involved. He also had difficulty in dealing with the impact of AIDS, believing it to be a direct product of sin.

Altogether, it was not possible, despite his huge intellect, for him to have an open mind about very much at all. In that, he was strikingly different to The Man.

You may still be wondering why I have devoted a chapter of this book to commenting on the life and work of a man who did so much to demean Christianity.

I have done so because he has been a major influence in convincing me that Churches are not in any way worthy or qualified to be the vehicle to promote the ministry of The Man and his power to create a better world. Communities of followers of Jesus will achieve much more than organised Christianity could ever hope for.

He also caused me to question whether or not we need professional priests when lay pastors would be much better advocates. I will say more about this later as it is a crucial issue in any advance of the stature of The Man. Indeed, a new reformation is needed, so long as it happens outside of the Church.

My final comment about George Pell is found in the Gospel of Mark, 8:36: 'What shall it profit you to gain the whole world but forfeit your own soul?'

*THE GEORGE PELL GUIDEPOST*

***George Pell eminently represented the imprisonment of souls by organised religion. But the violation of souls was not the exclusive haven of the Catholic Church. All Churches have practised abuse.***

*I recently read* Crimes of the Cross, *a shocking record of the Anglican paedophile network of Newcastle. They were ghastly predators.*

## 6.14 ZELMAN COWEN

Zelman Cowen is one of three close personal friends whom I have included in this book because of their unique contributions to enhancing the quality of society.

Writing about Zelman Cowen also enables me to comment on Judaism as he was a very influential leader of the Jewish community in Australia and internationally.

Among other important issues of my life experience, he introduced me to the Jewish faith and its rich but controversial history.

Especially, he taught me the art of clear thinking when faced with crucial decisions. I always valued his wise counsel.

I first met Zelman when he was vice-chancellor of the University of Queensland and we worked together to establish a college of the university in Toowoomba. Then we met again in Townsville when he became governor general of Australia and officially opened a nursing home called The Good Shepherd for which I had raised the finance. Our friendship grew and when he became provost of Oriel College at Oxford, we worked together closely in raising funds needed for a long overdue restoration of the fabric of the college which had been first established seven centuries earlier.

I often stayed at the college as the guest of Zelman and Anna. On several occasions, he invited me to accompany him to religious and social functions of the Jewish communities in Oxford and London. He even went to the trouble of giving me a skullcap to ensure my head was covered when required for appropriate purposes that respected his cultural heritage. I learned much during our decades of friendship about the relevance to his life of the Hebrew Bible.

Later, when I was visiting Israel on business, he arranged for a Jewish friend to escort me to the Wailing Wall in Jerusalem. I respectfully placed my hands on the wall and listened with consternation when my escort thanked God for not having been born a woman. Then I looked at the many other men at the Wall and noted the intense passion of those who were dressed in the special garments of ultra-orthodox Jews. This made me ponder the issue of any form of ultra-religiosity and its impact on society. I have always regarded any form of zealotry as a negative.

Whenever I spent time back home in Australia in the company of Jewish leaders, I noted their deep commitment to actively fostering our national acceptance of the heritage of Indigenous Australians and their right to justice in recognition of their unceded land. Jewish people believe that much of the land in Palestine and Jordan is theirs by right as they have not ever ceded it. It is quite clear that Jewish people regard Aborigines as a persecuted race in the same manner that the world has always persecuted those of Jewish descent. This is an important issue as it challenges Christians like me to review our sense of justice for all people as a genuine conviction of our faith.

Zelman and I discussed on a number of occasions the never-ending debate that is contested worldwide about the long-term hostility between Israel and the Arab world, especially Palestine, and what may be possible to bring about an end to it. Clearly, the Israelis will never forget that this is the land of the Hebrew Bible, the land of their heritage, faith, and culture. But they too often overlook the fact that they lost the land to the people of Islamic faith 1,600 years ago and this is a long enough period for Palestinians to justly and legally claim ownership. The dispute is regularly aggravated and widened by the clearly illegal establishment of far too many Israeli villages in the occupied territory of Palestine.

In recent times this has blown up into outright war following the cold-blooded murder by Hamas of 1,200 Israeli citizens and the brutal response by Israel that has killed far more civilians than those who are involved with Hamas. It will not finish well. Had he been alive now, the bloodshed would have caused Zelman Cowen huge grief as he was a very talented negotiator who had no doubt that negotiations made more sense than wars.

What Zelman and I often talked about was the issue of when does our faith have precedence over laws and justice. While Zelman was a devout Jewish person, he was never in doubt that as a lawyer he must always uphold the law first and foremost and if we believe that a law is wrong, we must seek to change by legislation and not by force.

I have often studied with amazement the history of the endless persecution of Jewish people over thousands of years, more so than any other race and wonder why this has happened. I asked on many occasions why it was that it has often been Christians who have led the persecution, far too often with extreme violence. The general folklore is that this happened because Christians have blamed the Jews for the crucifixion of Jesus. That is not only quite odd, but untrue, because without the crucifixion there would be no traditional Christian Faith.

THE ZELMAN COWEN GUIDEPOST

***Zelman Cowan was another of my friends who conveyed peace and calm in all that he did. When he was governor general of Australia, he became known publicly as 'the healer'.***

***He won this accolade for the huge effort he made to calm down the Australian people after we became hugely divided when Prime Minister Gough Whitlam was dismissed by Zelman's predecessor as governor general. He firmly advised me that is always wise to act with grace and dignity.***

## 6.15 POPE FRANCIS

He is the only pope I have ever admired or am ever likely to have the opportunity to admire as I doubt that priests or any other professional pastors of any rank will have a meaningful future in either Church or society. Their influence is diminishing rapidly.

Many earlier popes have been varying versions of George Pell. Most were cold-hearted administrators and powerbrokers who showed little indication of having any genuine love in their souls whatsoever. They have really only filled the role of emperors who ruled a religious fiefdom.

To the contrary, we can be very sure that the first pope, St Peter, had no intention whatsoever of ruling a religious empire.

Despite my respect for Francis as a decent human being, it has been a huge disappointment to millions around the world that he has not become the reformer we hoped he would be.

The curia at the Vatican, as they usually do with all popes, has overpowered him, and forced him into the role of a figurehead while giving him little room to move in expressing his own thoughts. This is shown by the fact that most of his reforms have been about changes to the way it which the Church manages its own administrative affairs rather than shedding ancient dogmas and reaching out to the world with compassion to give leadership in the care of humanity.

As the first pope from outside of Europe since the eighth century, and the first pope ever appointed from the southern hemisphere, he has had a unique opportunity to become the bright, shining light of a new era of enlightenment for our world but this has not yet occurred. It may not ever occur as his health is in decline, his mobility is considerably impaired and his Church is once more steadily and relentlessly focussed inwards.

My hope has been that he would stage a peaceful but purposeful campaign to rid the Church of all paedophiles and have them put in the hands of the lawmakers of every nation so that justice would be served. Sadly, he has failed to take decisive action on this matter.

This could have been followed by the implementation of a worldwide campaign of caring for victims and the restoration of the lives of sexual abuse victims by Catholics everywhere. Such an outreach would have placed Francis in the same realm of compassion in which Francis of Assisi had walked and loved. Little has been done.

Then, he should have changed the ancient attitude of the Church that denies the right of women to become priests. I cannot find one single justification for the male domination of any Church. It is a crude exercise in blatant misogyny that is utterly primitive.

He has also set aside many petitions made to him by Catholics in several nations that married men should be eligible to become priests. This has been personally difficult for him as he once publicly acknowledged that as a young priest, he had fallen deeply in love with a fine young woman who dearly wanted to spend her life with him. His decision not to give up his vows as a priest so he could spend his life with her was, in his own words, 'a very painful time in my life.' His Church should never have required him to make that decision.

I find his current leadership on all of these matters to be out of character from the inspirational courage he showed when he began his ministry in Argentina in 1969. When he was elected pope, he declined to live in the Apostolic Palace at the Vatican and took up residence in a guesthouse. I cheered him mightily.

His high-profile record in Argentina showed that he spent his priesthood as an outspoken critic of unbridled capitalism, corrupt free market economics, consumerism and over-development as well as being an opponent of capital punishment. He had also been an advocate of urgent action to combat climate change and had actively supported and assisted refugees in overcoming their plight of a constant struggle for new life.

His courageous presence in his home country of Argentina did much to deter the plunder and aggression of a succession of corrupt and regressive dictatorships who had done their utmost to destroy democracy there. On many occasions, he was the sole defender of the civil rights of the people in an era of the history of Argentina, accurately recorded as 'The Dirty War'.

Even as I write about my disappointment in his lack of action as a reformer at the Vatican, I note that in the years before he became an archbishop, cardinal and pope, the Jesuit order to which he had joined early in his priesthood had at one point suspended his membership of the order because they opposed his many radical reforms. They were particularly concerned by his close relationships with leaders of other Christian denominations and those of other religions.

In noting these great acts of humanity on his part, we have a responsibility to ask what happened to the radical reformer when he left Argentina to take up an enormous opportunity to save the world from the immense power base of a soulless Vatican.

Nevertheless, most of us will remember him fondly for his personal humility, his concern for the well-being of the poor and his commitment to social justice, attributes that most of his predecessors rarely displayed.

He has brought before all Christians a challenge to remove the causes of poverty as opposed to keeping the comforts of luxury and this is an important issue when we consider the rapid rise of the prosperity Gospel as a core belief of Pentecostal Protestants who are growing in numbers and are exercising their influence in fostering the politics of greed.

What is clear to me is that he is fighting a losing battle in Rome against the power of all who all those who want to preserve the Church at all costs. The priority in the minds of far too many Christians is to give this preference for survival over the call to spread the faith.

I am reminded at this point in the long history of the Catholic Church of the continuing punishment and demeaning of anyone who questions their declaration of what the Word of God really is.

Let me give you a small but compelling example of this. I believe that it is repeated every day by Catholic priests and teachers around the world.

Recently, I was riding in an Uber with a driver who asked me about my books. When I told him what I was writing, he told me that as a young lad at a Catholic school he had, during a lesson on the basics of the Catholic faith, asked whether Adam and Eve were real people or just a myth to describe how the world began. He was asked to immediately leave the room and attend confession to repent of his gross insult of the Church.

This is why Churches are dying.

While I am regrettably disappointed with Francis as pope, I tremendously admire the Francis of earlier years who was the compassionate pastor of the oppressed. May he be able to revive this compassion and spread it to the world from the Vatican.

*THE POPE FRANCIS GUIDEPOST*

***Pope Francis was once a caring revolutionary of great courage who could have lead a modern reformation. Sadly, his huge value to humanity has been smothered by those in the Vatican curia who have never walked meaningfully with The Man. They are simply bureaucrats.***

## 6.16 A J CRONIN

What a superb novelist of faith-based literature this uniquely talented man was! His ability with words and his skill in creating very human stories captivated his readers.

A J Cronin began his professional life as a respected medical doctor in rural Scotland who took up writing books as a hobby and became successful as an amateur author, much to his personal surprise. I am a beneficiary as I have read every one of his books and have never ever been bored or disappointed. While enjoying his books, I was constantly challenged to do some serious thinking about the circumstances of my own life.

His career as a writer began by accident. He was suffering acute abdominal pain from an ulcer, caused by excessive tension in his life as a doctor. He got involved in caring far too much about the mental health of his patients in a small community of people who lived close to poverty.

He decided to take leave from his medical practice for six months of rest in order to recover. He became bored and started writing short stories to occupy his mind. He loved it and, after one was published in a news magazine, he decided to write his first book, *Hatter's Castle,* never expecting that any publisher would become interested. Its instant success encouraged him to take up writing as a hobby that would eventually cause his medical career to cease. Writing happily consumed his life, gained him international fame, and made him a wealthy person.

My favourite of his books is *The Keys of the Kingdom.*

It tells the story of a young inexperienced Catholic priest from Scotland who was sent by an arrogant bishop to a remote and hostile region of China to begin a new mission with no back up support. He overcomes incredible difficulties, including a massive language problem, but never managed to gain genuine converts. So his bishop ordered him to come back to Scotland declaring he had failed in his priestly vocation. This book clearly raises the question of whether missionaries can ever have a long-term effect in areas of hostile religions and culture.

But this book's main purpose is to motivate us to identify with people who totally commit their lives to the advocacy and advancement of their faith with huge passion. Are we willing to make a similar commitment and should we, in fact, ever do so? Should our religion take us to extremes? Are we entitled to inflict western culture and religion upon the rest of humanity?

This leads us to a crucial fact about Cronin.

Every one of his books has a clear message about either religion or morals, values, ethics and commitment to a calling or a vocation. His continually makes the point that life is pointless without a clear purpose.

Apart from *The Keys of the Kingdom,* others I enjoyed were: *Hatter's Castle*, *The Stars Look Down*, *The Green Years*, *The Citadel*, *The Spanish Gardener*, *The Northern Light*, and *The Judas Tree*

There was also *Dr Finlay's Casebook* which became a famous television series. It was based on his own experiences as a doctor and was a forerunner to many of his books also becoming films that I enjoyed in cinemas.

Most of his novels specifically deal with events centred on religion,while the others contain a strong religious element as verified in his autobiography, *Adventures in Two Worlds*. This relates to his life- changing decision to gradually retire from his career as a doctor for which he did not have a genuine calling and spend his days writing novels that revealed to him and his readers that he had been born with very special literary skills.

Cronin was an agnostic while at medical school. At that time he said: 'When I thought of God it was with a superior smile, indicative of biological scorn for such an outworn myth.' However, after practising as a doctor in mining communities in Wales where most people held a deep religious faith, he gradually changed his mind. He then said: 'I lost my sense of superiority and this became my first step in finding God.'

A vivid memory of him as a person is focussed on a small article that he wrote in *The Readers Digest* called 'Quo Vadis?'

In it, he describes at length a visit he made to Rome. While driving around the suburbs of the city, he became aware that he had become lost and so he pulled up outside an ancient church, hoping that the priest would be a friendly soul who would give him some guidance.

As he entered the imposing building, he noted that it was the church of Quo Vadis, one of the most famous in Rome.

It is built on the spot where, by legend, Peter, The Big Fisherman, made a compelling decision that would lead to his death. He was fleeing along the Appian Way from a huge persecution of Christians that was being carried out by the Romans when he heard challenging words from the Lord asking him the question *Quo Vadis* which means 'Where are you going?'

At that moment, Peter remembered that he had personally denied Jesus three times in the last days before the crucifixion and realised he could not continue to repeat this weakness. He knew that he could not leave his Christian friends to die while he fled to save his own life. So it is that he turned around, walked back to Rome, and was captured by soldiers who crucified him upside down.

He was not to know that, centuries later, he would be declared to be the world's first pope and have a cathedral named after him in which his statue would be the centrepiece that would be reverently touched by millions every year.

Cronin spent a quiet hour of meditation in the church of Quo Vadis, pondering how many times he had walked away from his responsibilities to humanity. He accepted that far too often he had been guilty of leading a good life of constant accolades as a world-famous author and so he recorded the challenge of *Quo Vadis* quite often in his future writings.

There can be no doubt that Cronin used his books as his own quiet form of evangelism, constantly pricking the conscience of his readers without them ever feeling he was preaching a sermon or trying to save their souls.

I try to follow his example when writing my own books, knowing full well that I do not have his superb skills as a storyteller. But I enjoy the task of trying to do so as all forms of evangelism are an undeniable calling for every partner of The Man.

Despite being occasionally estranged from him, his wife proofread every one of his books and did critical editing of them. He does not appear to have publicly acknowledged this devoted commitment, a blot on his record.

Sadly, the truth is that there are many women, scattered around the world, who have often experienced the pain of being taken for granted by their husbands throughout their lives and yet have chosen to remain silent in the belief that it was is their personal calling to be a servant.

THE A J CRONIN GUIDEPOST

*A J Cronin was a talented storyteller, one of the finest ever. More writers of his quality are needed in the ranks of followers of The Man.*

*There is a special lesson that Cronin has passed on to us all when he gave up his work as a doctor to become a writer. He taught us to have the courage to decide whether we are in the wrong profession and face the risks involved in making a total change.*

## 6.17 MARY BAKER EDDY

She was a controversial reformer of the Christian religion and founder of a religious denomination known as Christian Science, the mother church of which is located in Boston USA and is still influential around the world in moderate numbers.

A person of huge Christian piety, Mary Baker Eddy began her work in creating a new Church in 1866 and continued with it relentlessly until her death in 1910.

From her earliest days, she rebelled against the tough and rigid rules of Calvinism as the generally accepted legitimate brand of Protestant Christianity at the time. I can relate to her on this issue as John Calvin is not on my list of inspirational people. Indeed he depressed me enormously. Steadily, she extended her personal theology to question the validity of the theology of many Christian denominations, finally leading to the creation of her new religion which closely linked Christianity with science.

The basis of all of her initiatives to reform Christianity began through tough experiences with her personal life and its considerable tragedies that occurred far too often.

Her first marriage lasted just six months before her husband died. Her second marriage was a disaster that ended in divorce and her third ended with the passing of her husband. Her son from her first marriage refused to live with her and her favourite brother died. She was seriously ill for many years with a variety of ailments and suffered considerable injuries from a severe fall which restricted her movements. Despite experiencing distress from the mental tension of all the personal criticism she endured throughout her life, she lived to the ripe old age of eighty-nine, passing in 1910.

Her massive health problems led to her taking an avid interest in science and its relationship to religion. Her views on this were strengthened by the controversy that surrounded Charles Darwin's scientific studies about evolution of which she enthusiastically approved.

Importantly, her study and advocacy of spiritual healing played an important role in fostering understanding of it and its relevance to believers from any faith. But she failed to take into consideration the inevitable consequences of extremists misusing spiritual healing in a way that put human life in danger through false interpretations.

Debate still rages as to whether or not people are cured via divine help or whether this occurs from the limitless power of a positive human mind. We can be certain that this debate will continue forever and that the very frequent discussion about it is a good thing.

When she founded the institution she called The Church of Christ, Scientist in 1879 with just fifteen initial members, it was a notable moment in the history of religion that has led, one and a half centuries later to the presence of a worldwide Church that continues to grow and have influence in both religion and politics.

The newspaper that she founded in 1908 and named *The Christian Science Monitor* just two years before she died, remains alive to this day and is an international publication of recognised journalistic excellence that is read by many who are not of her faith.

Nevertheless, her personal ministry in founding a Church has drawn many critics, some of them being eminent leaders of other Churches who could not tolerate the thought of a woman overstepping the mark by establishing her own Church.

The most notable of her critics was Mark Twain, a famous non-Christian, who wrote a book about her in which his disapproval was severe. Even so, he remarked that some of her teachings were worthy of respect. Because of his celebrity, his criticism brought her to the attention of many who would not otherwise have learned of her.

She also drew criticism for being a crusading feminist as she was a leader of the campaign to give long-overdue voting rights to women and gain them the right to own property, two issues about which she continues to be greatly praised in today's world.

In addition, some of her modern followers have betrayed her cause by establishing breakaway groups from her Church via fostering ridiculous controversy on fringe matters. One high profile example was the very public disturbance that has allegedly been created by film star Tom Cruise when he joined the controversial Church of Scientology that was set up in 1953 by L Ron Hubbard to discredit Eddy and which led to a high-profile court battle over its religious trivia. Had she been alive at the time this saga would have appalled her.

To me, she represented an important human trait that many of us can adopt.

The formulation of the ground of our being is a constant journey of discovery. Otherwise, our journey is a lost cause.

It is quite wrong for us to accept dogmas and creeds and rules for life perpetuated by too many insecure Church leaders who simply want to feel strong by controlling our minds and making us perpetuate an institution in which they constantly strive to maintain personal power.

Our personal journeys are all about asking questions and seeking answers that uplift our minds in ways that may often be different to those of others, but we have the opportunity to inspire others.

For this reason alone, Mary Baker Eddy has my admiration.

Just like the attributes of The Man, she had the mind of a lifelong crusader.

### *THE MARY BAKER EDDY GUIDEPOST*

***Mary Baker Eddy was an influential leader in the battle to cure Christians of our primitive fear that science will destroy their faith.***

***Fear of anything has no place in our lives when we walk with The Man. He neither protects nor saves us, but is a source of our inner power.***

## 6.18 MAHATMA GANDHI

An eminent historian, who closely followed the journey of Gandhi throughout the great man's long struggle to gain freedom for the people of India from the oppressive domination of 'Christian' England, has reported that Gandhi once said:

'The only thing wrong with Christianity is that no one has ever practised it.'

This statement vividly describes my thinking as I enjoy writing this book.

It reflects Gandhi's frequent observation that Christians from the United Kingdom would not have unlawfully plundered India for three centuries had they been genuine followers of The Man. His powerful observation was correct. The British were just power brokers and financiers, occasionally at prayer.

As an ardent student of history from my earliest days at school and throughout my life, I spent many happy hours reading everything I could find about great historical events that shaped the world. I constantly wondered how it was that the so called 'Christian' nations of Europe could in any way justify their appalling theft of land on every other continent, plunder the resources of those countries without ever paying for them and then make slaves of the people while pompously endeavouring to convert them to their superior religion called Christianity.

It represented hypocrisy of the lowest possible type. Absolutely disgusting.

No wonder Gandhi, without showing any malice towards the British, regarded them as absolute frauds. They were prime examples of it in every way and it is noteworthy that they have never ever apologised to India or the rest of the world for their brutal pagan theft.

All of my anger about the curse of colonialism caused me to read as much as I could about Gandhi and his struggle for the freedom of his people. I was fascinated by the way he organised a genuinely peaceful revolution that totally non-plussed the British to the point where they did not have even the vaguest clue of how to handle him. He was a devout Hindu who was closer, in all that he did, to The Man than any of the fake Christians who were trying to exercise their diminishing power in India.

Initially, Gandhi began his crusade for freedom from British rule when he decided to live in South Africa after his family had arranged for him to study law in London. He went to South Africa to help a relative who had lived there for a long time and was in legal trouble. Once there, he decided to open a law practice of his own.

This eventually led him to become involved in civil rights when he found that his relatives and many of the Indians who lived there had been sent to South Africa by the British to be farm labourers and became victims of apartheid. Restrictions were placed on their lives and their movements that were quite simply primitive, all inflicted by Christians. He spent a lot of time in jails for his role in organising revolts, leading marches, and deliberately going to places from which Indians were banned.

After twenty-one years of being defied by a fearless Gandhi, the British decided that they must get him out of South Africa and send him home to India. In doing so, they made yet another one of their many hugely stupid errors. They had set into train the founding by Gandhi of a cause that would inevitably ensure that they would be kicked out of India.

I won't outline in detail the fascinating history of how Gandhi peacefully removed the bewildered British from his homeland except to say they could not even remotely understand how to fight a peaceful revolutionary who could never be provoked to fight them.

There are countless books written about how Gandhi totally outmanoeuvred them. The most readable and authentic in my view is *Freedom at Midnight*, a bestseller for the ages, by Larry Collins and Dominic Lapierre.

There are several powerfully Christian attitudes that Gandhi the Hindu practised as a fundamental belief. They are compelling:

'Always turn the other cheek.'

He practised this every day no matter how he much he was abused, whether by the British or by traitors within his own ranks, who were worried that the nation would descend into bankruptcy if the British were kicked out.

'Thou shalt not steal.'

Gandhi did not ever cease to remind the British that they had stolen untold wealth from his people for centuries without even remotely considering that they were persistently breaking a Christian commandment.

'You cannot serve God and money.'

While British Christians lived in comparative splendour, Gandhi lived in poverty and did so happily along with hundreds of millions of fellow Indians.

Clearly, there are more fundamentals of Gandhi's Hindu faith that ally themselves with those taught to us by The Man. However, I reckon I have said enough to create a debate to determine who was a finer Christian at the time of the Indian revolution.

Was it Gandhi in the slums of India or was it the archbishop of Canterbury who was living in a palace in England financed by money stolen from the colonies?

When he was assassinated by one of his own people not long after India had gained its freedom, a great soul was momentarily extinguished. But his spirit, like that of The Man, will never be extinguished while sincere Christians and Hindus seek justice for all.

His humility was powerful and incredibly inspirational.

This is proven by the fact that his funeral in Delhi brought together the largest crowd ever to assemble at a funeral in the entire history of humanity.

I lament that militant Hindu leaders in India are now actively seeking to turn the faith taught by Gandhi into an exercise of power, suppressing Muslims, Sikhs, Buddhists, and other faiths in a lamentably ruthless manner. Their modern version of their faith is quite clearly not that of Gandhi.

Similarly, I abhor the way the so called Christian Right in Australia and USA are seeking to take the same path to power.

All of the above frauds do not walk the pathway of either Gandhi or The Man.

Both have taught us that Christianity and Hinduism are compatible for people of goodwill and peace and both have some similarity with every other mainstream faith in the world.

Interfaith relationships are now an important element in the future history of this century and I am pleased that I have been able to take a small role in fostering interfaith advocacy in Australia.

THE MAHATMA GANDHI GUIDEPOST

***Ghandi inspired me to love peace as a priority of life.***

***The British Christians who plundered India for centuries could not cope with Gandhi when he staged the greatest peaceful revolution in history. Their faith was based entirely on exercising power over others, with no idea that Jesus was a man of peace.***

## 6.19 THE DALAI LAMA

Helen and I were privileged to attend the Parliament of World Religions in Melbourne a decade ago as Uniting Church elders.

One of many reasons for choosing to attend was that the Dalai Lama was a keynote speaker. From the moment he arrived on stage he quietly and compellingly took over the conference hall with as a powerful an expression of peace as I have ever witnessed. He generated an enormous audience response that bordered on rock star proportions while he did nothing more daring than smile happily and talk quietly.

Until that occasion, I had been an interested observer from afar of his life and faith and his role as a leader of a great religion. After listening to him in Melbourne, I decided that it was time to learn more about his spiritual relevance in a changing world.

Firstly, I had to do some serious thinking about how to separate his political life as the leader of the former nation of Tibet from his role as the spiritual leader of the majority of those who follow the Buddhist religion. This proved to be not too hard a task as I was aware that

Mohammed also held political and spiritual roles and this has not diminished his powerful presence in the world.

Nevertheless, I was somewhat disturbed when I first took a serious look at the history behind China's takeover of Tibet in the era of Chairman Mao. However, further studies showed that Tibet from the beginning of time had never been a democracy. It had always been governed by whoever happened to be in charge of China or by who had ruled the Mongolian empire from way back in the days of Genghis Kahn. Mao's action, though brutal and wrong, was almost inevitable especially as all the previous thirteen Dalai Lamas had never been elected by the people but by a complicated and ridiculous process of determining incarnation.

However, it is important to remember that Tenzin Gyatso, the current and fourteenth Dalai Lama, wisely gave up his political power as leader of the Tibet Government in Exile, that is based in India, a couple of years ago, mainly due to his age of eighty-four years. Nevertheless, he still travels the world in his role as spiritual leader of the Buddhist religion and is more revered in this role probably because most people no longer regard him as a politician.

This brings us to consideration of what there is in Buddhism that bears a clear relationship to Christianity. There are certainly elements of the Eightfold Path, the Four Noble Truths, The Five Precepts, and the Three Marks of Conditioned Existence that relate to the basics of Christianity, particularly with regard to our attitude to suffering and compassion and discipline. But we have different views about whether we should eat meat or drink alcohol and there is a difference in the liberal attitude of Christians to sexual relationships.

Traditional Christians are poles apart from Buddhists concerning the existence of God but this difference is narrowing as I will talk about in a later chapter.

Strict adherence by some Christians to rigid dogma and creeds instead of seeking enlightenment on every issue of life is also a huge divide but not an insuperable one.

It is on most of these issues that I find myself more personally in alignment with Buddhism than I am with fundamentalist Christians.

I firmly believe that every word in the Christian Bible is open to debate.

I always read any passage of Scripture with an open mind, then ignore the exact words while I debate with myself what spiritual or practical message this page of the Scriptures is trying to convey. Then I can quietly work out what action I may be able to take about the principle, not the words, that will make me a wiser person who is able to help create a better society.

As in a later chapter, I seriously ponder as to whether we have any spiritual need of a mythical God when we have the huge spiritual power of The Man. I lean heavily on the latter but will be debating the issue with myself and others until the day I die.

I respect our current Dalai Lama as a person and as a spiritual leader of humanity who is able to reach the minds of people with simple but profoundly meaningful messages. He has the priceless gift of being able to convey with simplicity the wisest version of common sense and practical discipline as well as giving us a feeling of genuine peace and a huge calling to practice compassion even for those whom we feel do not deserve it.

Working partners of The Man can benefit from a continued relationship with Buddhists and vice versa. I aspire to having a role in helping to foster it.

It is also evident that all humanity will benefit from the continued influence of the very long life of Tenzin Gyatso, the leader we call the Dalai Lama.

*THE DALAI LAMA GUIDEPOST*

***The Dalai Lama is quite simply a great soul who has great skills to teach us how to live in peace with our fellow beings in a more meaningful way.***

***He also convinced me that it is possible to be an influential leader without exercising political power.***

## 6.20 JOHN ROBINSON

John Robinson turned the Christian world on its ear when he wrote and published *Honest to God* in 1963. In doing so, he established one of several crucial turning points in the never-ending, but exciting, challenge of determining my basic values.

Robinson was ordained as a priest of the Church of England in 1946 and, at the time of writing *Honest to God*, he was bishop of Woolwich.

Previously, he had written two books, *In the End, God.* and *Jesus and His Coming.*

They were moderately controversial but nevertheless caused the archbishop of Canterbury, Geoffrey Fisher, to question whether Robinson was theologically fit to be a bishop. However, he refrained from taking steps to stop his appointment as bishop of Woolwich.

Even so, John Robinson drew the ire of a subsequent archbishop of Canterbury, Michael Ramsey, when *Honest to God* was published. Ramsey subsequently and gracefully let it be known that he had not handled his criticism of Robinson very well.

Whenever anyone ventures beyond traditional theology, many insecure church people have a highly predictable capacity to lash out and tell the world how pure and godly they are in comparison to the latest infidel.

In reality, *Honest to God* provided little to get outraged about.

All that Robinson had done was to expand debate on the writings and teachings of Paul Tillich and Dietrich Bonhoffer. What he had honestly said was that we should no longer believe that God was a supernatural being who is out there. We should think of God as the ground of our being in this world. I have not the slightest problem with accepting Robinson's comment except that I regard The Man as the ground of my being, not God.

Nevertheless, many fundamentalist Christians still believe that Robinson had unnecessarily and irresponsibly capitulated to modernism. I can't work out what is wrong with modernism anyway. It solely highlights the fact that Christians have open minds as a natural asset.

The debate around Robinson's right to be a priest became very intense immediately after he published *Honest to God*, to the extent that later in that year (1963) another best seller was published by David Edwards entitled *The Honest to God Debate.* It contained a collection of essays by a wide range of theologians both for and against what Robinson had written. Robinson cooperated in its publication by commenting on the essays. A majority of theologians agreed with him.

Nevertheless, such was his continued infamy that in 1969 Robinson made a personal decision to resign as bishop of Woolwich and was appointed dean of chapel at Trinity College, Cambridge, as this would enable him to work exclusively as a theologian and author.

While at Cambridge he published in 1976 another book that he called *Redating the New Testament.* In it he questioned the traditional belief that the New Testament began to be written in 70 CE. He put forward his research arguing that the Gospels were published twenty-five years earlier.

He was finishing his final book *The Priority of John* when he was afflicted with a terminal cancer in 1983. He died quite quickly at the relatively young age of sixty-four. The usual fundamentalists publicly declared that God had caused him to have a terrible death in punishment for ever putting pen to paper to publish *Honest to God.*

His creative theology did not die with him.

An Episcopal bishop in the United States, John Shelby Spong, announced that he would take up Robinson's work. He wrote many bestselling books that expanded on Robinson's thinking in a far more radical way.

Robinson had become a public figure before his controversial book was published. He appeared as a witness for the defence in a high-profile obscenity trial of Penguin Books for their publication of a raging bestseller *Lady Chatterley's Lover* by D H Lawrence. Robinson declared it to be a book that every Christian should read so as to come to understand the moral issues of the day. It was wise advice and he generated headlines everywhere.

The only memorial to him is a school named in his honour at Thamesmead.

But his books are his permanent memorial. In fact, there were eighteen in all, most of them written for students of theology, but four of them drew widespread community interest.

His contribution to my life was to help me to compare the roles that God and Jesus have had in my life and determine that Jesus is the solid ground of my being.

*THE JOHN ROBINSON GUIDEPOST*

***John Robinson was a great thinker who offers another example of being persecuted by fundamentalist Christians for having an open mind.***

***He convinced me how sensible it is to have an open mind about everything that I encounter in life not just religion .***

## 6.21 WILLIAM BOOTH

How could I possibly leave out the founder of the Salvation Army?

William Booth was a man who spent most of his life in a spartan existence because he devoted his time to reaching out to people who did not go to a church and who lived through tough times in the shadow of the rich who treated them as economic and social slaves.

Born in Nottingham, England, in 1829 and living a full life for eighty-three years, he had little formal education as his parents were too poor to support him with anything but the bare basics. This meant that for many years, he worked as an apprentice to a pawnbroker as he had no skills training. Despite this, he was clear in his mind that God had called him to be a preacher devoted to evangelism.

Seeking to find a way to achieve his destiny, he started life as an occasional lay preacher with the Methodists, then the Congregationalists. Quickly, he became disenchanted with both Churches and decided to create a Christian movement that would have no church buildings but do all its preaching and caring out in the streets.

Firstly, he called it the Christian Revivalist Society, then the Christian Mission, and finally the Salvation Army. The title does not switch me on as the concept of salvation is of little relevance to me, but titles really don't matter very much. There are millions of people throughout the world who at one time or another have said: 'Thank God for the Salvos.'

He was certain that no democracy was needed to advance his army. It needed leadership in the form of a general in full command, making decisions and moving forward constantly seeking to conquer souls and care for their physical wellbeing.

So he became the first general of the Salvation Army, appointing officers to organise and command its foot soldiers throughout England. His plan worked and eventually spread to the whole world, with huge effectiveness.

He rarely had much money and so everything was done on a shoestring budget. The team, including himself, often did without food because they were broke. However, they regarded this as a core element of a solid commitment to their calling.

He began by concentrating primarily on bringing people to Christ but soon found this ministry alone was insufficient for the needs of humanity. He was certain that God was calling him to confront the economic and social evils that contaminated society.

He worked hard at raising money so he could establish soup kitchens for the poor. Then he extended this outreach to establish places of refuge for prostitutes and released prisoners as well as founding centres for education in essential basic skills that would help people to find work. He then began to pioneer other much needed social ventures.

He had no doubt that alcohol was a curse that was destroying countless lives so he regularly organised for protest meetings to be held outside hotels and breweries and did his best to encourage governments to close them down. Often, he would be punched and stoned and verbally abused by hotel keepers and their drunken customers, but not once did he ever retreat.

He became a widely revered public figure as the media were mesmerised by his commitment, zeal, bravery, and obvious achievements in uplifting humanity. They had never before come across anyone who worked with such vigour in helping those who were down and out.

It surprised no one when his tireless endeavours began to take a heavy toll on his health but this did not slow him down.

Eventually, he lost his sight and his vigour collapsed, So it was a tragedy when he died a blind and exhausted person who had given his life utterly to the cause of his Lord and those of his flock who were stricken.

His body was placed in Clapton Hall where the public could come to pay their respects. Some 150,000 people filed past his coffin and an immense crowd of 40,000 attended his funeral at the Olympia Stadium.

King George V and American President William Taft sent condolences to be read while Queen Mary attended anonymously as she did not want her royal presence to distract from the reverence of the tribute to as great a Briton as ever lived.

When the cortege moved on towards the cemetery, 10,000 Salvationists marched behind in full uniform with their band playing his favourite hymns while the crowd sang along with them with a passion that could be heard and felt miles away.

Two things we should especially note.

He had revived the great work of compassion that John Wesley had begun centuries before, but he took it to another level. He worked at the lowest pits of human suffering and lived as close to them as he could, very much in the mode of Francis of Assisi.

Booth and Wesley had vividly shown to established Churches that the Gospel message was primarily needed out in the world where the suffering was, not hidden away in Church buildings where a faithful few could worship as an exclusive club. Worship on a Sunday or any other day was for Booth quite simply a refuelling moment to fire up his army and himself to serve humanity with even greater zeal and better results than ever before.

The second notable comment is that his life's work had a co-founder.

His devoted wife, Catherine, was as wonderful a partner as any man could ever have hoped he could be blessed with.

She was at his side from day one and never left it. Her work was tireless but always in his shadow often unnoticed and when he was hungry and poor, so was she. Yet rarely was she acknowledged publicly mainly because she did not ever seek recognition. She was a saint and I salute her for her enormous love of people in need.

As I mentioned in the subchapter on A J Cronin, history has often ignored the thousands of examples of women who worked with huge devotion to support the leadership their husbands were giving to their life's calling.

There are very few examples of this happening in reverse. This is not something that the males of society can be proud of. I stand guilty like many others.

Nevertheless, I salute William and Catherine Booth as shining lights of compassion.

*THE WILLIAM BOOTH GUIDEPOST*

***William and Catherine Booth lived out their caring convictions 100%.***

***They were powerfully effective working partners of The Man, personally caring for every one they can find who were suffering out in the dark places of life..***

## 6.22 MITT ROMNEY

The Mormon faith has always intrigued me, so I want to say a few words about it in this book as it has an extraordinary history that has some positive messages for people of all faiths.

To achieve this I want to write about the life and achievements of an American politician, Mitt Romney, who may have become president of the United States had it not been for the fact that he was a practising Mormon. His life highlights the reality that throughout the world Mormon leaders in all walks of life have had to overcome the prevailing thought that there is something a bit odd about their religion.

The correct name of their faith is The Church of Jesus Christ of Latter-day Saints and its headquarters are located in Salt Lake City in Utah, USA.

It was founded by Joseph Smith in Missouri in 1830 when he published *The Book of Mormon*. It outlines a set of values that highlight the importance of family life, a belief in continuing revelation by God, a desire for an orderly society, respect for authority and a devotion to missionary work as a fundamental priority for believers.

Strangely, it banned the consumption by its members of alcohol, tobacco, tea, and coffee. I can relate quite easily with the banning of tobacco, but not the other three.

The Mormon faith is based on a vision that Smith had of an angel appearing to tell him to seek and find engraved golden plates that were buried in a hill near his home. He did this and translated the messages into English. He discovered their revelation that a family of Israelites had travelled to North America in 600 BCE, long before the birth of Jesus Christ and ages before Christopher Columbus supposedly discovered the New World. The family had been taught by Old Testament prophets who conveyed to them the true faith, not the traditional one adopted by Christians.

Smith declared that the plates, after he had studied them, were taken back to heaven by an angel, a highly unlikely event but one that most Mormons accept without question.

Years later, Smith was murdered by a man who felt very threatened by the Mormon faith. He was succeeded by a more famous leader, Brigham Young, who led thousands of believers away from persecution in Missouri on a long trek to Utah to establish a new home in Salt Lake City where a solid and long-lasting cause was established.

Without wanting to belittle or demean those who practise the Mormon faith, I find all of their history to be more than a bit hard to accept as having actually occurred. Nevertheless, there are millions of Mormons around the world who are devoted to it, as they are entitled to be.

Mitt Romney is now the most famous of them and I hold the view that he is also one of the most intelligent people to serve in the United States Congress in recent times.

Let me emphasise his commitment to his faith.

As a young man, before he entered politics, he spent thirty months living in France and working full time as a Mormon missionary. He called on homes every day seeking interest in establishing Mormon communities in France. He reported that in all that time he had enlisted only twenty new members but he did not ever give up. There have been few Mormon missionaries anywhere in the world who knocked on as many doors as Romney did.

(Incidentally, if you want to enjoy a light-hearted view of Mormon missionaries at work, go to see the highly successful Broadway musical 'The House of Mormon' which tells a delightful tale of young Mormon missionaries at work in Uganda. Helen and I immensely enjoyed it).

This poses the question as to how many Christians share the same missionary zeal that Romney has. The answer is not many. And I am a prime example of the slackers. I have participated only in a few lay evangelism campaigns in my ninety years of church-going. People like me are prime examples of why Christianity is in danger of becoming a dormant religion all around the world.

In all the time he has been in politics, Mitt Romney has found that his religion has cost him lots of votes when competing in elections but he has not ever hidden from the fact that he is a devout, believing Mormon.

When he first ran to become a Massachusetts senator in Congress in Washington, his opponent was Edward Kennedy, head of the powerful Kennedy Roman Catholic dynasty. Romney lost because Kennedy constantly asked voters whether they really wanted a Mormon in Washington or a good Catholic. He depicted Mormons as a strange religious cult who could not be trusted.

Romney subsequently won election as governor of Massachusetts but by a much closer vote than had been expected due to many voters being frightened of his religion. Nevertheless, most now rate him as one of the best achieving governors of their state.

The same thing happened when Romney ran for president.

He lost to John McCain in the primaries for the Republican nomination in 2008. He won the primaries in 2012 and became the Republican nominee but lost to Barack Obama in the general election even though a majority of polls on the day before the election predicted he would win. Even though Obama had not commented on Romney's religion during the election campaign, far too many voters could not bring themselves to vote for a Mormon president, so Obama won narrowly.

Polls afterwards showed that many voters thought Mormons still practised polygamy even though they had ceased to do so a century previously. Those polls also showed that the anti-abortion stance of his faith was a vote loser.

Overlooked was his vast involvement in community causes wherever he lived and his lifelong practice of giving away 10% of his income to his Church every year. Voters also forgot his excellent leadership as chair of the Organising Committee of the 2002 Winter Olympic Games in Salt Lake City which was run without causing any debt to the city, the first ever to do so.

After the crushing disappointment of not having had the opportunity to lead the United States to a better way of life, Mitt Romney quietly returned to his old home in Utah, the Mormon stronghold of America.

There he easily won election as their senator in Washington where he won fame as the only Republican senator who twice voted to impeach Donald Trump, earning Trump's bitter hatred. Romney said that he voted as his faith dictated. His Mormon conscience told him that it would have been morally wrong to follow the decision of the Republican Party to back Trump when he believed that the man was a liar, a cheat, a denier of democracy, a misogynist, and a creator of political violence.

While I have no intention of ever joining the Mormons, my relationship with those who live in my community is one that I value.

I have been involved in the North Brisbane Inter Faith Group as one of the representatives of the Uniting Church and, at those meetings, I welcomed the presence of the local Mormon community who are active participants and who go out of their way to build good relationships. In particular, I liked the fact that there is no distinction in their faith between priests and laity and I have been privileged to worship with them at their church.

Their missionary zeal and their obvious generosity are positive examples that Christians can follow and receive considerable benefits instead of ringing our hands and lamenting why more people don't come to our churches.

Mitt Romney is a prime example of a leader who has restored my hope that politicians of stature have the capacity to get their act together as faithful representatives of their communities and enhance their service to humanity to a quality not yet obvious worldwide.

*THE MITT ROMNEY GUIDEPOST*

***Mitt Romney has proved to me that religion and politics are not a natural mix. He did not use his faith as a means of gaining political power. Neither should you and I.***

***He showed the world of politics how to gain and use influence without involving religion.***

## 6.23 MORRIS WEST

Morris West is one of the finest novelists Australia has ever produced. If I look on a world scale, I would rank him among the finest whom I have encountered in my time, along with Lloyd Douglas and A J Cronin.

He was a fascinating character.

He studied to be a Catholic priest but had a sudden change of mind about his vocation just before he was to take his vows. He felt that he could have a greater impact on humanity through the written word rather than the spoken one. It was a decision that led him to considerable fame and fortune as an influencer of our faith, morals, and politics.

Having enjoyed reading all of his books, let me tell you a little about some of those that I enjoyed the most and which influenced my thinking more than the others.

*The Shoes of the Fisherman* is a powerful commentary on the clash of religion and ideology. It was published in 1963, long before the election of a Pole as Pope John-Paul II and the current war in Ukraine. It is the tale of a cardinal from Ukraine who is unexpectedly elected as pope. His life had been a long history of active revolt against communism, especially in the Soviet Union, of which Ukraine was part back in the era in which the book was written. His opposition had led him to be tortured and imprisoned for many years until the regime decided that they could safely let him free on a good behavior bond.

His elevation to the Vatican as pope put him in a position of power in which he could actively oppose the oppression of Christianity by communism worldwide. This raised a much-debated question. Was he a pope or a politician. Could he be both? Can you and I be Christians and politicians at the same time? Many have tried, but the record shows that politics usually wins.

After reading this, I came to the clear conviction that we can be both so long as we do not use Christianity as a weapon to win elections, gain power and use it. However, it will take enormous discipline as to be effective we have to spend a lot of time making sure we don't lose our political power, a process that by necessity could lead us to play 'rotten politics'.

*The Devil's Advocate* is a cracker of a book that powerfully raises the question of whether it is possible for anyone to be declared a saint or whether there is any need at all for us to revere saints in the Christian life. If we do, how do we go about creating a saint, as happened with Australia's Mary MacKillop.

In principle, you and I could go to any priest we know and convince him that our nominee is a worthy saint. If he agrees, he can then persuade his bishop who must then sell the idea to his archbishop who must convince his cardinal plus key figures in the curia at the Vatican who will finally place the matter before the pope. If he is impressed, he is then required by Vatican law to appoint a Devil's Advocate. This person must be a person of high intellect who is asked, not to find out whether the nominee has clearly displayed the qualities a saint, but to find valid evidence that the person is unworthy of appointment.

So it is in this fine novel by Morris West that the pope appoints a dedicated and intelligent English priest who is suffering a terminal illness to be the Devil's Advocate for a nominee for saint who once lived in a remote community in Italy.

He finds that the deceased man was a deeply religious person who selflessly gave his life in successfully stopping the German army from destroying the village where he lived and killing all its inhabitants near the end of World War II. He was also a man of many human sins, enough for the pope to deny the man sainthood. The Devil's Advocate has to make a decision. It will be the final decision of his own life as his cancer grows by the day.

You must read the book to find out what happens. The questions it raised with me are these. Is there anyone anywhere at any time who is qualified to be a saint and do we as Christians really need saints to inspire us or be our mediators before God?

My answer is No. What is yours?

*Eminence* is another Morris West classic.

This time it is about a priest from Argentina who openly and actively opposed the takeover of his nation by powerful fascists. When they win, he is brutally punished to the point of death as the vicious regime try and fail to force him to give them the names of those who were his allies in opposing them. Friends of great courage save him and take him to a remote refuge where a very devout and caring woman nurses him back to health, a process that takes a year. They develop a close relationship. When the regime tracks him down, her influential parents arrange for him to escape to Rome where he serves as a priest in the Vatican.

He is regularly promoted up the ladder of the hierarchy of the Church until he is appointed a cardinal with the specific task of being a special assistant to the pope who places great trust in him. His job is to travel the world on behalf of the pope to solve the many problems and crises facing the Catholic Church everywhere. He becomes famous and popular within the Church on every continent.

The pope dies and the cardinals gather to elect a new pope. He is the favoured nominee of many and the media forecast he will win easily.

In the days immediately prior to the election, the woman who cared for him back in Argentina many years before in his time of huge pain from torture, and whom he has not seen since, arrives in Rome. She contacts him and with great joy he eagerly agrees to meet her. She tells him that she is dying of cancer and wants him to meet her beautiful adult daughter. She reveals to him that this young woman is his daughter whose existence she has never told him of in their correspondence down the years.

He is elected pope by a huge margin over the second choice but remains in office for only five minutes when he dramatically resigns, telling his fellow cardinals that the Church will be hit hard by the scandal of a pope who has a daughter.

This however is not the real reason for his dramatic resignation. He happily makes the powerful inner discovery that he cherishes life with his daughter more than ministry to the world as its pope.

This raises a question that I comment on elsewhere: 'Is it theologically valid for any Church to declare that a priest must be celibate and what evidence can anyone find that will prove that celibacy is a sign of spiritual depth?'

Does celibacy make a person more like Jesus the Man? There is no direct evidence in his life that Jesus was celibate. We have just assumed that he was. I have not the slightest doubt that celibacy is absolutely unnatural. A celibate person has not experienced life to the full and is unable to counsel the human race about the basic challenges of life. Surely there are better ways to make sacrifices to God than via celibacy.

There is a second issue raised by *Eminence*.

Why would a pope give up his powerful role and the fame that goes with it so as to spend his remaining days with a daughter whose life he had not shared for a quarter of a century? The answer seems to me to be that love is of far greater value to a human soul than power.

*The Last Confession* is another Morris West book that I enjoyed and learned much from. It is very different to the others.

The story happens a few centuries ago. A priest is charged with heresy and is about to be killed for his sins. The book gives a very thoughtful account of his personal agony, as well as highlighting the viciousness of some of his accusers and outlining the growing doubts about his guilt in the minds of the others who sat in judgement of him.

The purpose of the book is to debate what constitutes heresy and is there such a thing as heresy in the first place. Back in the era that West's book covers, the book you are now reading would have had me burned instantly at the stake without a trial.

Morris West wrote many other books that have made a deep impression on my soul but space won't allow me to comment on all of them here. I strongly recommend that you buy them online and enjoy them as much as I have done.

I remember that I really did enjoy reading *Cassidy*, a great tale about corruption and power in Australian politics and the hypocritical role played by the Church.

*The Ambassador* was another powerful one which laid bare the absolute folly of the war in Vietnam and will inspire you to read his other fine books.

What actually occurred as the result of my reading of his novels is that each one of them pricked my conscience in a meaningful way that made it both a joyful experience and a challenge. They all forced me to open my mind to new challenges and possibilities.

All books should do this for us. I do hope that this current book of mine fills the bill for you as a mind expander.

Morris West died of a heart attack while sitting at his typewriter completing the final chapter of *The Last Confession*.

What a great way for an author to go. What a wonderful manner for anyone to go. He was happily writing away when he just fell across his typewriter into a permanent sleep. His long-time publisher completed the chapter in the way in which he thought that West would have gone about finishing it and then proudly published it as a final tribute to the best client he ever had.

Vale Morris West. Good bloke. Great author. Expansive thinker. Evangelist of a different kind whom we all can use as a guideline for our own evangelism.

The massive sales of his books prove that he was a powerful and successful evangelist who spread the message of faith via the written word with mind-boggling success.

*THE MORRIS WEST GUIDEPOST*

***Morris West rejected his calling as a priest, yet he had a greater and more positive influence on the minds of people than a thousand priests could ever dream about.***

## 6.24 HARRY EMERSON FOSDICK

Harry Emerson Fosdick was as fine a preacher as America has ever produced. I make this statement after taking into account the enormous impact that the preaching of Billy Graham had even though they were preachers of starkly different theologies.

Martin Luther King publicly declared on many occasions that Fosdick was 'the greatest preacher of the century.' He quoted Fosdick extensively in his sermons and speeches.

Fosdick was a modernist in his theology and in all of his thinking about life. He stirred up huge condemnation from within the ranks of fundamentalists and was consistently involved in advocating a social gospel which was relevant to the present, not two thousand years ago.

He upset the traditionalists most of all when he preached a famous sermon in New York in 1922 called 'Shall the Fundamentalists win?'

In this sermon he said: 'The Bible is a record of the unfolding of God's will. It is not a literal word of God. The history of Christianity is one of development, progress, and gradual change.'

Predictably, fundamentalists in their millions were outraged. In their narrow little world, not one word in the Bible could be doubted in any way or reinterpreted in any circumstances.

At the time, Fosdick was minister of the First Presbyterian Church of New York, a hugely significant church that was packed to the doors every Sunday. However, after much public turmoil at the highest levels of the National Presbyterian Church over a long period of time as to whether he should be tried for heresy, he resigned from his parish. He was not willing to apologise for the sermon or make any admission that he may have been misguided. Nor was he willing to join his Church in its opposition to the teaching of evolution in schools or recant from his public rejection of the creationist dogma of the Church.

A highly unexpected ally stepped into the breach at the moment of his controversial resignation.

John D Rockefeller, was the wealthiest person in the world, then and now. A devout fundamentalist Christian of rigid beliefs whose remarkable life I have covered in an earlier chapter of this book, Rockefeller invited Fosdick to meet with him. He told Fosdick that he was more hated for his wealth than Fosdick was despised for his theology. He strongly suggested that they should get together to do something very special for Christianity.

He provided Fosdick with a huge financial grant to establish a new independent interdenominational church in Manhattan that they agreed to call the Riverside Church. It was a very special moment as under Fosdick's talented ministry it would become the most famous church in the United States. People from all over the world flocked to hear him preach there. He drew larger crowds than Norman Vincent Peale and that is quite a feat.

The key factor in Rockefeller's decision to fund Fosdick was based on his belief that Fosdick could reach and involve the intellectual element of society in a way that Rockefeller's ultra-fundamentalist church would never influence. In his view, Fosdick had been given by God the ability to add a different type of Christian to the kingdom of God. Rockefeller actively promoted the Riverside Church as the spiritual gathering place for people involved in universities, schools, hospitals, courts, skilled professions etc, that is people whom he reckoned, quite accurately, would reject fundamentalist Christianity as below their intellectual capacity.

Intellectuals flocked to the Riverside Church in their thousands. In order to cater for their need for learning, Fosdick would spend at least fifteen hours a week preparing his sermons for church and radio. He would carefully choose exactly the right words and ensure their logic was sound so he could stimulate debate among academics while ensuring that his message still made common sense for the ordinary person.

This to me is a prime example of a much-needed change that must happen to evangelism right now in the 2020s. There is no such thing as one set of beliefs for all

Christians or one market of people to whom the faith is relevant. Rockefeller could understand this readily as he had achieved his wealth by his acute commercial understanding that for every product he chose to put on sale, there are many potential markets. Those products must be marketed in ways that suit the needs of widely different elements of society. He was indeed one of the most astute marketers the world has ever produced.

What is also fascinating is that Rockefeller provided not just enough capital to build a splendid church at Riverside, but a twenty-two storied tower beside it to provide social, recreational, and educational facilities for the broader community as well as a centre for outreach and care to the poor and marginalised in the community. Quite revolutionary. He too wanted the world to be aware that Christianity was not just about preaching sermons.

Also noteworthy is that Fosdick and Rockefeller came to a deal in that despite Rockefeller offering to pay all the costs, Fosdick wanted Rockefeller's agreement that there must be other significant donors so that it was not just Rockefeller's church as this would mean that it would be widely regarded as another money-making venture for Rockefeller, this time finding a way to make money out of religion. Fosdick went even further. He involved all levels of society in his fund-raising which meant that he asked the poorest people in the city to contribute their share as well so they could feel that it was a church for all.

Indeed, Rockefeller agreed that he would never tell Fosdick what he should preach about or criticise his sermons in public. In response, Fosdick agreed not to attack capitalism as an ideology. He would only ever attack individual capitalists who had done something that was of outrageous greed that had unfairly damaged society.

Fosdick was minister of the Riverside Church for twenty years, retiring in 1946 after becoming a very high-profile preacher and pastor as well as a famous author and broadcaster. His weekly nationwide radio broadcasts on Sunday evenings that were called 'Vespers', and had an audience of many millions, were also organised and financed by Rockefeller. In addition, Fosdick became a prime example of a Christian at work beyond the doors of his church by becoming a high profile and formidable opponent of racism and injustice in all its forms. Of special note is that he pioneered the establishment of Alcoholics Anonymous throughout the US in the same way as Gordon Powell did in Australia.

All of his sermons advanced the modernist theology that was the basis of his controversial sermon on fundamentalism of 1922. Each week those sermons would be printed and mailed in large packages to churches everywhere for distribution to parishioners at church doors every Sunday. It won't surprise you to learn that those supplies consistently ran out.

Fosdick was also fired by profound humility as he never failed to point out that his theology was not his original thinking. He built upon and expanded the work of others who had inspired modernism over a long period of time.

Theological liberalism had first come to light in the seventeenth century through the work of French philosopher, René Descartes. He called it rationalism and enlightenment.

In the eighteenth century, Rousseau developed it further and called it romanticism and this led on to the modernism that Fosdick and Dietrich Bonhoeffer embraced. After Fosdick, it would be carried forward into more revolutionary theology by three theologians to whom I have also devoted a chapter, John Robinson, Lloyd Geering, and John Shelby Spong.

What is fascinating to me is that Fosdick had the ability to challenge the minds of people who were nominal Christians and who only went to church on occasions such as Christmas and Easter. This was revealed by the publication of his bestselling book to the world beyond the Church. He named it *Twelve Tests of Character*.

Readers were fascinated by these chapters of the book that set out a practical, sensible, and inspiring blueprint for wise living:

- First things first. Work out what your priorities of life are.
- Use long ropes and short stakes. Make sure you have solid foundations before you reach out into the unknown.
- Have a high opinion of yourself and your ability without losing your humility.
- See the invisible. Study all the risks and create a strategy to handle them.
- Recognise that living is a privilege. Don't abuse it.
- Mind your own business. Don't waste time lecturing people about your successes and their failures.
- Be obedient. Stick to the tasks before you. Don't divert your attention to trivia.
- Don't try to be an average person. Set goals above the average

- Harness the caveman. If you have a wild streak in you give it a go occasionally.
- Be magnanimous.
- Possess a past tense. Be willing to learn from the past in planning a new future.
- Have the power to see everything through.

Thousands read this book and marvelled that a Christian could be so wise in producing words that would motivate them to chart a better life without getting pious.

Perhaps the best of Fosdick's message to the world is captured by powerful words from a sermon preached by the man whom I said earlier was his greatest admirer. Martin Luther King publicly attributed this compelling message as being based on the teachings of Harry Emerson Fosdick:

'The Christian Church should be a fountainhead of a better social order. Any religion that pretends to care for the souls of people but is not interested in the slums that damn them, the governments that corrupt them and the economic order that cripples them, is a dry passive do nothing religion in need of new blood.'

Hear, hear. Those words have hit me hard. Let's see them put into practice.

The fundamentalists who forecast that God would strike him down at an early age for his dreadful heresies were stunned when Fosdick lived to a ripe old age of ninety-one.

Rockefeller lived even longer, despite being criticised for 'contaminating the purity of his faith by forming a controversial and formidable partnership with a proven heretic and blasphemer by the name of Harry Emerson Fosdick.'

While I don't believe in miracles, the partnership of Rockefeller and Fosdick was as close to one as we can get.

*THE HARRY EMERSON FOSDICK GUIDEPOST.*

***Fosdick and Rockefeller were wisely aware that there are many Christian markets. There is not just one version of the faith that is embraced by all Christians.***

***I also learned from Fosdick that there are many and varied messages about the life of The Man that can become cornerstones of our lives. He convinced me that fundamentalism in any realm of life is a curse on humanity.***

## 6.25 JOHN SHELBY SPONG

Here is a high-profile American Episcopal bishop whom you either loved with devotion or hated with passion. Debates about his life and work were always polarised as he chose to live on the extremes of religion.

His writings as a radical theologian are in a different sphere to those of William Barclay, Harry Emerson Fosdick, Lloyd Geering, and John Robinson. This is not because they came from different religious denominations. Spong always ventured into dangerous territory, generating considerable controversy which he appeared to enjoy, whereas the other three were never headline seekers even though they generated lots of headlines.

My comment on Spong is not meant to denigrate him but indicates that while I can live comfortably with the words of Barclay, Geering, and Robinson, Spong quite often leaves me behind with his extremism which can at times come over as being invalid.

He is almost my twin. We were born only four months apart in 1931 and, in my later years, I have been a fellow traveller consistently and respectfully. I was saddened by his death two years ago in his ninetieth year.

I was able to identify with his firm belief that there is no such thing as a God who is in charge of everything and I am pleased that he powerfully questioned the validity of traditional doctrines and creeds. Like me, his early years were spent in fundamentalist Churches and we were heavily influenced by the faith of our mother. I regret that I did not ever have the privilege of meeting Spong as this would have been a memorable experience.

Spong was extraordinarily well educated, studying divinity at universities in North Carolina, Virginia, New York, Boston, Edinburgh, Oxford, and Cambridge. Even his staunchest opponents acknowledged that he was not an unqualified amateur.

He served as rector of three Episcopal parishes, then was elected as a bishop at Newark. He was the first Episcopal bishop to ordain a woman into the clergy, and the first to ordain an openly gay man. He was a close friend of the British Anglican bishop, John Robinson, and regarded him as a powerful mentor, while declaring Paul Tillich to be his favourite theologian. It is interesting to note that the Humanitarian Society of America awarded Spong the honour of Humanitarian of the Year in 1999 as his words made sense to them as being human and caring.

His personal theology was such that, as it covered so much religious territory, it is difficult to describe in a few sentences. However I reckon it will be sufficient for me to highlight here some major issues that he either highlighted in sermons or included in his many books.

- He rejected the virgin birth, a bodily resurrection of Jesus and emphatically stated that a physical ascension up to heaven did not ever happen.
- He affirmed we do not have to literalise words of Scripture to perceive their meaning.
- He was a hard-hitting critic of the doctrine of faith of the Catholic Church.
- He argued that St Paul was a homosexual.
- He did not believe in the supernatural.

Many of his book titles concisely describe his theology. They include:

- Rescuing the Bible from Fundamentalism
- Jesus for the Non-Religious
- Why Christianity Must Change or Die
- A New Vision of Eternal Life

He was a prolific author and possessed an extraordinary mental capacity.

He was not universally loved and was hugely hated or passionately despised by his critics. Some Anglican bishops created headlines by publicly banning him from preaching in their dioceses, none of which caused him even the slightest concern as it proved to him that he was on the right path. In particular, the more they denigrated him, the more they boosted the sales of his books, so he had no reason to complain.

My hope is that his contribution to advocacy of a new reformation outside the Churches will not be forgotten just because of the controversy he created everywhere that he preached.

He passionately believed that his words needed to be said, loudly and clearly.

I remember Spong as someone who constantly caused me to think deeply about everything he conveyed through his powerful words even if I did not adopt them.

He enhanced my spiritual journey simply because he did not ever fail to cause me to reflect on my own reason for being and work happily on the ever-fascinating task of making it clearer and more meaningful to me.

*THE SPONG GUIDEPOST*

***John Shelby Spong was a preacher and writer of huge courage. He thrived on the endless personal insults that were hurled at him***

***His critics motivated him to constantly move powerfully forward with his new messages of reform.***

## 6.26 TIM COSTELLO

I have included my friend Tim Costello for several sound and solid reasons.

Initially, it was because it was important that a Baptist should be included in my book. I think it is an honest assessment to say that he is the most famous Baptist pastor that Australia has ever produced. But primarily I have chosen him because he is a fine example of how a Christian can reconcile faith, politics and community service in an honest and meaningful manner while making a huge contribution to the advancement of humanity.

He is also a personal friend whom I greatly admire and whose friendship I hugely value. I will never forget the time he was a guest in my home for an overnight stay after speaking at a dinner of the Aspley Uniting Church. I greatly enjoyed the hour we spent quietly discussing the challenges of life and their potential solutions.

Let me first take you for a look at his incredible life journey.

Firstly, he came from a devout Baptist family from where he began his life's work as a lawyer operating from his own one-person practice where he specialised in family law. He then made a life changing decision to become a Baptist pastor.

His studies in divinity took him to the International Baptist Seminary in Switzerland and the Melbourne College of Divinity, graduating as a Master of Theology. When he was ordained as a Baptist pastor he became minister of the St Kilda Baptist Church, then the Collins Street Baptist Church from where he was elected as president of the Baptist Union of Australia.

His groundbreaking ministry at St Kilda was a unique success which is a blueprint for the revival of dying congregations.

The Baptist church there had only a handful of ageing members who met in old deteriorating buildings, had insufficient funds to pay his salary and provided him with a house that was barely liveable. He turned this church into a caring ministry to the suburb by establishing a drop-in centre which directly helped large numbers of people in crisis situations, especially those in legal trouble. It is now widely regarded a model for injecting new life into fading inner city congregations.

At the Collins Street church, he established a Christian not for profit organisation called Urban Seed which actively responded to the needs of people doing it tough in situations of homelessness, drug abuse and being marginalised from society.

Then he became chief executive and chief advocate of World Vision Australia for thirteen years. It grew extraordinarily under his leadership raising more than $100 million to fund and manage 480 humanitarian projects worldwide that gave help to more than ten million people. He also served on the international board of World Vision where he led their work in underdeveloped nations, mainly located in Africa.

He retired from this great work only when its constant toll severely affected his health.

Nevertheless, he has remained actively involved in society. He is executive director of Micah Australia as well as having leadership roles in Ethical Voice, the Centre for Public Christianity, the Community Council of Australia, and the Alliance for Gambling Reform.

In all, this is an astonishing example of community service powered by personal Christian conviction, a feat honoured by an award of Officer of the Order of Australia and an honorary doctorate at the Australian Catholic University.

Interestingly, he also had a brief political career.

While at the St Kilda Baptist Church, he became so involved in the community that he was elected mayor of St Kilda in which role he initiated many long overdue community reforms that made it a more cohesive society. He had only one term as mayor as the city council was disbanded when the Victorian Government decided to merge many local governments. St Kilda was absorbed with neighbouring councils.

Then, he was offered a Senate seat to represent Victoria in the Australian Parliament. This occurred because he was an active member of the Australian Democrats advocating matters of social conscience when a casual vacancy occurred because one of their senators resigned. He declined the invitation for a number of reasons, one of which was that it would have put him into a situation where he would have been politically opposed to his brother, Peter, who was at the time Treasurer in the Liberal Party government in Canberra led by John Howard.

In addition to all of the above, he is the author of six great books.

The last, *A Lot with a Little*, is an absolute cracker of a read. I strongly recommend that you buy a copy right now and be inspired by it.

I have learned much from Tim about the relationship of faith to the challenges of life that face humanity as well as learning from him the skill of being an evangelist triumphing in an almost impossible situation.

His visionary work during his time at St Kilda Baptist Church has revealed to me how it is possible for a small and dying congregation of quite old members can be motivated to venture into a totally new and different mission of service. All that they needed was a leader who was able to inspire them to give up their quiet routine of church life and reach out personally to others whom they knew and invite them to join a challenging outreach to those in need out in the community.

People who had only remote church connections were personally invited to take part in this inspiring mission and they did so in steadily growing numbers. They grew in faith by working side by side with Tim in reaching out to people they did not know and involving them in the way that the original disciples of Jesus did long ago. Their active personal outreach was far more effective than if they had only encouraged people to do the traditional thing and just come to listen to his always challenging sermons.

With Tim Costello as their leader they proved that there is no such thing in the world as a dying congregation. There are just too many leaderless, visionless, and lazy congregations happily dying in peaceful slumber.

Tim has set us a visionary example to follow and I am very aware that I have learned a vast amount of inspirational wisdom from a fine human being.

I grow in stature every time I reach out to do work similar to that which he did in meeting face-to-face with people giving them a challenge to become fishers and carers of souls.

May it continue. May it prosper. May it continue to change our world.

*THE TIM COSTELLO GUIDEPOST*

***In the realm of ministers, pastors, priests and elders, Tim Costello is a giant.***

***Absolute quality, enormous vision, and humble attitude.***

## 6.27 SCOTT MORRISON

Only after much careful thought did I make the difficult decision to include Scott Morrison in this account of my journey. In doing so I want to emphasise that I do not question his honesty or integrity in politics or his strong belief in his personal theology. I hold the view that a study of his life and work can lead us to discover new and better pathways in our missionary journey.

Nevertheless, he, more than any other Australian prime minister, has highlighted the use, misuse, and misrepresentation of Christianity in politics and government to an extent that I have never before experienced.

I have devoted this chapter to him for the same reason as I have elected to talk about George Pell and Brian Houston. There is much that we can learn from all three that will be of value on our journey as we navigate the challenges along the pilgrim way.

Morrison took his belief of an indivisible link between Christianity and politics to extreme lengths while electioneering when he invited the media to photograph him singing and clapping at worship at his Pentecostal church during the 2019 Australian election campaign. Clearly he wanted the voters of Australia to know that they would be electing a deeply committed Christian prime minister if they voted for him. As he had already publicly announced his devout Pentecostal faith to his electorate of Cook long before the election was ever called, there was no need to deliberately use it as a specific weapon to win an election.

He had already made it clear that he embraced the prosperity gospel as an article of faith to the extent that it has now become a permanent political landmark that is now constantly advocated by the Christian Right.

He is widely reported to have proclaimed that the Bible says that if you genuinely believe in God and accept Jesus as your Saviour and Lord you are destined to become prosperous if you work hard, smartly, and honestly. This proclamation created an image based on his personal belief that if you are a recipient of government welfare you are not really a genuine believer as you only need welfare if you do not implement God's word about prosperity. I have no doubt that he holds this belief sincerely, but the very existence of it within his faith troubles me enormously as it is quite simply not a doctrine that can be attributed to Jesus of Nazareth.

No disciples of The Man were prosperous people so they would never have made it into Scott Morrison's team had they lived in the same era.

The Pentecostals are a growing army of believers who are now a significant force in modern society, which they are entitled to be in a genuine democracy. I am delighted to have friends who are Pentecostal and I admire their enthusiasm for their faith and their willingness to live by it and bring others to it. However, Scott Morrison's interpretation does not ring true in the minds of many voters, especially those who identify as traditional Christians.

Having raised those issues of concern, let me comment on some known facts.

Scott Morrison is a significant person in Australian history, having served as our thirtieth prime minister for four years from 2018. His victory over Bill Shorten in the general election of 2019 was one of the most unexpected, but extraordinary, election wins in the history of Australia. He campaigned with a powerful simplicity, repeating over and over again several blunt one-liners about the leader of the opposition such as 'Bill Shorten will lose all your money. Don't trust him.' He believed utterly that God had called him to stop Shorten from being prime minister and never doubted even slightly that he would do so. His win will forever be a template for aspiring politicians on how to win an impossible election so long as you are willing to go to extremes.

What was striking about him was that he had an unimpressive record on his pathway to the job of being prime minister.

The media have reported regularly that on two occasions in his earlier life he had been asked to resign from executive positions that he held because of inadequate performance.

It is alleged that he won preselection for the seat of Cook in the Australian Parliament by spreading fabricated rumours about his favoured opponent that were totally disproved by subsequent investigations. Then, he became prime minister by working behind the scenes to undermine the then prime minister, Malcolm Turnbull, while blaming his opponent Peter Dutton.

When he became prime minister, he absented himself from Australia during intense nationwide bushfires in an arrogant manner that appeared to be uncaring as he took a family holiday in Hawaii. He was entitled to take that holiday but it gave a selfish look.

This was followed by his mismanagement of the national response to floods and Covid. He also grossly offended his ministerial team by having the governor general swear him into ministerial posts that they already held without advising them he was doing so. None of the above conveyed a traditional Christian outlook.

He believed that it was his God-given destiny to become prime minister and that it was therefore okay to do anything that would make this happen. He was certain that when you are doing God's work whatever you do will be okay with God.

He is not the only person who has ever believed this or to have carried this out relentlessly. Countless numbers of people have done so for thousands of years and more will do so in the future. God can always easily be blamed for requiring us to sin in his name.

In fairness to him, he did not deliberately become a Christian for the specific purpose of getting himself into Parliament and becoming prime minister. He has been a lifetime believer and is not a political opportunist.

Before his political days he went to study theology in Canada, and on another occasion at the University of New South Wales he did a thesis on the Plymouth Brethren. So there can be no doubt that his understanding and acceptance of Christianity is a basic core of his existence, not a fabricated public image to win votes.

Verification of the biblical basis of his life is indicated by his action as Australia's prime minister to recognise West Jerusalem as the capital city of Israel. He unswervingly believes that Christians and Jews owned Jerusalem as their holy city, certainly not Muslims, even though it was totally controlled by Muslim people for fourteen hundred years. They are entitled to believe it is also theirs.

His commitment went even further into more very dangerous territory as the years passed.

While prime minister, he arranged for a room in the Parliament building to be set aside as a prayer room for the use of his select group of core Christian believers from his governing cabinet. No important legislation was passed without it being placed before the Lord in prayer in this room and in seeking His guidance.

The policy that created the infamous Robodebt scandal was a matter of fervent prayer in this room. It was seen as a calling from God to punish people whom he believed were unchristian welfare thieves. The media has claimed that the impact of Robodebt caused several Australian pensioners to take their own lives while others had serious breakdowns in their mental health. This allegation has not yet been proven in a court of law and so he is entitled to a presumption of innocence.

However, allow me to emphasise that he did not deliberately set out to do physical and mental harm to anyone. It is an unintended consequence he now must live with.

This raises the question that has always concerned me.

Can any politician make decisions based solely on his or her faith, especially the Christian faith, given that less than 50% of the population of Australia believes in God and many other faiths have a significant voice in the land? Decisions can be made only on the basis of what is best for the entire population. A politician can then present it as the core of a personal Christian commitment but not as a Christian policy.

So, there it is. Is Scott Morrison a committed Christian?

Yes, undoubtedly yes, within the narrow confines of his understanding of it.

Did that make him a prime minister of quality?

I don't think so. He appears to have fallen far short of the qualities required to walk with The Man to create a better nation. Having said this, I wish him a happy life ahead, beyond politics. In doing so, I must also confess that my life has not been without sin. I am in no position to throw stones at anyone.

*THE SCOTT MORRISON GUIDEPOST*

***Scott Morrison's public record has convinced me that no person has the right to use their Christian faith as a weapon to get themselves elected to Parliament, nor can we use our faith as a political reason to have legislation passed.***

***Our morals, ethics and values should be obvious by the way we live day by day. There is no need to glorify our holiness in or out of politics.***

## 6.28 BRIAN HOUSTON

I choose my words carefully in this chapter as there are several court cases underway that involve the work of Brian Houston as leader of a significant Christian enterprise called Hillsong. He is entitled to a presumption of innocence until proven guilty. That which is alleged but is not yet proven and may not be.

However, I want to comment on two factors about his life that are important for us to look at in the context of this book.

One is the role of music in evangelism. The other is the question of whether any Church should be founded and controlled by one family when it has thousands of devoted members.

Houston and his father founded Hillsong Church in Sydney and, as the result of their personal leadership, it became the largest and most powerful congregation in

Australia. It spread to other Australian cities and then to other nations, especially the United States. Partly, this has been due to his considerable influence in political and financial circles.

This has been especially due to Brian Houston's extensive use of music in the life of his congregations. There, he masterminded the composition of new hymns and songs that became hits with the public far beyond Hillsong and became a significant generator of money for his cause. Many people came to worship at Hillsong just to hear and sing the music.

This reality is not an oddity as many Christian historians strongly claim that a prime reason why John Wesley drew such large crowds was that they loved the hymns composed by his brother, Charles, who in fact created over two thousand hymns during his shared ministry with John. This was a phenomenal achievement.

Some make similar claims about Billy Graham as many are said to have come to his rallies just so they could hear the famous Gospel singer, George Beverly Shea, who was an essential member of Billy's team. Indeed, Shea always held the crowds in raptures.

Music, art and poetry are grossly underused as powerful weapons of evangelism. Personally my skills in any form of art are barely above nil, but I do hope that those with these talents will hear the call loud and clear and foster a greater use of all the arts to inspire us along our pilgrim journey.

So we come to my second point in this chapter and it is a crucial one.

Down the centuries, too many people have blatantly used their Church as a pathway to personal power, influence, and authority. A person like George Pell is a prime example of this, closely followed by Brian Houston who used a different pathway to get there.

Should one person or one family control a Church, especially a large one? My answer is a very firm no. I am reminded of the actions of the children of William Booth immediately after his death. They insisted they had the right to take control of the Salvation Army when their father died. It caused a huge rift that irreparably divided its members.

The problems that Houston now faces have been generated by his use of personal power. Many of his accusers have publicly alleged that he became drunk with power, lived an extravagant lifestyle, took liberties with women, bullied his co-workers, misused government grants, etc. He denies it (as he is entitled to) but it seems to be the genesis of his huge fall from grace.

The story of Hillsong is a tragedy.

Houston's fall, combined with other experiences of religious empire builders of a similar nature over my nine decades, have caused me to come to the firm belief that Churches have reached the point where they do not need professional priests and pastors. Elders serving in a voluntary capacity are more than adequate to be able to lead any gathering of Christians.

I will expand on this vital matter in a later chapter.

My hope is that Brian Houston may be able to find a better way in which he can use his considerable leadership skills in walking with The Man.

*THE BRIAN HOUSTON GUIDEPOST*

***Brian Houston's ministry is alleged by news media to have been based on gaining personal***

*power, using Church funds to finance a lavish lifestyle and having inappropriate relationships. The courts of the land will eventually determine whether or not this is true of false.*

*The message for you and me is that participation in mega churches is not the pathway for working partners of Jesus the Man.*

## 6.29 BILLY GRAHAM

At the funeral in 2019 of Billy Graham, who was within just a few months of making it to his century, it was observed in eulogies that he preached face-to-face with more people than any other person in the history of Christianity.

I reckon that this estimate is correct as, while popes have drawn larger crowds for a few days during state visits, they have never assembled them night after night, week after week, month after month, year after year, in the extraordinary manner that Billy Graham did. His cumulative audiences can be verified in countless millions.

The question to be debated now is how he achieved it and whether it can be repeated now by another evangelist of his quality.

His crusades were organised by a talented professional team in a way that used every modern communication skill that no one else had ever before put together in Church life. Now, digital technology should be able to expand on this skill mightily for any of his successors.

Helen and I turned up at the Brisbane Exhibition Grounds in 1959, along with 50,000 others, to see and hear him in action, and I was impressed. The point that hit home the strongest was his personal charisma and his simple direct messages, conveyed with convincing power of unshakeable belief. I was concerned that he talked solely about our sins but he did not leave anyone in any doubt about what their personal challenge was. Were you or were you not going to give your life to Christ?

Helen and I did not go forward when Billy gave his call to do so. From my point of view, I have not ever wanted to be saved from my sins as I don't believe that being ashamed of my sins is a reason to become a Christian. I became a committed follower of Jesus of Nazareth very early in my life because of the simple faith that my mother gently instilled in my soul every day. The entire issue of sin and salvation has never ever gripped me. I just grew up wanting to do all the compassionate and courageous things that The Man did.

Many of the friends who were with me at Billy's rally that night and went forward to answer the call, were not doing it because they were accepting Christ for the first time. They were making a re-commitment so I am not sure how many of those who went forward were genuine souls saved for the first time.

Nevertheless, I was impressed with the evening and thought highly of Billy as a person. I had no doubt that he was a genuine believer and a great leader of the Christian cause.

I followed his career as an evangelist from that time onwards.

His success no matter where he went convinced me that every person who becomes a follower of The Man really does have a responsibility to be an evangelist. Billy taught me that, no matter what brand of Christianity any one of us may embrace, we must all be out there in public enlisting new people into the ranks with whatever modest skills we may have. The task of convincing people to be followers of The Man is not the realm of conservative evangelicals alone. It is also the task of wild-eyed radicals.

When I heard the news of Billy's death, I felt once again a need for some self-examination of my lack of performance as an evangelist, a matter that I raise frequently throughout this book.

I had to confess that, even though I had throughout my life always spoken positively and publicly about my pride in being a believer, I had only occasionally directly asked people to join me in the Christian team. I have let the side down. This has caused me, late in my life, to make a commitment to become a reforming evangelist, a matter that I will talk about later in this book as I have achieved some modest success.

In addition, the way that Billy Graham very professionally used top quality marketing skills to sell thousands on the idea of coming to his crusades also had a big impact. Now, without in any way attempting to do any preaching, I daily use Twitter and Facebook to convey simple messages of faith, ethics, values, conscience, and integrity to the growing number of people who follow me. I respond with direct messages designed to create debate.

My impression at this moment is that there are many people in our social circuit who are willing to have The Man as the role model of their lives but have no intention of going to church and could not care less about whether or not they will ever go to heaven.

There is one other aspect of Graham's life that we should carefully note and this is that he became the private pastor to every president of the United States of America in his lifetime except for Harry Truman (who thought he was a slick salesman).

On many an occasion, he was an overnight guest at the White House and a regular invitee to state dinners. Two presidents in particular called on him to spend quality time with them during their darkest hours.

The first was Richard Nixon who invited Billy Graham to come urgently to the White House at the time of his resignation as president of the United States for corruption revealed by the Watergate scandal. Nixon was in torment by the disgrace that caused him to lose his political power.

Years later, he was followed by Bill Clinton when Clinton's sexual prowess hit the headlines and caused him considerable humiliation. He sorely needed Billy's advice.

All the presidents regarded Billy as pastoral carer whom they could trust totally, a skill that many modern priests and pastors either go out of their way today to avoid or deliberately neglect their responsibility to be a trusted carer. Too many simply want to be preachers and communicators. They fear the challenges of helping people in need.

The prime thing is that when Billy Graham put his hand to the plough early in life, he never looked back.

Clear in his mind was an unshakeable conviction that reminded him daily of his divine calling to save souls: 'This one thing I do.'

He did it exceptionally well.

THE BILLY GRAHAM GUIDEPOST

***In terms of the life and times of my era, Billy Graham was the most famous and successful of all Christian evangelists. He created headlines for The Man, more so than any other person.***

***His was an incredible talent of top quality communication.***

## 6.30 ROSA PARKS

Her story is the final chapter of this segment of my book, deliberately out of chronological order, even though she lived several decades before most of those whom I have mentioned above. As most characters in this book are male, I hope that you will decide that Rosa outranks them just a little. It is an honour she has earned.

Her life was so dedicated to her search for justice for her people that Rosa Parks deserves special acknowledgement here even though she was a nominal Christian. She had great hope in the decency of humanity and that, no matter how bleak life may become, justice would eventually prevail.

She was a respected patriot for the recognition of civil rights, crusading powerfully beside Martin Luther King. Many times she marched with him and thousands of Christians on the long path to the achievement of a meaningful recognition of equality for her people. Most of their ancestors had come as slaves from Africa in inhumane conditions on boats owned by Christians who earned enormous profits from their evil trade.

Rosa first came to public notice in her peaceful advocacy for civil rights when she famously refused to give up her seat to a white person on a bus in Montgomery, Alabama. Her action is now a never to be forgotten part of the folklore of America. Subsequently, she was abused and jailed consistently, and dragged through many unjust court cases before finally making her point when the highest courts in the land at local, state, and national level all ruled that bus segregation was a breach of the constitution of the United States of America.

Despite her ultimate victory, she was a constant victim of discrimination and degradation in all of its forms, especially by white Christians who inflicted physical abuse on her and tried to destroy her mental health. But she survived. When she died of exhaustion at the age of ninety-two, she was awarded the belated honour of being the first woman in the history of the United States to lie in state at the rotunda of the Capitol building of Congress in Washington, so that many thousands could file past her coffin to pay their profound respects to a genuine hero.

Throughout her entire life the vast majority of those who abused her and vilified her were white Christians who believed that they were the chosen race and that African Americans were beings who were 'hewers of wood and bearers of water' who had no rightful place in decent society.

Another prime reason why I have given Rosa a place of honour in this book is that she represents the demise of the unjustifiable belief that there is such a thing as a chosen race. It disturbs me that the world still contains millions of Christians who with profound bigotry persistently try to restore the idea that they are the chosen people and all others are a lower version of humanity.

Christians have not only used this falsehood racially, they have done it also to people whom we refer to as LBGTQI+, divorced persons, those who marry a person of the same sex, and those who choose voluntary assisted dying or have had abortions. And Christians continue to do so.

Christians can no longer deny that it was their own flock who ran the evil slave trade of the world for centuries earning countless millions of dollars and pounds of blood money for their inhumanity, as well as providing huge sums of money to Churches in return for guarantees from religious leaders that they would keep quiet about their horrible abuses. We must never forget that it was slave money that financed the Church of England for a century as it prolonged the abuse of helpless Africans caught up in an exercise of utter degradation.

Rosa Parks was a quiet working partner of The Man to a much greater extent than 99% of the Christian leaders of history. Indeed, she leaves them far behind.

She had an extraordinary humility expressed in a way than most of us could never imagine or emulate and she displayed a willingness to face depravity, humiliation, and death in a way that we could not ever think about, let alone practise.

What a feeble person I am in comparison to her presence in my era. I have never been persecuted for following The Man and I don't expect that I ever will be. Obviously, I am a person of privilege.

I pay her my profound respects to a follower of The Man. Her name is high on the list of those who are prime examples of commitment to the dignity of humanity.

Vale Rosa.

### *THE ROSA PARKS GUIDEPOST*

***Rosa Parks is a prime example of the power of humility. She was a humble servant with whom The Man would identify.***

***She pointed me towards a path of humility. I am still finding my way.***

# 7

# Giants Who Led Me To The Light On The Hill

**OF ALL THE INSPIRATIONAL** people who influenced me on my journey there are five whom I believe had the greatest impact and I have highlighted them here. They were giants of huge stature: William Wilberforce, Lloyd Douglas, George McLeod, Dietrich Bonhoeffer, and Martin Luther King. Absorb their power and use it wisely and well.

## 7.1 WILLIAM WILBERFORCE

Here is a statesman of enormous stature who led a long crusade to have the British parliament pass legislation to outlaw the slave trade throughout the Empire. In doing so, he delivered a huge blow to the standing of the Church of England whose money hungry leaders declared him to be an undisciplined radical.

As I mentioned briefly in my comments on Rosa Parks, it was a huge act of hypocrisy and a generator of outrage that the largest and most powerful Church in the United Kingdom, headed by the monarch, relied heavily on the large financial offerings of wealthy slave traders to finance its daily operating expenditure for more than a century. In return for this blood money, the bishops of the Church agreed never to speak out in the House of Lords against the evil of human trafficking or even privately to express any reservations about its brutal and disgraceful inhumanity.

To make this matter even more deplorable, while the Church was practising this deceit, their clergy were, in an act of significant hypocrisy, preaching regular sermons about what they argued was a lamentable decline in moral standards in British society.

As an elected member of the British Parliament for fifteen years from 1791, William Wilberforce regularly moved motions requesting that a permanent ban be placed on British ships and their owners from being involved in slave trading. He lost every one of them despite making speeches that many of the newspapers in Britain declared to be the most eloquent in the history of the parliament.

At the same time, he was publicly and privately abused by Church leaders. They justified their lust for money by constantly and emphatically quoting those verses of Scripture that said that God's people were the chosen race and the pagan slaves were lesser beings doomed to hellfire. They claimed that their actions were biblically correct and any critics were heretics, especially Wilberforce.

Finally, by sheer perseverance, Wilberforce won the day in a dramatic vote in parliament that banished slave trading on all British ships and shook the national conscience mightily. The Church of England bishops, all of whom lived in palaces, lobbied hard to have the legislation defeated. They berated the parliament for causing them such a huge loss of income.

Wilberforce was not only a politician, but also a philanthropist. He had been converted to Christianity in 1784 by a former slave trader, John Newton, who had sincerely repented of his sins. It is fascinating to note that Newton went on became ordained as an Anglican vicar after removing the blot of slave trading from his life. Eventually, he served as vicar at the same parish church as the Wilberforce family had attended since William was a child.

In the process of his repentance, Newton composed 'Amazing Grace,' one of my favourite hymns. He fired up the natural aversion that Wilberforce had about slavery and turned it into a crusade that they jointly led despite suffering huge physical and verbal denigration.

Wilberforce formed a team of seven Christian friends to help him fight the good fight against slavery. They were famously known as the Clapham Sect as they regularly met in the London suburb of Clapham Junction. After they won the battle to make it illegal for British ships to participate in the slave trade, they fought valiantly to win freedom for all slaves in British colonies.

This struggle went on for a long time, but victory was finally won in parliament in 1833, three days after Wilberforce died. His death stirred the conscience of many of his political opponents to the extent that they had the decency to change their votes from No to Yes in his honour. The bishops remained silent. They could never forgive him for destroying their huge income stream from the profits of the slave trade.

It must also be noted that Abraham Lincoln acknowledged that Wilberforce had led a pioneering crusade in England that laid the groundwork enabling him to lead

America to follow the Wilberforce example and free slaves in 1860. This cost Lincoln his life as well.

William Wilberforce has been an inspiration to me to take up compelling causes of justice as an undeniable calling. He convinced me that there are no such people in our entire planet as God's chosen people.

Sadly, there are still far too many bigoted Christians who think in this way.

They are so selfish that they are mostly unaware that they are the ones causing their churches to die.

History will eventually tell us that in continuing their pomposity and flouting their irrelevance they are actually doing humanity a huge service.

*THE WILLIAM WILBERFORCE GUIDEPOST*

***Wilberforce ranks with Abraham Lincoln as a revered leader of the quest to rid the world of slavery.***

***His life is a clear example of how to achieve positive outcomes despite the intense negativity that inevitably flows from politicians, church leaders, and moneymakers. He took it all on the chin and kept going forward with huge determination and charm.***

## 7.2 LLOYD DOUGLAS

A century ago, this remarkable Christian pastor from the United States wrote challenging books of compelling inspiration that have made a long-lasting impact on my life and the lives of millions of others worldwide. I enjoyed them immensely as they added significantly to my continuing discovery of my reason for being.

Three of his books in particular were so influential that I happily read each one several times and discovered new messages of enlightenment each time I did so.

*The Magnificent Obsession* was the first. It stirred my entire understanding of generosity.

It is based on this famous passage of the Gospels from Matthew 6:5: 'Whenever you give alms, do not sound a trumpet before you as the hypocrites do in the synagogues and in the streets so they may be praised by others. Truly I tell you they have received their reward. When you give alms, do not let your left hand know what your right hand is doing so that your alms may be done in secret and your Father who sees in secret will reward you.'

It is a compelling tale that taught me how a power for good can grow in my life as I genuinely strive to become more generous more quietly. He convinced me that the constant practice of giving is a life changing experience and I have tried to practise it as a way of life, while now understanding that I should have tried harder.

The key message of the book is revealed in the character of the prime person of the story, the revered Dr Hudson, a famous surgeon. He believed and practised a belief that if you make a significant gift to a person who is in dire need, relative in size to the income and assets that you have, and you do so in secret, a power comes into your life that enables you to achieve extraordinary things for the enhancement of humanity that others cannot aspire to.

There are powerful words in the book that are spoken when one of the people whom Hudson had helped and who had recovered from his financial crisis deliberately sought him out and endeavoured to repay him.

Hudson said: 'You can't pay it back. I have used it all up.'

Often have I pondered on the belief that Hudson regularly put into practice. He had gone on to say that if he had ever allowed anyone to pay back what he had given them, his personal skill and power as a surgeon would begin to diminish from that moment.

On reflection, it would be easy to argue that no one should benefit in any way from making a gift, but the fact is we feel better within our souls after we have made a gift that makes someone happy. The Hudson theory and his action is just an extension of this.

*The Robe* was another splendid Lloyd Douglas book. Set in the Holy Land at the time of the crucifixion of Jesus, it gave me clear evidence that even an executioner can become a genuine follower of Jesus the Man. Its main character is a Roman tribune, Marcellus, who was the officer whom Pontius Pilate had placed in charge of carrying out the crucifixion.

Minutes after Jesus died, the Roman soldiers under his command, feeling triumphant for having killed the king of the Jews, held a lottery to decide who would get the robe that Jesus had been wearing on the cross and keep it as a noble souvenier.

Marcellus won it and took it back to his dwelling place with a feeling of triumph. However, from that moment onwards, his mind became troubled, and he fought a long mental battle within himself by trying to determine what had made this man so powerful. He set out to search for and find followers of the man he had crucified. He was so inspired by them that he joined their ranks. When he returned to Rome he told his shocked family and the emperor that he was a Christian.

The final pages of the book are as convincingly dramatic. The emperor has him executed. The last act of Marcellus is to throw the robe to the Christians who at great risk to themselves had come to support him. He called out to them: 'Give it to the big fisherman.'

This dramatic action opened the door for Lloyd Douglas to write *The Big Fisherman* as a dramatic sequel to *The Robe*.

It is a powerful depiction of the tumultuous life of St Peter who was crucified by the Romans, upside down. The Roman Catholic Church would eventually declare him to have been the first pope, even though the great man was never aware of it. They also placed his statue at the centre of St Peter's Basilica so millions of pilgrims could touch his feet.

This gripping tale of his life as told by Lloyd Douglas convinced me that it is highly possible for even an uneducated fisherman like Peter to become the founder of a great faith if your will and commitment is strong enough.

Those three books, together with A J Cronin's great novel, *The Keys of the Kingdom*, have had more influence on my life than all the sermons I have heard over nine decades of listening to some great preachers and far too many hopeless ones. As I relate in another chapter, *The Keys of the Kingdom* offers a prime example of how a humble believer can find a huge sense of calling in walking and working with The Man.

Lloyd Douglas enjoyed an interesting life. He commenced his ministry as Lutheran pastor, but then later moved to the Congregational Church without giving any public explanation. In all, he served in ten parishes, the final one being in Quebec, Canada.

He did not write his first book until he was fifty, but then wrote twenty-one books before his death at seventy-three. This prodigious writing works out to be one book a year for every year. It put him under great pressure as his many readers had great expectations on his ability to produce yet another best seller.

*The Robe* was the most popular of them all by far, selling in excess of two million copies. After Douglas died, *The Robe* was made into a highly popular film with Richard Burton acting the young tribune Marcellus.

*The Big Fisherman* became a successful film also with Howard Keel having the role as Peter, but neither this book nor the film, good as they were, matched the popularity of *The Robe*. It was, and still is, quite special.

I am certain that the most important message I received from Lloyd Douglas is the importance of having an inner power in my life and yours.

These three books of his that I have briefly described above are all about the powerful influence that The Man has, or can have, on you and me as we feel a calling to achieve extraordinary goals.

Indeed, becoming a working partner of The Man can become a magnificent obsession for all of us.

### *THE LLOYD DOUGLAS GUIDEPOST*

***The books of Lloyd Douglas taught me the power of generosity, the strength of being a genuine disciple and the cost of being an active partner of The Man.***

***I thirsted for his books, and grew as I read them.***

## 7.3 GEORGE McLEOD

Yet another giant. There really are a lot of them.

George McLeod was huge presence who left a significant footprint. Clearly, the finest leader the Church of Scotland has ever produced.

He is a prime mentor to many. His life and work alone is sufficient to send this book out to the world on a high.

McLeod is best described as a spellbinding preacher of the traditional faith and valiant reformer from a mould that is not likely to be cloned for a long time.

He will long be remembered as the creator of the now world-famous Iona Community which has become the spiritual home of true believers who want to learn about how to have a practical faith and act on it by getting personally involved in the tribulations of humanity.

Iona has worldwide membership and a high-profile international stature. In all of its history, the Church of Scotland has never produced another leader who stirred the entire Church to the core by taking its focus out of church buildings and into society in a way that had an enormous and lasting impact.

However, beyond the world of religion, it is fair to say that George McLeod was one of Scotland's greatest sons in any walk of life. He changed the manner in which Scotland did its thinking about its values and its future.

A young war veteran from the battlefields of France in World War I where far too many of his friends had died, he returned home convinced of the futility of war and the importance of peace. He chose to study theology in Scotland and the United States and eventually became an ordained minister of the Church of Scotland.

After serving here and there as an associate minister in large parishes, he was called to lead a rundown congregation in an economically poor region of Glasgow known as Govan which he transformed dramatically into a powerhouse of faith and community service. This occurred, not just through a massive growth of attendance at his church, but in its social outreach to the poor, lonely, homeless, hungry, and rejected in which hundreds of members became personally involved as active volunteers. Its success caused people to come from all over the world to come to hear him preach and study why his humanitarian outreach and care had succeeded so magnificently.

Later in his ministry, he felt called to create a new Christian community because he was certain that it was necessary to take Christianity to a greater level in enhancing its impact on a caring society. He deliberately created a haven where ordinary people who did not aspire to become ministers of the Church could study the Scriptures every day and learn how to devote their lives to enhancing any community cause of their choice that created a moral and ethical improvement to the state of humanity anywhere in the world.

He began this vision on the tiny Island of Iona, just south of Mull, among the most southerly of the western islands of Scotland. The community exists to this day, many years after his passing, despite constant attempts by the hierarchy of the Church of Scotland to close it down because it did not adhere to their rules and regulations about how a Church enterprise should be managed.

The Iona Community, as it is now called, occupies the entire island, and has thousands of pilgrims coming and going all year round even though it misses the personal magic that McLeod inspired.

His contribution to the ethics and values of humanity has been honoured in many ways. He was awarded doctorates at eminent universities and was appointed chaplain to Queen Elizabeth, as well as elected moderator of the Church of Scotland despite the controversies he had caused in trying to lead it to new ground.

Just after World War II, he visited Australia on a preaching tour which drew record crowds. I was working in rural Australia at the time and so I missed the chance to hear him in person. I regard this as a tragedy, a hugely missed opportunity, as I would have learned much from the experience of listening to his wisdom and then trying to put his thoughts into action.

One indication of the impact of George McLeod on my life is the role I now have at the Aspley Uniting church in Brisbane in leading our community arm that we call ACTS. We give direct cash grants to people beyond our church who live in crisis situations.

We base its work on the George McLeod model of service, that is we learn as much as possible about the social issues that cause crises and then help to change the causes of the crises in addition to just giving money to those in need.

Just as Thomas Jefferson did, we carry out our work from the foundation of our studies of the ministry of Jesus as set out in the Four Gospels of Matthew, Mark, Luke, and John.

George McLeod led the world in all of this. He taught us to highlight three things in our lives:

- Physical work that helps to provide the daily needs of humanity.
- Study of the Gospels to expand our minds.

- Reaching out to the world to directly help people in crisis.

This is powerful advice from a born leader.

When they heard of his death many Scots stopped wherever they were and wept.

Some background notes: The community on the Island of Iona was first founded by Saint Columba in 600 CE as the hub from which he and his brethren took the ancient Gaelic version of the faith to all the clans of Scotland.

All of us who despise the way in which the hierarchy of Churches smother initiatives to expand the outreach of the Church so they can retain their power, will be inspired to act, and persist by the example of George McLeod. We will be heartened by the way he defied the Church of Scotland in its efforts to stop his visionary work at Iona. He consistently and emphatically told them to get lost. He just stared them down. They retreated in shock. Let's have more of it.

Closer to home, I am remined that in recent years, several committed lay leaders of the Uniting Church in Queensland invested much time and personal money to begin a movement they called Milpara which challenged church congregations to take their ministry out into the community and try to conduct more of their mission there than in their local church. Hard as they tried, they were not able to generate any genuine interest in breaking established traditions. The movement lies dormant. George McLeod would understand their frustration.

THE GEORGE MCLEOD GUIDEPOST

***George McLeod was one of the greatest working partners of The Man who ever walked the pilgrim way. He was as powerful an advocate for positive change as one could find in a long day's march.***

***He motivated me to join the Iona Community as an associate member serving from afar. Hopefully some of his magic has rubbed off on me.***

## 7.4 DIETRICH BONHOEFFER

A modern martyr and a brilliant theologian.

Dietrich Bonhoeffer became a professor of theology at the very youthful age of twenty-five. From there he grew in stature to become a world figure in his calling via his regular lecturing appointments in the United States and the United Kingdom. His incredible talents led him to become a compelling author of outstanding literature that never failed to stir his many readers.

He will always maintain his eminent stature as a martyr as he was one of very few German Christians who had the courage to publicly oppose Adolf Hitler and bravely suffer the deadly consequences.

In one of the greatest and most appalling acts of hypocrisy in the history of Christianity, most German Church members, whether clergy or laity, quietly went along with everything that Hitler did, including the shame of remaining silent while he massacred millions of Jews. In truth, far too many of them backed the tyrant with huge enthusiasm, some even fawning to him as they declared him to be the modern Christ.

Bonhoeffer did the exact opposite.

He resisted everything that Hitler did and paid for it with his life in front of a firing squad in 1945 when he was only thirty-nine. He was not married, his engagement having been announced only days before he was arrested.

He was an inspirational Christian, cruelly and pointlessly chopped down in his prime. The witness of his life is a blueprint of faith that I have indelibly printed in my mind long term. I learned that his faith was not just in his mind and his powerful words, it was planted deep in his soul to the extent that he was willing to die in his quest for justice to humanity. And he did. I doubt that I would have had the conviction and the courage to follow his example. I think I would have found a compelling excuse to run away from Hitler or crawl in his presence.

What I found to be inspiring was the painstaking and dangerous work he did to set up a chain of safe houses between Berlin and the Swiss border where Jewish families could be hidden while his dedicated team of voluntary helpers found ways and means to take them at night to safety in Switzerland. When the houses were discovered by the Gestapo it gave Hitler a further reason, on top of others, to have Bonhoeffer shot.

An even finer example of his courage came at a time when war was imminent and he was lecturing in the US where he had been given a permanent professorial appointment at Harvard University. He chose to give it up so he could return to Germany to do what he could to help save his nation from Adolf Hitler. He did so knowing that his chances of survival were remote.

In time of peace, his ministry was highlighted by his conviction that Churches of every denomination in the world should unite and work together as a committed team to spread the word to all nations instead of competing with one another to determine who was the most holy. He was probably the strongest advocate of ecumenism the world has ever had, especially in his relationships with Jewish people for whose survival he gave his life.

He was an immensely intelligent theologian with a distinguished academic record. He studied theology at the universities of Tübingen and Berlin as well as at the Union Theological Seminary in New York. He then became a pastor for German speaking congregations in Barcelona and London before becoming a professor of theology in Berlin.

His stature was evident when he courageously established and led what he called the Confessing Church which became the centre of opposition of Nazi ideology in Germany, He and his fellow confessors courageously opposed the persecution of Jewish people. In doing this, he developed and advocated a powerful theology of justice, something that visionary Christians can easily revive in today's troubled world.

I found it interesting (and noteworthy) that when Kevin Rudd became prime minister of Australia, he made a statement of his faith in which he said: 'I am a disciple of Dietrich Bonhoffer.'

Many eminent persons worldwide threw their full support behind Bonhoeffer both before and during World War II.

A valiant one was George Bell, Anglican bishop of Chichester, who actively helped Bonhoeffer to establish the Confessing Church in Germany. He had a resolution passed by the House of Lords at Westminster declaring that Hitler's National Socialism was incompatible with Christianity. Bell paid a high price for his involvement with Bonhoeffer as he had been hot favourite to be appointed archbishop of Canterbury when a vacancy occurred. Sadly, he was blackballed by the hierarchy of his Church who declared that his partnership with Bonhoeffer had made him a political figure not a religious leader.

Bonhoeffer's most famous statement of faith rocked the Christian world to its very foundations as it was a commentary of shameful truth:

'The Churches of Germany were silent when they should have cried out because the blood of the innocent was crying aloud to heaven. They are guilty of the deaths of the weakest and most defenceless brothers of Jesus Christ.'

I am certain that his finest moment was in the final minutes of his life when all around him were weeping in fear as they faced death.

He told the members of Hitler's firing squad that he forgave them for what they were about to do as he knew they were simply carrying out orders.

He taught me that followers of The Man cannot ignore the never-ending challenge of having an influential role in a secular world, especially a world of regular conflict and we can do it without becoming politicians.

I stand in awe of him as I recall the words of Scripture from John 15:13: 'No one has greater love than this, to lay down one's own life for one's friends.'

THE DIETRICH BONHOEFFER GUIDEPOST

***Bonhoeffer defied his Church when he refused to follow their pitiful decision to form a fawning relationship with Adolf Hitler. His extraordinary bravery in organising a system of shelters that enabled so many Jewish people to escape to Switzerland inspired me to the core of my being. His influence on me remains huge.***

## 7.5 MARTIN LUTHER KING

What a spiritual powerhouse.

What an incredible colossus of the cause of justice.

What an orator.

What an achiever of change.

What a courageous person.

Yet he was also a sinner like the rest of us.

Embedded in my memory forever is Martin Luther King's spellbinding speech to the many thousands of African Americans who gathered for the Great March to Washington and its enormous gathering at the Lincoln Memorial when he said words that reached the entire American nation and much of the world and which will ring down the ages.

'I have a dream that one day my children will not be judged by the colour of their skin but by the quality of their character.'

As I heard these words that historians will never cease to record and will always quote, a tear trickled down my cheek. I was ashamed as a white man that he was ever placed in a position that he felt that he was compelled to say those words.

I experienced the same emotion when I learned of his death by an assassin's bullet in Memphis, Tennessee.

An insane racist gunned him down as he stood on the balcony of his modest motel room talking with his music leader about what they would sing at a rally scheduled to be held that very night. It was organised as part of a crusade he was leading to eliminate poverty, having moved on from his great battle for civil rights.

He had just said, 'play that song real sweet' but he was dead before he hit the concrete balcony on which he stood.

My next comment may cause concern.

A powerful reason why I became an admirer of Martin Luther King was because he was occasionally frail in character just like you and me. He had personal weaknesses side by side with his greatness. No-one is exempt from human errors even though our failings may be totally different from his frequent sexual transgressions.

Through his handsome countenance and mesmerising personality, many women found him irresistible. He took advantage of that throughout his life.

Shortly before he died, he had the courage to confess his transgressions to his ever faithful and forgiving wife, Coretta, just before his lifelong enemy from the FBI, J Edgar Hoover, was about to reveal it publicly.

This placed him in the same league as other noted sexual predators of his era such as John F Kennedy, Robert Kennedy, and Lyndon Johnson, and subsequently Bill Clinton and Donald Trump. For most of those mentioned, such relationships were an exercise in power.

King's friends said it was a quest to reduce some of the enormous tension out of his life. Who will ever know the truth? Will many care anyway?

Coretta did not ever condemn her husband despite the fact that the public knowledge of his indiscretions had humiliated her to the very limit of her capacity to handle it. She was a humble human being who had never sought a place in the public limelight.

After the two Kennedys and King had been assassinated, Lyndon Johnson had civil rights legislated in an incredible display of political arm twisting of Southern Conservatives such as the political world had not seen before. No-one other than Johnson could ever have achieved it. He had the good grace to acknowledge that the legislation would never have been debated and passed without the compelling power and influence of Martin Luther King.

Let me mention a personal incident.

I once enjoyed morning coffee in London with Eric Evans, dean of St Paul's Cathedral and Andrew Lloyd Webber, the famed musician, son of an Anglican vicar and a regular worshipper at the cathedral. I asked them who in their opinion was the greatest preacher ever to give a sermon in St Paul's Cathedral.

Without hesitation both said in unison: 'Martin Luther King'.

He had given another of his spellbinding binding sermons on his way home to the US after receiving the Nobel Peace Prize at Stockholm. There was standing room only in this huge cathedral and many felt that he shook its very foundations with the electricity of his message.

No wonder that America observes a public holiday that they proudly call Martin Luther King Day. It is a day that honours the birth in our time of a powerful leader in the fight for justice for all humanity.

## *MARTIN LUTHER KING GUIDEPOST*

***Martin Luther King's 'I have a dream' speech still brings tears to my eyes. He convinced me that a right to justice for all is a core activity of those who walk and work with The Man.***

***This is a hundred times more important than having my soul saved.***

# 8

# Guideposts To A Partnership With The Man

**IN THE CHAPTERS ABOVE** I have highlighted the inspirational leadership that many great people have given to me. I feel confident that many of my readers will agree with my choices as I am very sure that their powerful messages are more relevant to us today than those which have come from many of the great biblical figures.

Through my words about these special leaders, I have attempted to convey my thoughts on the many lessons I have learned from them as they have earned the right to be described as extraordinary prophets. They were trailblazing innovators and committed activists who constantly opened and expanded my mind and yours as we have walked along the pathway of life. Mine has lasted ninety-three years and counting. Yours may be longer.

You will have noted that these unique human beings have been an invaluable resource from which I have been able to draw strength for my ceaseless endeavour to firm up in my own mind what is the basis of the creation, expansion and conduct of my personal reason for being.

Now, I am hugely grateful that they have led me to a point where I am able to make rational core decisions as to how best I can now walk with The Man as an effective working partner who actively seeks to enlist other working partners to the cause.

During my journey to discover my role in life, I have encountered twelve significant mind-changing challenges with which I have struggled, but about which I have remained positive. Now I feel that I have made sufficient and quite definite progress that will enable me to outline to you the ground on which I plan to tread using the lives of those great pilgrims as a solid foundation.

So let us share and walk through some personal thoughts in a way that is respectful, sincere, sensible and, I hope, visionary and inspiring, without in any way demeaning or ridiculing the faith and the beliefs of what may be the longstanding fabric of your own journey.

These are not decisions I have made on the spur of the moment as the result of any memorable experiences or dramatic revelations. They have been nine decades in the making and will certainly continue to further develop after the publication of this book as the sheer mystery of life will never be solved either in my lifetime or in the years to come.

Mysteries abound as we enjoy our search to learn more about The Man and expand our minds to discover how we can persistently grow as an effective partner of his.

So, let me begin with the core elements of my personal challenges, one at a time, as I want these words to be my humble contribution towards a modern revolution in the quality of life that is long overdue and absolutely necessary. I am certain that every one of them can be validly seen, not as a denial of belief, but as a guidepost that lights the pathway.

I am aware that five centuries have passed since Martin Luther nailed his theses on the door of his church at Wittenberg in Germany and created a revolution within Churches that slowly grew and eventually created a more inspirational impact on those who walk the pilgrim way.

Such a reformation is now due once more and it needs a considerable and profound upgrade of a totally different kind to Luther's.

My planned reformation will occur beyond Churches as they are solely focussed on survival at all costs. The thought of another reformation is not even vaguely on their minds. It will take place in society where people who seek a meaningful life will decide to follow The Man without ever going anywhere near a church.

So it is that many others are already enjoying my experience of going to the core of the matter by deciding that many of the old myths of religion are no longer the prime reason why you and I have chosen to walk with The Man. The changes we make are symbolic of new life.

So let us start by seeking to understand the existence and relevance of God in comparison to the presence of Jesus.

This question is clearly the most important place for us to start as we seek to expand our inner strength.

Then, I will discuss the relevance of the virgin birth, The Man, crucifixion, resurrection, ascension, the second coming, being saved from sins, life and death, eternal life, Churches, and hope. All of the above are highly relevant to us, no matter where we are in our journey.

May we all enjoy the open and honest debate that lies ahead.

Feel free to improve on my outlook.

## 8.1 GOD

In my world Jesus the Man is God. His personality is the Holy Spirit.

Allow me to explain how my journey led me to this solid and unshakeable conviction.

The existence of a God in any form, as well as the supposed powers of such a God, has always created a huge question mark in my thinking as I journeyed forth from my Sunday School days.

Many of my friends old and young, firmly believe that trillions of years ago, when the first atom appeared and began to divide and grow to create the universe, it had to have been created by someone and so it is reasonable to believe that there was a God who was the creator. I respect their right to believe this but I hold the view that it was just a first step of nature, not a religious event. Nevertheless, the debate will go on forever. May it be a challenging one that expands minds.

In debating this, it is important to note that out in Central Australia scientists have now found fossils of fish from the great inland sea that once was there. They have scientifically estimated that those fish swam there 500 million years ago. If God created them why did he wait until the last million years to create human beings?

However, to be more specific from the very beginning, let me make three observations about this that are similar to those of Thomas Jefferson when he created *The Jefferson Bible*:

'I have no place in my life for anything that is supernatural.'

'I am not influenced by miracles.'

'I am mightily impressed by Jesus the Man.'

In emphasising and agreeing with many of Jefferson's words, let us discuss several important issues.

I have never regarded Jesus of Nazareth as supernatural in any way even though I have influential friends who have told me regularly and emphatically that they are certain he is a fictional person created by religious zealots.

Nevertheless, I must emphasise that, while the myth of a God is remote from my being, Jesus is very real to me as person who actually lived in our world. This fact is the solid core of all that I have already said and will continue to say throughout the remainder of this book.

From the earliest days of evolution, human beings have believed in, and lived in fear of, the existence of a wide variety of gods and have had an essential personal need for those gods to be a powerful presence in their lives. Their chosen gods were widely presumed to have the ability to reward, punish, forgive, and make decisions as to who lives or dies, who gets ill and who recovers, who is poor and who is rich etc. But never has anyone ever found any evidence that the god they had chosen actually had those powers.

As is well recorded by historians and biblical writers, the number of gods whom people have imagined, or felt the presence of, can be counted in many thousands. The evidence seems to be that those gods have been accepted or rejected by people regularly, based on their performance.

In fact, in modern times, people have found a huge need to find gods as an essential part of life far beyond religious ones. So it is that their gods are sporting teams and their star players as well as singers and bands. There are gods such as Roger Federer, Bruce Springsteen, Taylor Swift, Pele, Manchester United, etc. People easily and enthusiastically identify with them. They are very real and they instantly inspire, far more effectively than a mythical Christian, Jewish or Muslim God.

People also worship gods such as gourmet food, fashions, shopping, money, power, status, as well as themselves Incredibly, some actually worship their favourite whisky calling it the nectar of the gods. All of the above are far more exciting gods than one whose prime concerns are our sins.

For some yoga and meditation are far more personal than a mystical God.

Be this as it may, it is firmly on the public record that at some point in Jewish history the Hebrew people declared that they had discovered the only one genuine God and there could be no further argument on the matter.

Subsequently, Christians accepted the same God as the Jews had done.

As the centuries passed, both Christians and Jews emphatically rejected and ignored the declaration by Muslims that they had found an even greater God whom they called Allah.

The harsh truth is that no person, no matter what their intellectual capacity or religious conviction, has found any physical evidence that there is any God anywhere other than in the minds of people. No one has any right whatsoever to say that their discovery of their God is the correct one and the only one.

Added to my personal dilemma is the frustration I have experienced of not ever having met anyone on my journey who has been able to give me a clear and convincing description of the God that Christians, Jews, and Muslims have chosen to follow through the ages. Similarly, they cannot convincingly describe what influence, beyond mystical, their chosen God has had on the entire world and its people and themselves personally.

Try as I might, I cannot satisfactorily describe God either, nor can I find an essential need for such a God to be part of my life.

So it is that decades ago Jesus the Man (not the Christ) became the God of my life.

I have absolutely no need for a mythical power beyond The Man but I will always defend your right to believe otherwise.

Throughout my long journey I have met cardinals, archbishops, bishops, deans, moderators, presidents, priests, deacons, and elders located all around the world. Not one of them has been able to describe God to me in any way other than the supernatural. They just tell me that I must have faith and all will be revealed. In other words, they have consistently fobbed me off. Mostly, they did so kindly and respectfully.

Central to my search for a God is the perplexing fact that never has anyone ever found a piece of paper with any words written on it by Jesus himself that personally stated his own views about God or any other matter. All we have are words written by many people who have sincerely claimed that they heard what Jesus said. This is not proof enough as all the biblical writers were people of limited education by modern standards and lived in a world of thinking that was heavily dominated by ignorance and fear of the supernatural and unexplainable.

Until recently, I have been unable to settle on the wording of an adequate description of an internal power, traditionally thought of as God, whose presence is meant to be an unshakeable element of my life, except for only one person, Jesus the Man.

This has led me to a personal conviction that the all-powerful presence that we, plus our ancestors for thousands of years, have referred to as God has not existed and did not create the earth, nor humanity, nor flora and fauna. But Jesus the Man exists.

I am concerned that we human beings may have created a God in our own minds because we have always felt that we needed in our lives a strong presence who will protect and prosper us. Indeed, we could quite deliberately have embraced God because we felt that we could not live without him and required him to fill in all the gaps that have been a mystery to us. A God of the Gaps could also take, very conveniently, the blame for every difficulty we encountered in life and every mistake we made in handling those challenges. We have too often declared, in a way that has could be described as quite fragile, that all of our mistakes are the will of God.

Of course, in modern times, we cannot ignore the fact that there are more than a few people in the world who believe that if there is a God then this God will be female.

Having a mother of all humanity makes far more sense to me than having a father. I hold the view that this debate should not be silenced. After all, it was males who decided that there is a God, not females, and it was males wrote 95% of the Bible. With incredible arrogance, males have not considered for one moment that a female could possibly fulfil any mission of such power and influence.

Gender is always a live issue. For example, some of my friends have told me that I should change the title of this book to *Jesus the Human*. I considered it, but I have not taken their advice. Jesus is not without gender.

Much more relevant now is the fact that, while people ask questions about the reality of a God, a majority of the world's population, including me, readily acknowledge a need in our lives for a guiding light beyond ourselves – a cornerstone of our existence.

However, we all have difficulty in envisaging just what this inspiration is and how we can harness it effectively so we can live a good and responsible life. For thousands of years, we have called this power by the name 'God' whom we have accepted as being a master personality whom every person on the planet (and presumably the universe) can identify with for the overall good of humanity.

A description that I have often used in sermons to describe such a master personality is 'The Great Spirit,' the same title that I first took seriously when I met with a tribe of indigenous Canadian Indians in Manitoba who are not Christians but whose forebears have followed a great spirit for thousands of years.

I find those words to be a meaningful description of a power that is within us and influential in our daily lives. I have not the slightest doubt that it is a substantial presence in my life that I hugely welcome and from which I can learn a lot more about the meaning of life.

Especially and thankfully, I am certain that the Great Spirit does not perform miracles, is not a judge who either punishes or praises us nor sits in judgement of us or decides who lives and dies and what is good or evil or who gets into heaven.

No one needs the presence in their lives of a killer God, or one who creates misery. Such a need could only be an influence of superstition.

So it is that in my mind there is not the slightest doubt that the great spirit whom I have described above is Jesus the Man, not a mythical God.

Our challenge, therefore, is not just to become friendly followers of The Man but to become his working partners, boots, and all. He is our internal power that enables us to do good.

I have a firm conviction that passive people who just dabble occasionally with the power of The Man in times of crisis or when an opportunity arises to achieve special things will never ever have a meaningful relationship with him as active working partners. The reality is that we have a need to be constantly inspired by him if we want to achieve great things.

May I add also that I can find no logic for there to be any place in my journey for the Trinity of Father, Son, and Holy Spirit.

I am certain that the Trinity is just confusing jargon that was designed by religious leaders after the crucifixion for the purpose of creating yet another mystery that would enable priests to expand their power over us so as to preserve and enhance the presence and domination of Churches in our lives.

There is one more matter of confusion that has become very obvious to me as the result of my years as a disciple of The Man. Most people cannot tell the difference between God, Jesus, and the Holy Spirit. They could not care less about trying to discover an answer. Indeed, they don't want to waste time understanding the difference as they regard it as trivia. They just think of them as one being, so why fiddle around with three?

However, if we want to play around with religious confusion, then let's agree that the Holy Spirit is clearly identifiable as the personality of The Man.

And it is The Man whom we are talking about, not the mythical Jesus Christ who was created by the disciples and the early Church just to add to the confusion they believed was necessary so as to keep a firm hold on our lives.

The Man alone leads us to enjoy all the many challenges of living when we walk with him through a meaningful life of service to humanity.

It is on him, and the example of so many his inspirational followers that my entire life focuses on as my reason for being.

In absolute reality, he is my God.

Even so, if the traditional God is the cornerstone of your faith, you will always have my total respect and my assurance that I am ready to talk with you regarding your evidence that a God other than Jesus the Man may actually exist.

My mind is always open. Indeed, it is a necessity for it to be open.

*GUIDEPOST ONE*

***The concept of a God arose when humankind had a huge need to find a protector from all fears and mysteries. This experience has eventually enabled us to now relate to a power that does not judge or punish us but transforms our lives.***

***This power is not that of a 'god.' It is the powerful influence of The Man. Jesus is my God.***

## 8.2 VIRGIN BIRTH

With respect and goodwill to all, I must say that I have difficulty in understanding why intelligent and rational people feel that it is a vital element of their faith to believe that Jesus was born of a virgin.

Nevertheless, I openly acknowledge that, no matter what I say, the virgin birth will continue to be a fiercely defended element of traditional Christian faith if only because so many of us love singing Christmas carols about it. Hopefully, we won't ever stop singing them.

Nevertheless, I want to convey some of my thoughts on the matter as they have been developing in my mind for a very long time.

I struggle to understand why, even if a virgin birth could be proven to be physically possible, it seems to have happened only once in human history and only for the benefit of Christianity.

It is especially strange when we know that Christians number only a fraction of the world's population and the matter of a virgin birth is irrelevant to the remainder.

It has all the elements of a contrived and fragile piece of mythology. Even if we believe in miracles, which I do not, and about which I comment elsewhere, the virgin birth really is not a core element in the building up of a meaningful personal faith.

It baffles me that so many sensible people believe that without a virgin birth there would be no such faith as Christianity. Strange that so many fail to acknowledge that Mohammed is not the Son of Allah. This has not destroyed the Islamic faith. He is quite rightly revered as their great prophet whom they passionately believe was sent to them as a direct messenger from Allah.

Nevertheless, while I defend the right of any Christian to believe what is spiritually important to them, I find myself bewildered that many are not mindful of the fact that their necessary belief drives many millions of people away from Christianity simply because it is an offence to their common sense to be asked to accept a belief that is based on an unnecessary fantasy. They are baffled as to why it is that so many Christians believe that for Jesus to be accepted as a cornerstone of civilisation, he must be propped up by a miracle.

Jesus the Man, unlike God, needs no propping up whatsoever.

Additionally, they fail to understand why it was deemed vital to Christianity that Jesus should not have an earthly father.

Why is Joseph, a solid responsible person, portrayed as just an honourable man who accepted what was a highly embarrassing personal situation for him when his wife became pregnant and he knew that the child was not his?

Could not God have validly proclaimed that he had chosen both Joseph and Mary to be the holy parents of the extraordinary person he had destined to be the Messiah?

It would have been a far more powerful reality for us all if Jesus had been born in abject poverty, with sinful people as his parents, so as to show us all how we can eventually rise above every disaster of life if we walk the pilgrim way with him.

I mentioned in an earlier chapter that a highly respected and devout Presbyterian minister in Australia, Samuel Angus, a significant theologian of international recognition, declared that it would have made a far greater impact on the world if Jesus had been born as the illegitimate son of a Roman soldier as this would have identified him more closely with the human frailty that most of us encounter sometime in our lives.

Angus was grossly humiliated by many of his peers simply because he had made a legitimate comment that deserved rational debate. They did not have the intelligence or capacity to face up to anything that challenged the ironclad certainties they desperately needed to remain Christian.

For many years, I have been involved in debates that have sought to find a valid reason why a virgin birth must be an essential part of my journey. I found most of these discussions to be quite shallow and pointless. In honesty, I must say that I am convinced that the very thought of the need of a virgin birth diminishes the stature of the life and work of The Man and unnecessarily hinders his mission to humanity.

The fact is that Jesus was an extraordinary person of incredible personal magnetism and spiritual power who naturally drew people to him. No miracles are needed to prove this.

Right now, so many years later, I am clearly aware that his presence still changes and uplifts the lives of millions of people of numerous races, cultures and ideologies who accept him as the prime cornerstone of their lives even though spiritual leaders falsely tell us that he is a secondary figure to an imaginary 'God'.

Many ancient religions that have now ceased to exist have had as their central figure someone who was claimed to have been born of a virgin. People who lived in the era when Jesus was born considered it mandatory to have a virgin birth as a fundamental of their faith so as to keep up with the others. Examples of some of the other virgin births are Romulus, Mercury, Krishna, Attis, Perseus, etc., none of which are proven.

The mysticism that has created a need for a spiritual elevation of Jesus from that of a rebel to that of a miracle man has resulted in Churches down the centuries failing to convey to their faithful attendees a clear and compelling message. It is that the lifetime calling of The Man was primarily for him to create a better life for the many millions who, in every generation, have been unjustly marginalised and left without hope.

His brother James did not ever forget it and did his best to make it happen.

It was a tragedy that Paul did not make a priority of advocating it. His role seems to have been to challenge people to think solely and selfishly about saving themselves from their sins.

The Man does not require a myth such as a virgin birth to make him a special person.

He, and he alone, is the prime pillar of my life and always will be. I have no need of an imaginary event such as a virgin birth to convince me otherwise.

My commitment to him is solid. I am not alone in this conviction.

### *GUIDEPOST TWO*

***The birth of The Man was not a miracle. It was an extraordinary event in the history of humanity that needed no supporting miracle.***

***The powerful personality and presence of The Man caused a revolution that has shaken the world to its core and will do so forever.***

## 8.3 THE MAN

From my earliest days, despite my doubts about the existence of any God, I was always captivated and inspired by The Man.

In my view, he is the undisputed leader of our world, morally, ethically, ideologically, and mentally, who has motivated us to create grand visions for humanity and given us the internal power to achieve them with excellence.

Here is a real person, not a mythical figure.

He has left clear and challenging footprints for us to follow as well as fine dreams for us to strive to achieve as his working partner in making our contribution towards the creation of a caring society of justice and peace and equality of opportunity.

The Man is far more real to me than the mythical Christ of the faith by a huge margin.

That version of Jesus as the Christ was created by religious people who used his name for their own gain after his physical departure. They sought to establish a doctrine that would enable them to create Churches and foster their control of society. They did so in a way that would ensure they would be able to dominate his followers via fear of punishment of sins and use this to sustain their own personal power.

In my early life, Churches had an overbearing presence in society which is now steadily diminishing. However, The Man has been my lifelong role model, not in the manner of traditional role models, but in the sense of being a powerful presence far above the standing of any other. His influence inspires me to try to better care for humanity than I could ever achieve alone, hopefully in a similar way to that which he constantly achieved around the shores of Lake Galilee. Especially, he provides an essential inner power. This enables every one of his followers to achieve that which is the best. It provides a clear link to the inspiration of his tremendous life which took the world by storm and has retained its impact for many centuries past, still does today and will never stop.

While I have considerable trouble in discovering the existence of a God and have no need for a God in my life, I have encountered no hurdles whatsoever in understanding who The Man is and why he has a very real and high presence in my life and that of millions of others.

After all, the sacrament that I regularly take with reverence is the body and blood of Jesus, not God.

Jesus had, and still has, a clear message to all humanity. It is a powerful one that advocates becoming a genuine reformer, exposing, and diminishing greed, fostering gender equality, calling out racism, exposing corruption, ensuring justice and equality, spreading a spirit of love in a selfless manner that rejects fear and hatred.

In learning all that I can about him, I now concentrate my Bible readings and religious education on the Gospel of Mark which was the first written and the most authentic of the four. Mark tells his story plainly and simply, whereas the remaining 99% of the Bible is just interesting background reading of his life and times and the long history that preceded him. It has little impact on my life except to set the scene for an understanding of the world before and after Jesus had his brief but powerful presence that spread from Israel to the entire world.

I reaffirm unequivocally that my prime goal in life is to be a working partner of Jesus the Man.

This sets out my role in compelling words within in one sentence but it means far more than this in reality.

I now never declare that I am a Christian except in generalised conversation as I find that the word Christ has no genuine meaning for me.

I proudly state that I have only one identity and this is what I have already stated above and now mention once more.

I am a working partner of Jesus the Man.

When I quietly identify myself with those words, it never fails to start a conversation about what the difference is between being a 'Christian' and being a working partner. It creates a splendid opportunity for me to upgrade my calling from that of being an occasional evangelist to one who advocates daily as an ambassador of The Man.

The first question of a conversation is usually this one.

'Everald, what is the difference between being a Christian and being a working partner of Jesus? Are they not both the same thing?'

My basic response is usually something like the words I mentioned in the opening pages of this book.

'Being a Christian usually implies adherence to a slavish following of the creeds and doctrines of Churches in the hope that these rigid rules will get us into heaven. Being a working partner of The Man cuts out all that unnecessary baggage and gets me to the point of affirming that Jesus walked the earth doing good to all humankind. I try to do likewise without aspiring to go to an imaginary heaven and gain eternal life.'

Almost always a positive and productive debate follows where we talk about the role of The Man in the key issues of life and talk about our potential to generate it further.

I find many who don't want to go anywhere near a church for countless reasons have a genuine interest in walking and working with The Man. They come to see this as potentially a huge positive, free of bigotry and with a capacity to open the doors to endless possibilities.

Some call me to say they now endeavour to live on the basis of asking one simple question when faced with the daily challenge: 'What would the man do in this situation that now faces me?'

Their calls challenge me never to forget to continue to do likewise, far more often than was my practice. It has proven to be a splendid decision-making process.

Often, people ask me if there is a book they can read, other than the Bible, which will give them an interesting view of Jesus.

My normal response is to recommend the wonderful William Barclay book, *The Mind of Jesus* but it is now difficult to buy it as he wrote it so long ago. I recommend another book by Barclay which is available, called *The Gospel of Mark*. It's well worth reading.

I have mentioned several times that it is a huge disappointment to me (and many others worldwide) that no one has ever discovered a document that was written by Jesus himself in which he records his life and his beliefs in his own words. This would add immensely to our power to do good.

No one can legitimately declare that Jesus the Man was not a literate person of considerable intelligence who could write. It is highly unlikely that he deliberately recorded nothing in writing as a legacy of his life and work. Some historians say that the Romans went out of their way to destroy all of his possessions so his words could never be used again to create another Messiah. This is highly plausible.

What we now have is hearsay about him from witnesses, much of it being written by people who did not ever met him. As the discovery of any document written by Jesus will be a miracle, one parchment in his handwriting would have a hugely energising impact on millions of his followers. Strangely, I have been unable to find any evidence that anyone has ever committed time and effort in trying to discover such a document.

I have the feeling that far too many leaders of the Churches of the world have a huge fear that a personal statement by Jesus relating to events and teachings may be significantly different to those written by the authors of the Bible. They are very aware that it has the capacity to blow their Church apart so they don't press the matter at all.

Nevertheless, I have always understood that our beliefs are a challenging leap into the unknown so my desire to walk and work with him is not diminished by the scarcity of historical evidence of his existence. Nevertheless, I never stop wondering what an inspirational experience it would be to read his own words.

I can only reaffirm the reality that his presence simply grows and grows in my life and is a huge asset in enjoying a happy and positive life of humble achievements gained in quest of creating goodwill for all.

I do have intelligent friends who believe that Jesus did not exist and is a figure of fiction. They have read widely and they are certain that no proof can ever be found that there was a person called Jesus who died on a cross.

While there is always a remote possibility they could be correct, let me say emphatically having read as widely as I can, that I unfailingly believe that he did live and his presence endures today and forever.

Discovering The Man is something like falling in love.

A line from that wonderful song 'Some Enchanted Evening' from that great musical 'South Pacific' gets it right: 'Who can explain it? Who can tell you why? Fools may give you reasons. Wise men never try.'

Perhaps the naysayers could be moved to sing another song from South Pacific: 'This Nearly Was Mine'.

*GUIDEPOST THREE*

***The Man is the greatest peaceful revolutionary in world history.***

***You and I walk with him to ensure his reformation creates a caring and cohesive society that will never die.***

## 8.4 CRUCIFIXION

I accept without question that Jesus was crucified and died on a wooden cross side by side with two thieves at a place called Calvary just outside Jerusalem at a time long ago.

This appalling murder occurred after he had been tormented and tortured during a farcical trial in which people who claimed to worship God knowingly convicted him of crimes he did not commit.

The crucifixion event is huge in Christian heritage even though its occurrence has been only sparsely recorded in public records. The main one is a reference by the Roman governor, Pontius Pilate, who briefly reported on it to his emperor on one occasion when he mentions that a man called Christos had been causing unrest and had been killed.

There are, of course the Bible accounts recorded by Matthew, Mark, Luke, and John in their Gospels written more than forty years after the event.

I note that none of the four Gospel writers personally witnessed the crucifixion, but I accept their accounts of it in good faith as having been conveyed to them by their ancestors and the disciples whom they trusted and who were present in Jerusalem on this unforgettable day.

To me, the crucifixion symbolises that Jesus died as a martyr for beliefs that he cherished and had conveyed powerfully and fearlessly as a great teacher in a manner that was so inspirational that it has been carried down through the ages.

His death, violently though it was carried out, was a symbolic physical end to a tremendous life that is unlikely ever to be forgotten.

It is immortalised in churches, schools, hospitals, religious institutions, museums, art galleries and the homes of the faithful. There must be at least a billion symbols that depict Jesus on the cross in statues, carvings, stained glass, pottery, wood carvings, paintings, and embroidery. These are far in excess of any symbols honouring any other life or event in all history.

However, as I have mentioned in an earlier chapter, I do have genuine difficulty in taking seriously the story that it was Judas who caused the death of Jesus by deliberately betraying him with a kiss on his cheek at the Garden of Gethsemane.

If we choose to accept that there is a God and that this God needed a traitor to bring about the death and resurrection of Jesus, then it is logical to presume that Judas was deliberately created by God as a fall guy. This would mean that his total destiny was such that he had no option but to do what was required of him or there would have been no crucifixion or resurrection to perpetuate the Christian faith.

We can assume therefore that Judas will always be a key figure in the history of Christianity.

I firmly believe that Judas unfairly copped the blame for the betrayal of Jesus whereas others who blatantly deserted him, such as Peter, are now honoured as saints.

Indeed, it could be validly claimed that most of us have betrayed Jesus as a role model at some point or another on every day of our lives without even being aware of it simply because we are frail human beings.

I suppose this means that we must all ask ourselves this blunt question: 'Who crucified The Man?'

Do we unwittingly crucify him by the way in which we live or the meagre manner in which we choose to walk and work with him?

The short answer is that we probably do. We are not much different from Judas and Peter in terms of human frailty.

However, there is no need for us to lament this.

We just have to face the fact that we have a constant challenge before us to keep upgrading the quality of our own performance in order to be worthwhile working partners of The Man.

## *GUIDEPOST FOUR*

***Jesus the Man was assassinated by people of fragile mentality who feared his presence and were threatened by his influence.***

*They failed to conquer him. His presence in my life remains very real and powerful.*

## 8.5 RESURRECTION

I have reached a point in my journey through life where I no longer feel that it is necessary, in all honesty of mind, to accept a requirement that my faith must be based on a belief that Jesus experienced a physical resurrection in the days after the crucifixion.

It was an event which was considered by the initial followers of Jesus to be necessary in order to provide a prime cornerstone in which to base the continuing mission of Jesus. They were certain that he had to be seen to have conquered death. I see their thinking as being similar to the need that was felt when they imagined a virgin birth.

Therefore, I face a huge difficulty in understanding why so many Christians firmly believe that a physical resurrection of Jesus is vital to achieve depth and credibility of faith so that we are able to firmly assert that he did conquer death.

I accept as an undeniable fact that Jesus the Man is present in my life today. He has never died as a source of inspiration.

Therefore, I have no problem whatsoever in believing that Jesus experienced a resurrection of his spirit, not a physical one, and I am conscious of the fact that his very strong influence now constitutes the cornerstone of the lives and values of many people.

Many millions of Jesus committed followers have had, and still do have, an impact on humanity long after their death because their example fires us all into action in a wide variety of ways.

For instance, I have no doubt that the spirit of Saint Francis of Assisi still motives us today. I experience his influence whenever I ponder on our need to care for the environment as well as our concern for those who live in poverty and others who are ostracized from society, such as the lepers with whom he lived.

There are others who gave their lives to the cause who never cease to inspire us. They include Father Damien in Hawaii, Mark who was killed for creating the Coptic Church, Wiiliam Booth who often lived in poverty in London as he cared for the poor, and Dietrich Bonhoeffer who gave his life in defiance of Adolf Hitler. We regularly experience the presence of many like them as we walk the pilgrim way.

My real concern is for the lives of people whose faith is founded solely on Jesus having experienced a physical resurrection and who believe that any questioning of this destroys their entire reason for being in the world. They seem to have missed the essential message that Jesus the Man remains with us forever with or without a physical resurrection.

If you would like to read a great novel on this very subject, I recommend that you read, *On the Third Day.*

Written by eminent British journalist and author, Piers Paul Read, it is based around the discovery by a Jewish archaeologist of a skeleton which he believes was the body of Jesus. Revealing the full story right now will spoil for you the impact of a superb novel written by an author who portrays what such a discovery would have on a wide variety of Christians and atheists. I had to read it twice so as to understand what shock waves would be set loose by a discovery of a skeleton confirmed by experienced archaeologists as being that of Jesus .

When I discuss this with friends, they often point out that I am denying what the Bible records about the experience of Mary Magdelene and her friends when they found that the tomb had been opened. Also, there are the occasions when some of the disciples clearly believed that they had met and spoken with Jesus in several places after the crucifixion.

I have not the slightest doubt that they acutely felt his presence at that time and that this experience led them to believe that he was physically guiding them.

I am also certain that the Romans had such a low opinion of Jesus that they would not have given him a special tomb. His body would have been thrown into a mass grave as was their normal practice after crucifixions.

If he had been given his own tomb, they would have guarded it so his followers could not make it a shrine. Governments down the centuries have done this with the bodies of famous people whose continued presence threatened them.

Many of us have often experienced a feeling of the presence of loved ones who have died and we often dream that they speak to us. We are not revering a body. We are honouring the personality of the loved one whom we will never forget even when the body turns to ashes. Indeed, we know that the personality that had its home in the body did not turn to ashes.

The key challenge for us is not whether we choose to blindly believe dogmas and creeds and regard them as being sacred.

We are called to work, day by day, with The Man in carrying out our role in his never-ending mission to the care of humanity.

We are never separated from him except by choice and we are very aware that we grow as we continue to walk and work with him on a purposeful journey that achieves good for the world.

GUIDEPOST FIVE

***Belief in a physical resurrection has been passed on down the centuries as a treasured symbol of the fact that Jesus the Man is powerfully with us in spirit today.***

## 8.6 ASCENSION

It is quite reasonable to assume that a logical person of sound mind will have the common sense to understand that an ascension into heaven by Jesus did not happen because it is impossible to have happened.

What's more, it is absolutely unnecessary for it to have occurred.

Speaking in the most respectful terms I can muster; it really is an insult to our intelligence and theirs to ask anyone to believe it took place.

This leads me to ask a polite question about the heaven that Jesus is said to have ascended to.

Without a hint of sarcasm, may I ask if any of my readers are able to describe to me where heaven is physically located and what does it contain? I have been searching persistently all my life to find its whereabouts without any success.

If we are inclined to believe that Jesus actually did ascend into heaven, how did he locate it after he took off into space. Decades of space travel by highly skilful astronauts have never found it despite being backed by the power of countless computers and telescopes that have had all of our known science and power to assist them. Neither has any unmanned spacecraft found heaven either, even though they have reached Mars and beyond.

If heaven is up there how did Jesus get there without being burnt to a cinder. Neil Armstrong required the greatest available lifesaving technology and protective gear just to get to the moon and back in a heat resistant space capsule.

Why have the hundreds of research and communication rockets fired into space over many decades not found heaven?

How can anyone just ascend into the heavens?

Belief in this event goes close to being declared a deliberate lie and an outright farce that, in the eyes of all humanity, hugely diminishes the power and stature of Jesus the Man unnecessarily. It should be perpetuated no longer despite its embarrassing situation of being a traditional belief of Churches whose leaders perpetuate it and expect us to say in their creeds.

I will never forget my first of several visits to the Holy Land.

After I had completed my meetings with the Christian and Jewish leaders to whom I had been given prior introductions, I decided to sign up for a day tour of Jerusalem to be led by a firebrand American pastor who turned out to be an ultra-fundamentalist egotist of huge vanity.

He took us to the place where it is generally accepted by long tradition as being the spot from where the ascension took place. There is a large rock there with a huge crack in it. He declared that the crack in the rock was created by the great pressure that Jesus applied to it, so as to get enough leverage to enable him to lift off and fly upwards towards heaven.

I should have been much more respectful, but I could not refrain from laughing rather loudly as it was so ridiculous as to be utterly childish.

The pastor was mortally offended. In a very loud voice, he commanded me to leave the group immediately for being such a primitive pagan as to doubt the eternal truth of what he had just revealed to us. In fact, he declared me to be beyond redemption (which is probably true).

I did. There was not one small scrap of repentance in my soul.

Allow me to re affirm here what you already know.

The Man is with you and me right here every day right now. Whether or not we choose to create a close link with him is a matter of our personal choice.

He is not in a place that is popularly called heaven, primarily because there is no such physical place and, if there was, he could not get there.

Heaven is the splendid state of creative life that you and I enjoy for every moment of our lives when we walk and work with The Man.

No search is required. His leadership has ascended into our hearts and minds.

*GUIDEPOST SIX*

***The myth of the ascension gives us a vision of Jesus giving us leadership over and above the tumult of our daily world.***

*He did not depart from our world. There was never any need to. His presence is always with us.*

## 8.7 THE SECOND COMING

Immediately after the crucifixion, the disciples of Jesus had not the slightest doubt that he would return to continue his ministry. It was an absolute certainty.

It has been recorded that they accepted as fact that the second coming of Jesus would happen almost immediately, certainly during their lifetime, more likely sooner rather than later, perhaps within days.

His return was very important to them as they had firmly and personally bonded with him before his crucifixion and were inspired by the visions they believed they saw of him in the days after that momentous event. They did not entertain the thought that his return might not ever occur. They would have been stunned beyond comprehension to discover that 2,000 years later he still has not physically rejoined the world and never will.

I have no doubt that the second coming is another myth that blurs the reality that The Man is with us now and always. There is no need for it.

It is similar to the belief in his physical resurrection and his ascension to heaven.

None of them have relevance to our relationship with The Man but there must be a symbolic message to discover in all three.

May I say respectfully to Church leaders that they should question their personal integrity if they continue to advocate any of the three as anything other than symbols?

The Uniting Church in Australia has the second coming as a basic belief within its Basis of Union. As a lifetime elder and lay preacher of the Church I am, theoretically, supposed to preach occasionally about the second coming but I have never done so, and never will, as it is never wise to commit perjury.

Nevertheless, let us for a moment forget the myth and make an honest appraisal for a moment at what actually would occur if the second coming happened right now. I have some practical questions to place before you about its immediate impact as it would be irresponsible of us not to at least consider the possibilities:

- Where on the planet will Jesus initially appear? Presumably, it will be in the Holy Land, which has been far from holy for a long time.
- How will he, at that precise moment, command the attention and repentance of the entire population of the world of more than 8 billion souls spread over five continents, 6 billion of whom are of other faiths and do not accept him as their leader.
- Will the lives of non-Christians cease at this point or will Muslims, Jews, Hindus, Buddhists, etc. instantly become Christians?
- What changes will he make to our daily lives from that moment onwards, and then day after day forever?
- Will every one of us who are supposedly saved from our sins be able and willing to lead totally sinless lives from that moment onwards?

- Will corruption, violence, theft, and depravity end instantly and never be practised again anywhere on the planet?
- Do we go to work every day as usual?
- Who continues to work at providing all the food supply and essential services we need to survive and will they do it with total honesty?
- Will anyone ever get sick again?
- Will every person on the planet love one another forever?
- Will we be allowed to enjoy any form of entertainment?
- Will we still have a Parliament and a Government and continue to pay taxes?

Obviously, there are thousands more questions we can legitimately ask, but there is no point it in pursuing the issue as the whole concept is unsustainable and impossible, indeed ridiculous.

There will never ever be a second coming for one very valid reason:

> Jesus the Man is right here in my life
> and yours right now.

It is our choice as to whether or not we accept or reject him. There is absolutely no reason why a second coming will in any way occur.

I know that the Man is already present in my life and has been for a long time. As I type these words that I am very aware of his influence in my life and gain strength from it.

It is sad that the continued advocacy of a second coming makes Christianity such a public laughing stock.

It is a huge deterrent to our witness and an enormous burden to our credibility as we try our very best to live out our calling as working partners of The Man.

GUIDEPOST SEVEN

***When the disciples declared that Jesus would return they were simply expressing their hope that The Man would be with them forever.***

***As he is with us every day and year, their hope and ours has been fulfilled.***

## 8.8 BEING SAVED FROM OUR SINS

It is bewildering to me and millions of others that Christian preachers have been so obsessed with sin.

I have never been able to understand why, except to determine that it was designed as a compelling sales pitch to allure people to accept the faith or suffer the consequences.

Fundamentalist advocates of ancient theology go to extraordinary extremes in almost every element of Christianity to create and sustain mystery, guilt, and fear in our hearts. Their prime message is that we will not be admitted to heaven and are headed for an awful destiny in hellfire unless we repent of our sins now and permanently.

This is a primitive way to sell Christianity to the world when it is obvious that followers of The Man are people who want to love and care and give and serve. We are not frightened little beings who live in fear of non-existent hell fires.

Seeking forgiveness for sins is in blunt reality a hugely selfish reason for anyone to decide to become a

Christian. It should be discarded, utterly and totally, as selfishness was never ever a part of the life of Jesus.

When I commit a sin, which I often do because I am a human being, my responsibility as an active follower and working partner of The Man is to go immediately to meet, face-to-face, with the person I have hurt. I must say with sincerity that I am sorry, apologise, and do all I can to repair the damage I have done. In addition, I must pay the social cost in repairing the damage to my reputation as well as pay the necessary financial cost of squaring up the ledger.

There is no way I can avoid this very clear obligation as a decent human being. There is no valid reason why I should even attempt to do so.

To dump the responsibility of my sins on to God and hide behind him is dishonest and cowardly in the extreme and gutless as well. In fact, it is an act of irresponsibility.

I wince every Sunday when priests or ministers assure their congregations that our sins are forgiven. I absolutely refuse to give the traditional response of 'Thanks be to God.' This pardon gives us all the opportunity to go out and sin once more as we are assured with utter certainty that we will be forgiven again next Sunday. It is sad in every way.

This opportunity to repeat sins is hugely welcomed by paedophiles and other predators such as thieves, thugs, and wife bashers. They are enabled to feel good about their evil as they know with certainty that all will once again be forgiven over and over again.

Of all the things that motivate people to walk away from fundamentalist Christianity, forgiveness of sins is the worst and most repugnant element.

The prime example of selfishness has its beginnings at the conversion of Saint Paul, not from Jesus.

Saint Paul's emphasis on sin had its origins in his own appalling lifestyle as Saul the murderer, as well as from the fact that he never met Jesus face-to-face and did not know him except by reputation. Paul chose to sell the faith to the world via fear of punishment of sins and had no justification for this whatsoever.

His theology of selfishness and fear makes me weep, even though I hugely admire his skills as a superb communicator. You will recall that I mentioned this earlier in the chapter on James.

I am very certain that we have no need to repent of our sins in any way in order to qualify to be working partners of The Man. As we walk with him, our sins steadily diminish as we are concentrating on achieving nobler deeds. In addition, we become intensely aware that we must make recompense for those sins all by ourselves and so we do our best to avoid repeating them.

I welcome the words of the Gospel account of the crucifixion of Jesus. It says that when he spoke to the two criminals who were nailed to crosses on either side of him, he said to them:

> 'This day you will be with me in paradise.'

He did not ask them to repent of their sins as a price to pay to get to paradise.

I have not the slightest doubt that he would have rejected the theology of Paul.

Loving people is our primary domain, not punishing them for being sinners or perpetually frightening them.

It is not difficult to do something positive about diminishing our sins when we walk with The Man.

### GUIDEPOST EIGHT

***The challenge of paying the personal price for my sins here and now is a motivation to lift my game. I diminish my sins by accepting my sole responsibility for them, paying the price for them, and recommitting my life as a servant of humanity.***

***The Man does not require me to be pure of heart. He challenges me to walk the pilgrim way with honesty and decency.***

## 8.9 LIFE AND DEATH

I have huge difficulty with the traditional belief that God decides who lives or dies.

Who indeed would want to worship a killer God?

Nor do I believe that God determines who gets sick and who recovers, or who becomes rich and who lives in poverty, or who is punished and who is not, or that floods, fires, wars, are acts that God designed to create fear in our hearts, punish us for our sins and force us to become more devoted and penitent.

Jesus was never a killer of people or a destroyer of health and welfare or a creator of misery or disability or a punisher of our sins. Such a being is simply not him. It is indeed blasphemous to suggest that he would have done so.

I know that his example helps me to open doors and gives me inner strength to face up to and handle and overcome whatever hits me in life.

I go to my death, walking confidently with The Man. I have no fear of punishment nor do I expect any reward in heaven or punishment in hell.

Death is a fact of life, simply inevitable.

So it is eminently sensible for you and me to welcome it and enjoy the experience as it is our final curtain call of life and must be our finest hour. There is absolutely no point in making the occasion miserable, either for ourselves or our family and friends. It is quite selfish for us to get an attack of the pitiful ailment called poor little me.

This is why I will choose to depart by voluntary assisted dying if I have a terminal illness. I refuse to put my family in a situation where they go through suffering while they watch me painfully waste away and die. I have lived for ninety-three happy years. Why drag it out for an extra couple of months, wasting money on doctors and hospitals when my grandkids and great grandkids have need of that money to get them off to a good start in life.

I will also discover a painless and dignified way to die when I sense I am about to become a vegetable or am aware that dementia is starting to hit me badly. My first thought is that it will not be hard to run around the room for an hour or so until I drop.

If the circumstances permit me to have 24 hours' notice of my death, I plan to invite my family and friends to drop by whenever they are free during the day and share a fine whisky with me (hopefully Lagavulin from the Isle of Islay) as we chat about happy memories and occasions of much joy, especially our shared achievements. I really do hope this will happen. What a wonderful occasion it will be. Looking forward to it so long as it does not occur too soon.

May I suggest that you read my book *A Beautiful Sunset*? Just go to my website *everaldcompton.com* and place an order for a signed book.

It is about a man who has a terminal illness and decides to depart via voluntary assisted dying. He makes his last three months the greatest of his life and on the day before his death he holds a party for family and friends just like the one I plan to have. It was a most difficult chapter of the book for me to write as I had to include conversations.

Exactly what should each person say to a man who has determined that he will die tomorrow. When you leave, you can't say 'Thanks for the drink mate. The next one is on me.'

Enjoy reading it and let me know what you think of the conversations I created. When I get around to doing a second edition, I want to improve it and will value your advice.

I do not believe that I was born with a destiny that had been prearranged by God. However, I am certain that we are all born with talents that we can use or misuse or neglect. We create our own destiny.

It is a tragedy that so many people blame God for so much that naturally occurs in their lives.

I am grateful that I was born with a few talents. There is evidence that many of them are hereditary. I thus have an unavoidable responsibility to use those talents in partnership with The Man as my role model. I can feel a sense of calling to use them by having a role with him in creating the better world that is desperately needed.

To not use those talents would mean that I am demeaning my role of a working partner. I would be a fake follower who had strayed from the pilgrim way, someone who does not maximise his capacity to develop the quality of my service of humanity.

So it is that I go to my death with complete faith in The Man thanking him for the chance he has opened up for me to do my best.

And I do hope that people will not pray for me and ask God to spare me. I am ready to go. The Man will give me the strength to handle it well.

I am reminded of an event that happened at St Stephen's Presbyterian church in Toowoomba while I was a regular attender during my World War II schooldays.

Around the same time, two families who were long time members of the congregation received telegrams from the military hierarchy saying their sons, who were both serving overseas in the RAAF, were missing in action, presumed dead. We all offered them comfort.

A few months later, one family received official advice that contained wonderful news. Their son had been found. He was wounded but would recover.

The following Sunday the father stood up in church to give us the happy news and amid tears of sincere rejoicing said,

> 'We thank Almighty God for answering
> our prayers and giving us back our son.'

The father of the other missing airman rose and quietly said: 'We prayed too.'

GUIDEPOST EIGHT

***Birth, life and death, are simple reminders to us that everything in life has a beginning and an end. It is vital that we enjoy all three.***

***The only fear we can possibly encounter is fear itself.***

## 8.10 ETERNAL LIFE

Yet again, I have difficulty in accepting a traditional Christian belief.

I regularly ask myself this genuine question.

Is there is such an event in my journey as eternal life?

In reality, I find it particularly baffling to comprehend as it is a near impossibility even to define precisely what eternal life is and why any one of us would want to experience it.

Every qualified scientist in the world tells us without hesitation that eternity lasts for countless trillions of years.

The very mention of it raises hosts of questions such as the basic query as to what purpose is achieved for anyone by wanting to live for trillions of years either on earth or in heaven.

How can we live as long as a trillion years without ever getting bored over and over again endlessly?

What does heaven actually look like?

Do we go to work on most days of those trillions of years and what do we do in our spare time?

What sort of houses will we live in and who produces our food and water?

How do I care for the many thousands of ancestors who are supposedly there already, and descendants who will eventually crowd around me after endless generations of them keep producing?

Are we all saints who are able to be totally sinless for trillions of years? It is all an unbelievable impossibility.

Of course, I know that any life after death will be in some type of spirit form as our bodies quickly turn to dust while our personalities survive in some form. Nevertheless, will our spirits float around for trillions of years?

It is because I am a solid non-believer in eternal life that I live in hope that circumstances will enable me to make my last day of life to be as happy as possible, because that is it. All over. I am certain that none of us will receive at death any rewards for the good work we have done. We did our good deeds because our relationship with The Man motivated us to do it and we have already experienced a genuine sense of happiness for a job well done. We need no more accolades.

My final day must not be a miserable experience either for me or anyone who shares my life. Unless I die suddenly, I have a duty to ensure that joy and happiness abound as I thank everyone for love they have given me and the wonderful times we have shared. Their last view of me must be with a smile on my face that fosters peace, joy, and goodwill all around.

Death is an absolutely certain life experience for you and me and so there is clearly no point whatsoever in fearing it because such a fear will achieve nothing but emptiness and gloom for everyone.

Living in hope of eternal life is in reality wishful thinking as we know it will not happen.

I am certain that heaven is a wonderful state of contentment. I often am privileged to enjoy it in the life I lead now as I experience the daily satisfaction of being a working partner of Jesus the Man.

Heaven is freely available to each one of us here and now. The best thing to do is to grab it in both hands and enjoy it as it occurs.

I have no fear of there being anyone or any being whom I will encounter who is called Satan or the Devil or the Evil One or any other title of fear. There is no such being or presence waiting to misguide us during life or punish us at death.

I have always believed from my Sunday School days that my teachers used Satan to scare me into being a good boy. Ministers in all churches have used Satan to frighten me into coming to church every Sunday and keep putting my money in the plate.

I reckon also that it is pathetically gutless to pass the blame for all my sins on someone called the Devil and claim that he forced me to do it. Such a thought or intention is the ultimate in disgraceful personal behavior as I would be actively seeking to avoid responsibility.

Let me add these words of truth. If I discover when I pass away that I wind up in hellfire with the Devil stoking the fire, I will be at peace because all of my mates will be there with me. It will be terribly horribly boring to be in heaven with a team of selfish do-gooders who think they are more holy than the rest of us and deserve to be saved.

I have no shadow of doubt that a heaven and hell experience after death are in the realm of either vivid imagination or forlorn hope or absolute nonsense.

Living now with The Man is the ultimate experience. I am enormously grateful for the privilege of walking with him.

In closing, I do hope that priests and ministers and pastors will stop telling people at funerals that their loved one is forgiven of his or her sins, is in heaven, and will be there forever. Every time they use those words they teach someone in the congregation to give up Christianity as being fake news. This occurs especially when we are the funeral of a person whom we know has not treated family and friends well.

Funerals where those inappropriate words are not spoken are an absolute delight to attend.

I recall the funeral of my old Aunt Joyce. She was a delightful rascal. Spent her whole life gambling on horses and consuming too much alcohol with too many doubtful friends. She did not ever darken a church door and loved to tell us juicy stories about the sex life of priests and nuns.

When she died, she was buried at a chapel at a crematorium with no clergy present, no hymns or readings or prayers and no mention of eternal life. It was just a happy event where all of us told wonderful stories about her.

When her coffin was slowly being moved to be cremated, we all stood and sang in rousing fashion that old American ballad: 'The Camp Town Race Track's five miles long.' Then we all clapped and cheered her.

I told everyone who was present, and lots of people afterwards, that it was the most beautiful funeral I have ever been at in my life. It was all so genuine and happy and captured perfectly the down to earth spirit of Joyce. Sadly, I have never again experienced such a happy celebration of the conclusion of a life.

So, let me tell you in advance of my funeral that if anyone says I am going to heaven to enjoy eternal life, I will kick my coffin open and yell out in my loudest voice: 'I'm not going.'

*GUIDEPOST TEN*

***Death is the final experience of life. Not one of us has the capacity to handle the boredom of an eternal life of a trillion years.***

***The spirit that is our personality will live on for as long as we are remembered.***

## 8.11 CHURCHES AND THEIR PRIESTS

There are priests, ministers, and pastors whose quality of life and work is above and beyond the critical comments I am now about make. I have met them on my journey and enjoyed their ministry and friendship. I continue to do so. Some of them whom I have not met personally have had a major role in the earlier chapters of this book.

For instance, there is no way that Father Damien identifies with the words I use below, nor John Flynn, nor Dietrich Bonhoeffer and many others.

So, let me proceed with some observations that relate with accuracy to the majority of Churches and their leaders who have not yet come to terms with the power of The Man, nor sought to have a close relationship with those who do not go to church or good people who have rejected Christianity in its current Church form.

There is a huge difference between the institutions we call Churches and the vibrant groups of believers who are working partners of Jesus the Man, most of whom regard the role of Churches in society as being without purpose and woefully negative.

A Church is a legal corporation, managed and dominated by an entrenched hierarchy who are devoted to perpetuating an institution that provides them with permanent employment, while enabling them to mouth platitudes about the faith that justifies their holy positions. Their maintenance of power and influence fosters an inevitable situation where congregations slowly die because they have been taken on a journey far from the real work and witness of The Man.

I have not the slightest doubt that genuine Christians can and will survive and grow. They will serve humanity forever as we walk with him along the pilgrim way.

You and I are able, capable, and willing to live and spread our life experience without going anywhere near a church.

We are more likely to more happily grow as caring persons when we join a home group of likeminded people. There we can constantly welcome newcomers into our groups and then form new groups without getting involved in a legal church structure or need help from any priest or minister who too often believes, absolutely erroneously, that he or she are special souls who are closer to Jesus than we are.

This is why Christianity is growing so strongly in China, where there are now in excess of 50 million committed believers. The vast majority do not meet in church buildings and have no desire to meet in one. This would require them to become a legal entity, something the communist government would frown upon as a means of creating potential political dissent.

The truth is that Churches and their congregations worldwide are steadily reaching their use-by date and deserve to do so. Refreshing alternatives to their rigid structures and creeds are now urgently needed but are unlikely to happen in time to save them.

As Churches fade away, free thinking partners of The Man will grow in numbers and give their money to help the needy, rather that it being used to sustain buildings and administrators. The absence of Churches will give us fresh opportunities to open our minds and use our skills to give justice to the oppressed and compassion to those in grief without being restrained by the closed minds of entrenched Church bureaucracies.

It will be an exhilarating experience for each and every one of us to be released from the suppression of religious dictators after 2000 years of tolerating their smothering presence and their relentless repression of our personal development as we search for our reason for being.

The fact that Churches have failed to do their job is shown by the fact in the nations where Churches have been large and powerful, even in the United States, there are at least 25% of the population who are atheists and another 25% are agnostic, while another 40% are simply fellow travellers. Only 10% have a genuine commitment to a congregation. If the clergy had held a similar positions in the secular world, and were reported to have a sales record like this, they would have been sacked long ago for being incompetent ditherers.

I have read a disturbing book on the decline of Christianity in the United States written by Tim Alberta, an enlightened Christian. He named it *The Kingdom, the Power and the Glory*. It is a powerful read. He says that the reason given by fellow travellers for not going to church has been that Churches are all too self-righteous. In recent years this excuse has steadily changed. Now Churches are increasingly regarded as being too 'wicked'.

A prime reason for this change is that people are appalled by the disgusting record of child sexual abuse occurring within Churches – the act itself, the cover up, the miserable recompense and the failure to offer pastoral care that can lead victims back to a normal life. They are also appalled by the opposition of Churches to same sex marriage, abortion, and voluntary assisted dying as well as persecution of divorced persons. These reasons are emphatically correct. Churches have given up all right to be the leaders of morality, ethics, and decency in society.

All this means that in my own life I will feel a genuine sense of relief when the day comes when I can put behind my years of being restrained by Churches from experiencing the privilege and satisfaction of walking and working with The Man in the way that I do now.

Even so, I remain loyal to my local Uniting Church congregation at Aspley in Brisbane as I was one of its founders and must share the blame for whatever is below what The Man expects of us.

I happily attend because the congregation involves decent people who are long-standing friends and whose company I enjoy. But as a group we acknowledge we have reached the point where we have to upgrade our sense of mission to the community that surrounds us. To use a cricketing term, we are at the moment just playing out time until stumps. Nevertheless, some of us are working purposefully on changing this.

While on this note, I hold the view that 90% of those who attend churches regularly do so because of the fellowship they enjoy within the congregation. The message they receive at Church is a secondary attraction.

A small footnote on what will happen when Churches lose their relevance. All of the robes and headgear that is worn by clergy to display their rank can be thrown into the dustbin.

When Churches fade away, Christians will be able to participate in the sacraments without any need of a priest. It is an act of vanity for anyone to claim that they alone must give as bread and wine are they are closer to God than you and I.

*GUIDEPOST ELEVEN*

***The world sees and accepts The Man as a shining light because he is a person, not a Church.***

***We do not need an organised congregation, a holy building, or a holy person to be our intermediary with The Man. We need only to enjoy the company of a group of friends who walk with us as we become active participants in a dynamic team led by The Man.***

## 8.12 HOPE

How can Jesus give hope to the world? How can we reach out to all humanity if Churches no longer exist?

If most of those ancient traditional beliefs and creeds and dogmas that once we accepted by rote without question for a lifetime are placed on the backburner, what remains of the faith and where do we go to from here? Are we left in a vacuum?

My answer is this: We are left along the pilgrim way with only Jesus the Man at the helm, unencumbered by religious baggage. We are ready to take on the positive task of changing the world for the better with hope, faith, and inner power as our prime assets.

It is refreshing to face the world unencumbered by rules and edicts and fears of the unknown, such as the nonsense of going to hell.

We will be refreshed and assured by the reality that working partners of The Man are never without hope. With this hope comes a capacity for new visions and finer horizons, plus a greater bonding of all humanity free from the many divisions and confrontations that religion has far too often created in society.

Wonderful days lie ahead of us in being expansive and creative in fostering compassion, justice, peace, and goodwill in a tough world where people live and move and have their being in stressful circumstances.

Our solid hope is that we will gain through our partnership with the greatest person who ever lived. He can expand our minds and our dreams to an extent that we are able to think beyond our normal capacity. We can acquire the courage to step out into the unknown without being dominated by fear or doubt about the consequences.

Our never failing power is the fuel of hope.

There is clear evidence that The Man is the brightest symbol of hope it is possible to discover and his presence helps us to keep on discovering the unlimited potential of hope.

So, how do we prepare ourselves for our walk on the pilgrim way?

It is wise never to forget the memorable words of William Barclay in his splendid little book *The Making of the Bible*: 'The Bible is the place where people seek to find Jesus.'

However, he also makes it abundantly clear that this does not mean that we cannot challenge the words of the Bible.

May we find him there without having our search destroyed by rigid fundamentalist thinking that closes our minds. May we be open to the breathtaking possibilities that we can discover for creating a wonderful new world led by a man who is a constant light on the hill that never fades and always leaves footsteps for us to follow.

I do all of my biblical study about Jesus through the four Gospels: Matthew, Mark, Luke, and John, especially Mark. I find that the rest of the Bible to be interesting background reading.

William Barclay also wrote another ground-breaking book as a guidepost for people who want The Man to be the sole cornerstone of their faith. He called it *The Mind of Jesus*. I find it to be an excellent personal reference book. *The Jefferson Bible* is another gem, discussed in the chapter on Thomas Jefferson. You can buy a copy on the internet and read with interest what he believed are the core elements of the four Gospels that highlight the life and good deeds of Jesus.

For those who want to venture deeper, I can recommend some others that are interestingly radical and quite thought provoking: *The Sayings of Jesus* by Marcus Borg and *Christian Origins* by Burton Mack, as well as *The Radical Jesus, the Bible, and the Great Transformation* by Dougas Oakman. Another is *Made on Earth*, a fine book written in 2015 with great courage by Lorraine Parkinson, a minister of the Uniting Church in Australia who suffered unjust criticism from some of her fellow clergy for committing the mortal sin of having an enquiring mind. The subtitle of her book is *How Gospel Writers Created the Christ.* These words disturbed some fundamentalists as did an honest sensible statement she made that she wants to: 'Remove the Christ and reclaim the teacher.' So do I.

An absolute classic is a famous book written in 1418 by a Dutch monk, Thomas à Kempis, *The Imitation of Christ.* As a bestselling book of Christian literature, it is second only to the Bible. Its volume of sales worldwide is still huge six centuries later. I bought a new copy this year. It is a deeply spiritual book but it's simply stated theme is that we must imitate The Man in every way.

As working partners, we are not just imitating him, we are actively doing what he has called us to do.

Keep your reading choices on your bedside table for regular reference. I can also recommend that you look for the many books written by Marcus Borg and Harry Emerson Fosdick. They are interesting and compelling page turners as are several splendid religious novels written by Piers Paul Read, especially one he wrote about a famous archaeologist who is certain he has found the remains of Jesus near Jerusalem, thereby causing huge turmoil. He calls it *On the Third Day*.

There are also those I mentioned earlier by Lloyd Douglas, A J Cronin, and Morris West. I especially hope you can find time to read at least some biographies of the lives I have briefly depicted in the chapters above. I have enjoyed great biographies on Martin Luther King, Francis of Assisi, John D Rockefeller and Mark Twain.

All in all, our reading leads us to an interesting question that is worth debating: Do we have faith in Jesus or do we have the faith of Jesus or do we have both?

When all said and done, it will be wise for us to keep learning how we can best follow him and be his effective working partner.

But to summarise the vision of hope gained through walking with The Man, the best words are found in Matthew 5:14. 'You are the light of the world. A city built on a hill cannot be hid.'

The Man cannot be hidden.

## *GUIDEPOST TWELVE*

***We know that without hope, life is impossible.***

***The prime hope of a meaningful life is to walk and work with The Man, gathering and growing our hope along the way.*** ***We serve humanity with hope.***

# 9

# Working With The Man

## 9.1 PARTNER

**WE HAVE THE OPPORTUNITY** to make positive changes as we move forward along our pathway from being a traditional or nominal or former Christian.

We can undertake challenging steps that will transform us to the status of being active working partners of The Man. This will become for all of us a stimulating and uplifting experience.

It challenges us to acquire a much deeper understanding of life than that of just being a fundamentalist who is propped up by rigid dogmas, unproven creeds and unbending theology that are just forms of ritual that are supposed to get us to heaven but in reality have no genuine meaning or purpose.

While I greatly enjoy this experience of new freedom that comes with signing up as a working partner, combined with the responsibility that comes with it, I have reached this point after having been regularly accused by well-meaning friends of too often straying much too far from the basics of the traditional faith. They claim that I am watering down treasured beliefs and demeaning the status of Christianity in society so as to make it cheap and easy to follow.

Of course, this is nonsense. Nothing could be further from the truth.

In reality, I am doing the exact opposite as I am talking the language of the 90% of Australians who have shunned Churches but now have the opportunity to start their new journey from where they are now.

I am convinced that I have watered nothing down. That would be a weak exercise close to the realm of cheap politics.

All that I have done is to strip away the myths and excess religious padding that has been passed down through the centuries, primarily as a means of providing certainty for 'believers' in a way that will lock them safely into a rigid faith for life.

There is nothing in life that is certain. Indeed, it is clear that there is no such thing as certainty in any form.

In contrast, I have found that the core of my being is embedded firmly in the life and work and power of The Man, not the pointless jargon of Churches whose leaders too often have robot minds and rigid discipline. I need nothing whatsoever in my life that will prop up my beliefs. I am sustained solely and confidently by the positivity gained by mentally conquering any sense of 'uncertainty' caused by venturing out on a limb.

I am simply shedding from my life all of myths that have closed people's minds for centuries while setting out on a mind growing experience.

This strengthens me, doesn't weaken me, gives me no reason for regret and sets me off on the search to find the inspiration who is The Man.

Becoming a working partner just means chopping away at all the so-called certainties of religion and enjoying facing the headwinds and perils with positivity.

This takes far more courage that blindly following Church ritual.

What I hope is important to my readers who grew up as Christians but found nothing of value in the experience, is the discovery of a vision that accepting The Man as the role model of life will be a step forward in creating a fascinating life of genuine purpose.

It firmly acknowledges that The Man is a person well worth following.

So, what are some of the key elements in the life of Jesus that form the foundations on which you and I can become his strong working partners.

Let me spell out just a few which for me are key basics of his personality, character, and core teachings:

- Honesty and integrity
- Ability to distinguish between right and wrong
- Absence of greed
- Justice for all, irrespective of financial status or political power, especially as regards race, gender, and religion
- Compassion for humanity and a willingness to suffer personally when standing with anyone who is in need
- Lifelong learning and fostering of wisdom
- Enquiring mind and uncluttered vision of how to achieve the impossible
- Ability to handle failure and rise above it with humility and strength
- No self-pity

- Commitment to accept blame for failures and misbehaviour
- Respect for views of others and an ability to tactfully upgrade and change their views and mine
- No fear of illness, pain, or death
- Unlimited capacity to love and to forgive
- Rejection of hatred and bigotry
- Limitless generosity
- Acceptance of a power beyond personality and ability.

All of these finer points of life make a pathway along which we can participate in the creation of a society that has a clearly definable purpose that will lead to the finest quality of life and achievement.

I will be delighted to hear from you with additional strengths that you believe will add to the stature and achievements of a working partner of The Man.

There are many others in our life journey who have left a legacy and who also hugely qualify as role models who can add depth to our journey with The Man. Many of them have been commented on above.

However, there are six who are special role models for me whose inspiration enhances my partnership with The Man.

I look forward to learning of yours.

James, brother of Jesus. Paved the way to the creation of caring and sharing communities before his vision was replaced by that of Paul.

Francis of Assisi. Not only taught us to care for the sick, hungry, and homeless. He showed us how to live with them and walk in their shoes as well as care for the environment in which we all live.

Gladys Aylward. As wonderful an example as can be found of complete commitment, courage, and perseverance, exercised with humility.

William Booth. Challenged the Churches of the world to get out of their holy boxes and into the dark places where they can serve humanity as their primary focus as well as valiantly attempting to remove social curses such as gambling, drunkenness, drug addiction, homelessness, prostitution, and poverty while replacing them with a better way of life.

John Flynn. Became my boyhood hero and advanced forward in my life as a splendid example of how a working partner of The Man can become a visionary nation builder of huge dimensions. His thinking and planning had no blind spots.

Martin Luther King. An absolute giant in the cause of defeating racism and poverty and giving justice and equality for all. Like Jesus, he was assassinated.

The act of writing about them inspires me to be a better working partner of The Man.

## 9.2 CORNERSTONE

Australia, like much of the world, is a nation significantly lacking in evidence of any cornerstone of values, ethics, beliefs, integrity, and enlightened action. We live in a vacuum of presumed community standards that few of us can identify, let alone describe.

My certainty is that working partners of The Man can pioneer, create, and sustain new and solid cornerstones that will remove our divisions while strengthening and sustaining our society while never being religious.

Here is what I understand to be the pathway we have trodden as a nation, where I think we are now and where we can head to if we have the clear mind and conviction of The Man.

Australia has had an unfortunate and pointless beginning as a colony of England.

Governor Arthur Phillip, leading what is now called the First Fleet, was instructed by King George III to establish a prison for convicts at Botany Bay. In carrying out those orders, he and his successors treated the convicts with huge degradation and inhumanity, especially those who were female.

At the same time they invaded then subsequently stole the lands and sustenance of indigenous peoples who had occupied the continent for at least 65,000 years. Eventually they shot and killed a conservative estimate of 30,000 of them whose sole sin was to defend their ancient lands. This led another 100,000 to die by the conveyance of diseases of civilisation. Then they treated them in the same manner as slaves who were not even regarded as human beings.

Nevertheless, the six colonies made steady democratic progress economically, socially, and politically. They federated in 1901 to create our nation. In doing so they made three crucial errors.

Firstly, the Founding Fathers totally ignored Indigenous Australians when creating the new nation. They gave them no recognition in the Constitution and did not recognise them as citizens for another seventy years. This failure is simply unjustifiable.

They also gave white women no role in the Federation negotiations and retarded their future role in politics, government, business, and the professions.

Disgracefully, we still do not give women the equal pay to which they are entitled. This can only be described as primitive.

In addition, they declined to create a preamble to the Constitution that could have concisely set out the values, ethics, ideals, integrity, and moral standards that would give our nation a clear and proud reason for being.

This failure occurred despite considerable efforts by Alfred Deakin.

He was a spiritualist, who had initially and sincerely tried and failed to accept Christianity as a meaningful basis of his own life, but strongly endeavoured to have such a preamble to the Constitution adopted. He failed because most Christians irresponsibly sat on the fence and were quite happy to see his efforts come to nothing. All Catholic and Protestant delegates to Federation meetings, with huge bigotry, bitterly opposed one another in attempting to write even the most basic of words for consideration in such a preamble.

This means that we established ourselves a nation of no conscience and we cannot with any honour or common sense continue in this manner.

Adopting a statement of values is therefore a cause that Australians who are working partners of The Man must take up without ever trying to form yet another Church or political party. We are undeniably challenged to undertake this important task as a calling of major importance that must be achieved as soon as is possible in this century. It simply cannot be avoided any longer.

Right now, it is embarrassingly ridiculous to continue with a situation where, when most Australians are asked what are our national values, the response usually is:

> 'A decent Aussie is a good bloke who will always pick his mates up out of the gutter and make sure they get a fair go.'

This is as weak as water.

We have the clearness of mind, quite separate from that of rigid Christianity, to build relationships with all faiths as well as atheists and agnostics to weld our society together in a manner that will achieve cohesion, noble purpose, and quality of life.

It is a compelling calling that in my view can only be achieved by walking and working closely with The Man to create a purposeful powerhouse of enlightened thinking. This would be an undeniable force for good.

Indeed, I hope that this book can help lead to the creation of a statement of Australian values in our constitution. Fundamentalists do not have the expanse of mind to bring anything remotely like it to reality.

Hopefully, it will become a similar document in stature to the Sermon on the Mount, though being far more challenging and expansive for a totally different society than that which existed in biblical times.

The quality of life in our society will be hugely improved if thousands of people across the nation become working partners of The Man, particularly if all religions, similarly, begin to take up a reformed working relationship with their central prophet, thereby enabling all Australians to live with respect for the values of one another.

It will be splendid if this can be achieved as most of the ills of our nation and the world have been created by the weak leadership of religions.

## 9.3 EPILOGUE

So where has this book of mine led us?

I hope that your answer might be: 'Somewhere that is life changing.'

How may it help to open doors that will provide you and I with opportunities of service to humanity far beyond the visions and challenges mentioned in the chapters I have written above?

We have discovered that treading the pilgrim way with The Man is a lifelong journey that keeps providing new insights, along with perils and challenges that will appear before us.

It will have been a pointless exercise in ego building for me to have written this book just as an exercise designed to create public debate beyond the realm of Churches through which I may gain some temporary notoriety.

It would be utterly opportunistic for me to write it in a manner that will just create enough controversy so that it achieves an aura that creates a smart means of selling lots of books.

This never has been my intent and never will be.

My plan for this book is that it will become an instrument of modern evangelism to bring more people into a working relationship with The Man as a prime step in their journey to create an enlightened meaning for lives worth living in a caring society.

This means that my primary and compelling calling as an author is to reach out to people who have quietly placed their Christian values and ethics on a back-burner mainly because they have chosen to be no longer involved in any Church.

I envisage that the initial steps of its impact will be to encourage readers to initiate social involvement in small groups of friends of like mind (absolutely nothing like a Church). There, you, and I can freely discuss together how we can walk and work with The Man as a basic role model of life in all its breadth and depth of love of humanity.

Then, each one of us can build on this experience to develop a deeper relationship that will cause the group to have a notable impact on society in a manner of significant social reformation.

This will enable you and I to actively and positively create a peaceful revolution outside of the current realm of Churches that will transform our world and make it a more enlightened community of achievers who are compassionate souls.

What we must not do is create a legal group called 'working partners of The Man' or anything similar. This will just evolve into another Church and this is what the world does not need.

***So let us take these seven initial steps along a fascinating pathway:***

- Make The Man our role model for life.
- Base our lives on the Sermon on the Mount.
- Using the ideology of common sense, face all challenges by asking+: 'How would The Man handle this?'
- Meet often for a meal with a small group of friends who have made the same decision.
- No matter what the personal cost, make a commitment to walk closely with others who face huge challenges and tragedies in their daily lives.

- Actively encourage the establishment of new groups of working partners of The Man (without ever creating a legal organisation or a political movement).

* Without becoming involved in politics, foster the writing and adoption of a preamble to the Australian Constitution that will forever record an inspiring set of values that are the cornerstone of our national life.

## 9.4 CREED, PRAYER, AND CHALLENGE

My walk and work with The Man has led me to enjoy the fascinating task of preparing a personal creed to replace in my life the Apostles Creed, the Nicene Creed and others that have no meaning for me in any way whatsoever as I strongly feel that they represent ancient theology and the advocacy of selfishness.

I am also led to write a prayer that has far more meaning and has fewer self-centred thoughts than the Lord's Prayer which selfishly focuses on you and me, not the whole human race.

This exercise has hugely deepened my sense of calling in a manner that has genuine meaning for me in an ever-changing world.

Here they are in the briefest possible form, quite the opposite to fundamentalist need for words that cover every possible thought.

I welcome your advice on how I can improve them as the upgrading of these words will forever be for me a challenging work in progress that has no end. I look forward to accepting your invitation to read and understand your own creed and prayer.

## *EVERALD'S CREED*

*I walk the pilgrim way.*
*I work with Jesus the Man.*
*He is my partner, the role model of my life*
*and the powerhouse of my endeavours.*
*He leads me to serve the poor, the oppressed, the*
*hurt, the lonely and those who suffer injustice.*
*He calls me to a positive role in saving our*
*society from domination by the practice of*
*personal greed and irresponsible pollution*
*of the environment in which I live.*
*He inspires me to search for new visions to achieve*
*that which provides a better quality of life for all.*
*He leads me to expand my mind as a lifelong learner*
*of all that it means to be a dedicated pilgrim.*
*Jesus said: 'Follow me.'*
*I do.*

## *EVERALD'S PRAYER*

*May my whole life be a visible prayer of thanks for the*
*privilege of being a committed follower of Jesus the*
*Man, working as one of his diligent working partners.*
*Each day, may I with conviction say*
*to myself these simple words:*
*'Lead me Jesus, onwards and upwards*
*to the light on the hill.'*
*Inspire me Jesus.*
*Empower me Jesus to be a responsible citizen.*
*Fill my heart with a total sense of*
*responsibility for humanity.*

***Help me through lifelong learning to build into my soul the finest elements of decency, discipline, justice, peace, generosity, compassion, and love.***

*THE CHALLENGE*

***Am I willing to discard the rigid props of traditional religious behaviour that have hitherto sustained my life so that I may walk freely to a rational understanding of the powerful bond between The Man and the human race that leads us all to a meaningful life? Yes.***

## 9.5 THANKS

Many valued friends have helped me to plan, research, write, edit, and publish this WALKING WITH THE MAN and I am forever in their debt. They highlight the undeniable truth that a genuine working partner of The Man always does so via a team.

I particularly give thanks to: David McGiffin, Michael Springer, Alison Courtice, Greg Cary, Peter Catt, Greg McMahon, Rodney Evers, Ken Gilbert, Beverley Bell, Madonna Stott, Rebecca Levingston, David Hetherington, Paul Inglis, Garth Read, Neill Florence, Bev Floyd and Maryna and Constant Mews. Their advice and encouragement has been incredibly generous and wise. I would not have made it without their input. They are in no way responsible, however, for the way I which I have finally chosen to write this book. All critics must direct their comments to me alone.

I will never forget the thousands of people around the world who over my lifespan of ninety-three years have quietly contributed to my growth as a working partner of The Man.

Especially, I express my loving gratitude for my partnership of sixty-six years with Helen who quietly tolerates my loud presence with infinite patience, never fails to get me back on my feet whenever I fall, and always wisely points me once more towards the realm of The Man.

My special thanks to Jason Smith and his competent team at publishers Clark and Mackay for the very professional manner in which they have made this book possible